Vor Forn Siðr:

(Our Ancient Religion)

A handbook for the
Living Einherjar and Valkyrjar

Casper Odinson Cröwell, Ph.D., DD

*I trade not myself for the follies of man,
I give thee my body and soul, my word
for all time. Judge me naught against
your standards, fair or otherwise, for all
to me that matters rests in Odin's eye.*
                                    - Rob Lowery

All written content of this book is the property of Casper Odinson Cröwell with the exception of: "Who is White" and "the 88 Percepts" by David E. Lane; "14 Codes of the Aryan Ethic" by Ron McVan and David Lane; Essay on Wotan by C.G. Jung, The Hammer Speaks by Friedrich Wilhelm Nietzsche, Hávamál translation by Carolyne Larrington, and The Runes translation by Unknown

ᛉVor Forn Siðr, A handbook for the Living Einherjar and Valkyrjar. Copyright ©2012 Vinland Kindred Publishing

ISBN: 9780985476007

This book is dedicated first to Allfather
Odin and to the Trú Einherjar And Valkyrjar thereafter...
Both living and in Valhalla.
Heil Allfather Odin! And Heil his Holy warriors!!!

Thanks & Appreciations go to my wife, Linda,
For her tireless efforts and undying love. And to
The Æsir & Vanir for never quitting on me..

Aso available by Dr. Cröwell, Ek Einherjar: Hammer of the Gods (978-0615330747)

Cover photo: Carved stone, Odin on his eight-legged horse Sleipnir, at Tjängvide, on the Swedish island of Gotland.

"Odhin" (1901) by Johannes Gehrts

Vor Forn Siðr: A handbook for the Living Einherjar and Valkyrjar

TABLE OF CONTENTS

	Introduction by Harvald Odinson Jones	viii
	The Hammer Speaks by Nietzsche	ix
	Preamble	x
	Forward	xi
1	Chronology	1
2	Odinist Fundimentals	5
3	Odinism vs. Ásatrú	9
4	Fundamental Odinism	14
5	Traditional Blótar-Ritual Tools of Fundamental Odinism	21
6	The Yule Tide Season	23
7	Jól Blót/Midvíntirblót	25
8	Sigr Blót (Summarsdagr)	30
9	Disa Blót (Veturnætur)	35
10	Odin's Blót	39
11	Rite of the Ancestors	43
12	Rite of the Martyrs	47
13	The Rite of Sumbel	51

14	Thor's Hammer Blessing for Protection of Vé	55
15	Rite/Ceremony of Consummation & Consecration of Marriage	57
16	Daily Meditations	61
17	Meditations & Musings	92
18	Daily Chants/Dagr Galdrar	99
19	Invocation to Odin	103
20	Invocation to Thor	104
21	The Hammer Sign	105
22	Runic Half Months	107
23	Weekdays & Months	109
24	Perpetual Calendar	110
25	14 Codes of Aryan Ethic by David E. Lane & Ron McVan	113
26	Æsirian Code of Nine	115
27	Nine Noble Virtues	117
28	Rede of Honor	118
29	Code of Northern Warrior/1519	120
30	Elder Futhark	123
31	Old Norse Vocabulary	130
32	Profile of 1519	135
33	Nine Nights in Harvest	147

34	Gothar Course	159
35	Hávamál	173
36	Who Is White by D.L.	199
37	The 88 Precepts by D.L.	201
38	WOTAN: An Essay by C.G. Jung	212
39	The Gods: Odin	226
	Frigga	240
	Thor	253
	Balder	274
	Tyr	289
	Heimdall	297
	Vidar	304
	Idun	307
	Vali	313
	Njörd	317
	Freya	322
	Frey	329
40	Rite of Self Profession for Odinism	340

Dr. Casper Odinson Cröwell

INTRODUCTION

Many who walk the Northern Road know the term of Einherjar, those spiritual warriors who after having lived a life dedicated to Odin and usually having died in battle, then go to Valhalla where they train and await Ragnarok.

There are few though that know the term, "Living Einherjar". For All-father Odin has chosen his host of Einherjar long before they ever reach the great Hall of the slain. When one has been born that Odin has placed his mark upon, that person's life from that moment on is never an easy one. The childhood is full of hardships and strife, as a young man he starts to prove himself as a warrior, as an adult and battle proven he often starts to reach out for more, trying to find answers to the questions that have always plagued him. All the while, though it may not seem that way, Odin was guiding, teaching and inspiring him the entire way to become more, to become great!

The lessons of life, that taught strength, courage, truth, and honor he has learned. Then the old familiar voice he has always known, that whispered ancient wisdom to him and always inspired him to become even greater whispers into his ear once more. Just when he thought that had he had reached greatness, "Have you done all that you could my son, or could you do more?" So, through meditation he begins to ask the question to himself.

It is through these meditations that one Living Einherjar has gained the answers that he has always sought and now they are in your hands.

When the great Roarer whispers into your ear will you be ready to hear what He has to say?

Harvald Odinson Jones, 1519-CGDC

THE HAMMER SPEAKS
by Friedrich Wilhelm Nietzsche

"Why so hard?" the kitchen coal once said to the
diamond. "After all, are we not close kin?"

Why so soft? O my brothers, thus I ask you: are
you not after all my brothers?

Why so soft, so pliant and yielding? Why is there
so much denial, self-denial, in your hearts? So little
destiny in your eyes?

And if you do not want to be destinies and
inexorable ones, how can you one day triumph with me?

And if your hardness does not wish to flash and cut
and cut through, how can you one day create with me?

For all creators are hard. And it must seem blessedness
to you to impress your hand on millennia as
on wax, blessedness to write on the will of millennia
as on bronze-harder than bronze, nobler than bronze.

Only the noblest is altogether hard.

This new tablet, O my brothers, I place over you:
become hard!

- Zarathustra, III, p. 326

Dr. Casper Odinson Cröwell

PREAMBLE

"When the world is pregnant with
lies, a truth long hidden shall
be revealed."
                - An Odinist Prophecy

The afore stated prophecy has been assigned numerous equations and translations by a myriad of self-acclaimed prophets of Vor Forn Siðr, (Our Ancient Religion), what we today call Odinism. I am no such prophet by my own account, though I have been called thus by several others. I am but a servant of my Gods and Folk... A holy warrior and Gothi (priest) in defense thereof. I am Herjan (Chieftain) of a Sacred Order of Holy men, sworn to live our lives in service to Allfather Odin and his noble Folk of the Aryan Tribes.

What follows on the pages of this book, are the very teachings which Allfather Odin has revealed to me in my own spiritual meditations. It is my own testament, for better or worse.

What value will this book yield for the people of the Aryan Tribes? Surely, I cannot say. For only time, Skuld and Allfather Odin shall decide both my fate and that of this book. For such is the decree of the Norns.

                The Honorable Herjan, Casper Odinson Cröwell, 1519-CCG
                          Fjoturlund (Fetter Grove) Lower West Vinland
                                          Circa 2262 RE (2012 CE)

FORWARD

"When the world is pregnant with lies, a truth long hidden shall be revealed..."

Such a time has come to be a reality, and that truth is now revealed; "Oðin Býr (Odin Lives)!!!"

I do not propose that the teachings of Odin which I commit to print hereafter are his only words or truth. Or that I am the only one blessed enough to have him reveal his sacred words to me. For this would be both a falsehood and a deception. On the contrary, Our God of primacy, Allfather Odin, speaks directly to the mind, heart and soul of all of his descendants, his progeny. Sadly so, far too few may descry this simple truth, or his sacred words for a myriad of reasons, albeit most are motivated by greed, selfishness, egocentricities and a host of self-accepted weaknesses.

The revelations which appear in this book are merely Allfather Odin's words and truths as he has revealed them to me in my own meditations via the medium of divine inspiration.

This book is offered as a handbook for those men and women of the Aryan Tribes whom have chosen to dedicate their lives in service to our Gods, Folk and the mission of the 14 WORDS!

"A life in service to something higher than oneself, is a life filled with genuine purpose. Unwavering conviction in that purpose is the catalyst for fulfilling it."

Dr. Casper Odinson Cröwell, 1519-CCG

"When you are in the host and you look around for the weakest link, but you cannot find it... you are it!"   *An ancient military maxim*

Dr. Casper Odinson Cröwell

1
CHRONOLOGY

2217 Runic Era (RE) (1967 Common Era (CE)

Allfather Odin first appeared to me at the age of five during the Yuletide (the Wild Hunt Season) and claimed me as his son. The experience was both terribly frightening and continued to haunt me with nightmares, until as an adult decades later, I finally comprehended the reality of this, "my", initial ordeal. From this night forth, my life would become a constant storm! I suffered from ADD, ADHD, Dyslexia and a host of other behavioral maladies. This plague seemed to be the cruelest of fates, until in retrospect, I was able to glean what a gift from Odin that it truly was. for that winter night in 1967 CE when he placed his hand upon me and claimed me as one of his mortal sons, he incited within my mind, the "Wode Fury", which my mind has seethed with ever since.

Unbeknownst to me, let alone my parents, family, doctors, teachers and others, the storm of hardships and heart aches associated with my hyperactive behavioral afflictions were simply Odin's way of initiating me. I would either fall by the wayside of life along the way, or I would overcome, thrive and grow strong from the tempest. Such strength in the face of the storm is a prerequisite of the Einherjar, Odin's holy warriors. For Ragnarok beckons. There can be no room or place for those whom cannot stand strong as the tempest achieves its apex. And so, there shall be none! For self-accepted weakness is the destroyer of man's majesty. This early experience in my life was to be the confirmation of my cradle song... The prophecy of the Norns writ large for me to discover.

2228 RE (Early 1978 CE)

It is at this time which I formally renounced Christianity in all of its forms as a faith and way of life. I began to call myself a Pagan/Heathen. The only old Germanic Gods of which I knew, was

Thor and Baldur, from my paternal grandmother, (Mein Oma/Nanna) and the stories which she had told to me as a small boy. Thus, I had begun my conscious journey on the road north. I was fifteen years old and had no idea what I was doing. I just knew that this was the direction in which I must wend and trust that Thor and Baldur would lead me to a place of greater understanding. And so, they have indeed.

2229 RE (middle 1979 CE)

I was stationed at Fort Knox, Kentucky in Shedding (September) when I met a fellow from Texas, whom had told me that he too was a Pagan. He had heard of the trouble that I had with the Army's administrators regarding my religious preference to be listed in my service record and stamped upon my dog tags. I had insisted upon being registered as a Pagan. But the Army had refused. When they had failed to change my mind, they simply listed my religion as "No Preference". And that is what was stamped onto my dog tags as well. When this other fellow had introduced himself to me, he had offered me his own dog tags to peruse as he quipped; "See, me too." His dog tags had also been impressed with the "No Preference" designation. He had informed me that he too was a Pagan. I asked what his religion was and he had replied that his God was Odin. Knowing only of Thor and Baldur at the time, I had asked him who Odin was. He told me that Odin was the God of his ancestors in old Germany. I enthused, My Gods too! He then asked about my Gods, and the more that we spoke, it didn't take long for us to realize that we were both on the same road north. We decided to call ourselves followers of the old Gods from then on and we did our first Rite to Odin, Thor and Baldur only a few days later on the Army post, where amphibious armor personnel carrier training took place on the banks of the Ohio River. By today's standards regarding Blótar, our rituals bore little resemblance, if any at all. But our intentions were Trú as were our hearts. And that is what was important. We had believed at the time that surely we must be the only followers of the old Gods. Neither of us knew of any groups, etc... Indeed, what groups did exist in mid-late 1979 CE, were both small and mostly unheard of. Never the less, a few did exist and in the early 1980's CE, I would meet my first and this led me to my biggest influence.

2223 RE (1983 CE)

I had met a biker from Glendale, Arizona by the name of 'Torch'. He was a member of an Odinist Motorcycle Club called the "Norsemen of Midgard." Their club colors were blue and black and their patch was a Thor's Hammer. Torch had given me some literature on the Odinist religion and he told me that all members of his club were members of the Odinist Fellowship, in Crystal River, Florida. He also gave me my Bind Rune (↑).

It was not long after that, he had put me in contact with the Folkmother Else Christensen. Else gave me my true Odinist foundation. She had educated me with books, her personal correspondence on a regular basis and of course, current and back issues of "The Odinist", which was the Odinist Fellowship's publication. Although I had long since been 'Self-Professed' by this time, it was not until Ostara 21, 2236 RE (April 21, 1986 CE) that I professed formally as a member of the Odinist Fellowship, through Else.

2239 RE (1989 CE)

I had initiated contact with an Odinist Order in Sweden called the SONS OF ODIN, Svensk Kindred, (Gottland). I had acquired their address from a fellow Odinist. The Svensk (Swedish) Kindred, Sons of Odin had sent me contact information on the SONS OF ODIN, 1519 -Deutschland Kindred. I began to correspond with Gunther Odinson Pflaum, a 4th Degree Court Elder of their Order.

2244 RE (1994 CE)

I, along with two others, chartered the Vinland Kindred of the SONS OF ODIN, 1519.

2246 RE (1996 CE)

In Ostara (April) I was Ordained as a Gothi (priest) in the Order of 1519, by Gothi, Manfred Odinson Bauer, 1519-8-CCE, the Chief Court Elder of the Deutschland Kindred (near Leipzig Germany.) I have since then been legally ordained by other Odinist & Ásatrú Churches/Hofs/organizations and Gothar.

2256 RE (2006 CE):

On 9, Merrymoon 2256 RE (May 9, 2006 CE) I co-founded, along with my wife Linda and two kinsmen, Harvald Odinson Jones and Brian Ganglare Simas, the HOLY NATION OF ODIN. On 17, Merrymoon 2256 RE (May 17, 2006 CE), we incorporated as a legal non-profit religious church/ministry organization. On 12, Fallow/Midyear 2256 RE (June 12, 2006 CE), we received our Federal EIN and 501(c) status.

2259 RE (2009 CE):

On 11, Fogmoon 2259 RE (November 11, 2009 CE), Feast of the Einherjar and 1519 Day,
my first book; "Ek Einherjar: Hammer of the Gods", was published and released. And so, the journey North continues.

What appears upon the following pages of this book hereafter is my own testament as are any errors in content or grammar.

This handbook is designed as a primer. It may best serve the reader by perusing its content from cover to cover, initially and thereafter, daily - as meditations.

> Dr. Casper Odinson Cröwell, 1519-CCG
> First Herjan of Sons of Odin, 1519
> And Chief Court Gothi of the
> HOLY NATION OF ODIN, Inc.

2
ODINIST FUNDAMENTALS:
Correcting the 'New Age' maladies of the 20th century

As the Living Einherjar and Valkyrjar (the defenders of our Gods, Folk & Sacred Way/Religion), here on Midgard (Earth), we find ourselves in the forward ranks not only in the physical, spiritual and litigation battles in defense of Vor Forn Siðr, but also wherefore correcting many maladies have and continue to afflict our sacred Way/Religion since the latter four and a half decades of the twentieth century.

As Fundamentalist Odinists, it is important to glean from history's annals just what truly constitutes genuine heathen/pagan fundamental rites and observances as opposed to those of a new age climate. Especially as they pertain to what we today call Odinism.

When Folk set out to either revive or reconstruct Vor Forn Siðr in the late 1960's in Vinland, their intentions were noble enough, albeit, the more educated many of these Folk became, regarding Vor Forn Siðr, via the Sagas and Lore, they unfortunately omitted to correct several errors within our Way/Religion as they advanced with it, thereby resigning both, themselves and our spiritual way to the realm of new ageism and cult like status.

Never the less, a great debt of gratitude is warranted for these revivalists. Just the same, these corrections are long overdue and to date, I am aware of no other religious ministry/Hof/Church/or organization beyond the HOLY NATION OF ODIN, Inc. whom has sought to effect such corrections which are in fact necessary to the clearly defined practice of Fundamental Odinism.

To begin with, it is important and equally germane to such sacred practice, to acknowledge the genuine Blótar (Rites & Ceremonies) from the new age, oriented ones, and thereafter, adhere to those Blótar and dates.

We have been taught, via the medium of general Ásatrú practices, to disregard the words of Allfather Odin in chapter eight of the Saga of the Ynglings in the Heimskringla, wherein Odin ordains the burial rites to wit; 'he ordered that all the dead were to be burned on a pyre together with their possessions, saying that everyone would arrive in Valhalla with such wealth as he had with him on the pyre'. We may elect to interpret such wealth today as one's accumulated wealth of honor and wisdom. The same may be ascribed to dying with one's proverbial sword in hand as well. The sword being one's loyalty, honor and virtues right up to the point of the Gods gathering he/she up to them!

Yet, new age Ásatrú has long taught that one may elect to employ whatever burial rites one so desires. Of course, this is true. One's business is one's own. However, why would any self-professed Odinist, elect to willfully disregard <u>his</u> ordained burial rite? Especially a traditionalist and/or a fundamentalist. They wouldn't of course! Odin further ordains that the ashes are to be buried in the ground or scattered at sea. And that memorial stones are to be erected in honor of/to the departed.

Another tradition, sacred and ordained by Allfather Odin, is the <u>three</u> true Blótar and dates for them. These too have been erroneously reduced in their importance in lieu of new age assigned Blótar and dates of significance, by the Gothard (Priesthood) of contemporary Ásatrú practice.

Once again I direct your attention to chapter eight of Ynglinga Saga in the Heimskringla; "A sacrifice is to be made for a good season at the beginning of winter (Veturnaetur/Winter Nights in the month of Hunting/October. This is the traditional Dísablót), one in midwinter for good crops (This is the Midvintirblót of Jól/Yule on the Winter Solstice), and a third one in Summer, for victory (This is the Sigrblót on Sumarsdag". This is the traditional first day of Summer in the old country, in Ostara/April.) The Heathen Yule Blót is described in the Saga of Hákon the Good, chapter 14, found in the Heimskringla.

These 'Three' Blótar are the <u>only</u> ones ordained by Allfather Odin in print in any of the ancient writings. Period! That renders them both traditional and fundamental to Vor Forn Siðr of Odinism. Additionally, it should be noted that with the singular exception of the Midvintirblót during Yule, the other two Blótar asserted herein this writing, have been reduced to rather insignificant status of only minor importance by both the Gothard and practicing body of contemporary Ásatrú and its myriad of religious organizations. Instead, they have replaced the mandated Blótar and dates ordained by Odin, with the two equinoxes and two solstices in addition to other Blótar which corresponds more rightly with new age paganism and Wicca, more truly than they do with Odinism. As Heathens/Pagans, the Solstices and Equinoxes are and should remain important to us. Albeit, they also should be considered in their proper context both spiritually and religiously as they truly exist in their 'solar' context, as opposed to "OUR" Germanic traditional 'Lunar' reckoning of time and the year!

Our Germanic Ancestors employed the lunar month to measure time. They counted nights, not days. Additionally, they counted years in winters, (the lunar/dark side of the year), not summers (the sun/light side of the year). One was said to be this, or that many winters old, and Mani (the male moon) was/is the measurer of time. If genuine, traditionalists and fundamentalists we would be, then by this ancestral tradition and design, must we abide in our own time, both now and in the future. It is long overdue that we adjust our thinking and correct the maladies which have retarded our approach to Odinism and arrested the development of Vor Forn Siðr as the valid and primary religion for the sons and daughters of the Aryan Tribes.

This is our time and it is our duty as servants and defenders of our Gods and Folk to correct the erroneous ways within Odinism which were heaped upon us by the weary and feeble minded proponents of politically correct and accepted ultra-liberalism cloaked in the guise of paganism. True heathens in Odin's name stand true and proud, based not upon either political correctness, or incorrectness, but rather, by the time tested standard of honor alone. Heil Allfather Odin! And heil his sons and daughters, the true Living Einherjar and Valkyrjar!!!

A footnote regarding Blótar; I opine that the most spiritual and productive Blótar which I have attended or led over the span of my own thirty-three years as a practicing Heathen/Pagan/ Odinist, have been those lasting no more than thirty minutes or less in length. I've bore witness on any number of occasion to the degree of short attention spans and lack of focus which supplant the genuine interest which is required if one would spiritually benefit. Blót must be more than just going through the motions and Blót form should be only as elaborate as is necessary to achieve spiritual advancement and provide a traditional and ritualistic vehicle to commune with our Gods, Ancestors and Wights.

In the end, it is of course, up to each individual to decide what is or is not productive to one's spirituality; what Blót design/form is too long or short.

Religion and spirituality are two separate qualities. Religion is the vehicle of observing and exercising ritual, liturgy and tradition. While spirituality is the relationship one enjoys with that which is divine and its ability to nourish, cleanse and fulfill one's Sál (soul).

Religion should be a productive means toward the ends of supporting and fulfilling one's spirit and Sál. And merely going through the motions of a long and boring Blót will not sustain one's spirituality from one Blót to the next.

I have found that after all the many avenues which I have employed over my years on the Road North, that synoptic Blót form has better served my own meaningful spiritual needs way more efficiently than many of the lengthy and verbose Blóts which I have attended and departed from feeling spiritually unfulfilled for the most part.

Better to attend meaningful Blótar from which you gain spiritually and live your life true to Vor Forn Siðr every day. For this, I have found can provide an even and sustained level of spirituality as opposed to the up and down spiritually draining rollercoaster ride which leaves so many feeling empty and may lead to their inevitable lack of interest in religious matters.

May you never be left feeling empty, but always left feeling truly fulfilled. Heil Odin! And Heil the Æsir and Vanir in his reverent and venerable name!

3
ODINISM VS. ÁSATRÚ
A Clarification

There is an erroneous perception going around these days, like a bad flu bug infecting our faith/folk community. In fact, it has been a malady which has beset upon and burdened us for nearly the past thirty years that I've been an Odinist. I am, of course, referring to the misconception that Odinism and Ásatrú are one in the same faith/religion. In fact, there are many whom share the common view that there is but one Northern Faith with several names ascribed thereto including, but not limited to: Odinism, Ásatrú, the Troth, the Way, Irminism, Theodism, Norse Wicca, Vanatru, Northern Dawn Revivalists, etc., etc.. Indeed, some of these are very much the same Theology/Philosophy while others are not. Odinism is most certainly not one and the same with any other denomination within the Northern Tradition. If you are one of the many whom believed this to be the instance, it is not your fault. Most have been erroneously taught this by another who was taught this way and another before him/her! Much in the same way we have been taught, or exposed to Christianity by those whom believed it to be so, and we in turn believed in them. Be that as it may, it is long overdue to correct this long standing error. No other faith or individual will ever take us seriously if we do not take ourselves seriously and seek to establish a liturgy of our own within the Northern Faith, which sets us apart from all other denominations. This does not render Odinists as elitists, nor should it. What it does do is allow us the space to practice our faith with like-minded folk devoid of the cancer of back biting which so commonly exists within the Northern Faith community today! This exists because so many insist that we are all following the same faith with different names all the while, excluding those we don't care for. This leads to a great deal of back biting, which in turn contributes to our faith's arrested development. Acceptance of this reality is the key element required here in order to cease this self-defeating nature we exhibit. If ever we would escape the fetters of retarded growth and ascend beyond 'cult' status, then we must face the inexorable facts.

Does Odinism share similarities with Ásatrú and other denominations of the Northern Tradition? The answer is a resounding 'Yes'. But to what degree? To some minor extent, mostly of mythological proportion and equivalency and deities, Odinism shares some basic similarities with all of the afore mentioned denominations within the Northern Tradition. And yes, more so it shares its greatest similarities with Ásatrú, albeit, the two are not the same.

Let us consider the realities predicated upon the facts: The dawn of our race may be traced back some forty-thousand years to date. In all of that time, Allfather Odin, has been either worshiped, prayed to, or honored in one form/name, or another, consistent with the qualities, attributes and archetypal concepts which we to this day can and do attribute to Allfather Odin as the primordial consciousness of the racial lineage otherwise discerned as the Aryan Tribes. All that we may descry in the echoes of nature's laws, including the personae of the other Gods and Goddesses, are manifestations of his divine will and thereafter his conscious thought 'to be'! And as such, the spark of that divinity resides within each one of us, whether we elect to acknowledge thus, or not.

On the other hand, Ásatrú is a relatively new entity in the history of the Aryan Tribes. Ásatrú is an Old Norse word which translates to "Troth, or loyal to the Æsir (ON Sky Gods)". Rooted in the (probable) century leading up to the era we today know as the Viking Age (Approximately 789 to 1100 Common Era). So too, do many of the Gods/Goddesses have their beginnings in the Scandinavia countries during this era. Along with the Vanir, these deities of the Old Norse Æsir constitute the corpus of the Northern Gods and Goddesses of Ásatrú today. Whether the Aryan Tribes migrated from Asia Minor is a matter of ongoing debate among scholars today. It certainly exceeds the allotted space afforded this essay. I merely raise the issue as it has been posited by scholars that the origin of the very word/name: Æsir, is of Asian origin and as thus, were we able to substantiate such a claim, then we would further thus be able to fix the origin of the Æsirian deities to that locale and the period of the inhabitants thereof as well. Yet, the Æsir came to be known as such in the Scandinavian countries only, in their infancy, and not in the Teutonic countries whose inhabitants (i.e. Germanic Tribes) would have most certainly made the same migration journey out of Asia Minor to Europe via the Caucus Mountains. Though, the Æsir as they were/are known, would have been foreign to them beyond Wotan (Odin), Donnar (Thor), Frija (Frigga), Paltar (Baldur) and Tiu (Tyr). They would not have known them to belong to the family of Gods known as the Æsir, or even what the Æsir were. Were this not the case in fact, then Cornelius Tacitus (56 CE - 115 CE), when composing his treatise: the Germania, surely would have named, or identified the Æsir, and/or other deities beyond those cited in his chronicle which predates the Viking Age by over six centuries. In fact he does wherefore Nerthus/Erde/Erda/Ertha/Erce, and Isis are concerned, and not more!

The knowledge of Odin as Allfather, or as "Thee" Allfather, predates the knowledge of the Æsir and Vanir within the memory of our race, by millennia.

So then, we whom profess ourselves as avowed Odinists, identify Allfather Odin as the primordial consciousness of creation and the progenitor of the race of people which constitute the Aryan Tribes and their descendants today. Furthermore, with all due respect to Dr. S. Flowers (Edred Thorsson) whom posits within many of his published works that the difference between an Odinist and an Odian, is that the Odinist worships Odin while the Odian seeks to emulate him. This I see and denounce as a preposterous employment of semantics in an effort by Dr. Flowers to create and employ verbiage created by himself and used by adherents of the esteemed Rune Gild. While I have the utmost respect for both, Dr. Flowers and the Institute which he founded to the dedication of Esoteric Rune Work, I must assert that I have been an Odinist for nearly thirty years and it has been my own experience, as I believe it to be the natural progression, that any and all whom profess themselves to be Odinist, will begin their own journey as I myself did, somewhere near the bottom end of comprehending Odin, initially via the vehicle of worship and then evolving through self-transformation on a continuum until one ascends to the place where one gives oneself to one self and thereafter seeks to honor Odin by emulating him and his own holy quest for wisdom. Anyone who would lay claim to just instantly and fully comprehending the divine consciousness that is Odin, from the beginning of their journey, is either severely confused, or suffering the delusions of some grand illusion! One thing is for certain, no such person truly knows Odin!!!

In concert with our theology, nothing else would be possible without Odin first, all else follows thereafter. And as thus, Odin warrants our supreme respect and honor as we ourselves seek to emulate his own quest for Ascension via the vehicle of self-transformation on a continuum. Do we still honor the Æsir and the Vanir? Absolutely! They too are our beloved Gods/Goddesses as well as our ancestors and friends. Albeit, they would not "be", any more than we would "be", save for Allfather Odin`s desire and will thereafter.

I know of no Ásatrúar who perceives walking the road North in the same manner. For them, **ALL** Gods within the Northern pantheon are equal, none greater than the other. And there is nothing wrong with that at all. It's just not who we are, or the way we do it. Even more, I am a fundamentalist Odinist, as are all of the members of the SONS OF ODIN, 1519 - VINLAND and the overwhelming majority of the HOLY NATION OF ODIN. That is to say, we live, eat and breath our beloved faith in Allfather Odin, to the extreme wherefore troth/loyalty is in regard. The mantle of zealot quickly comes to mind, and for me - rightly so.

That this issue has up till now, not been addressed within our faith/folk community only further solidifies the sad evidence that we incur too much unacceptable squabbling and fail to enjoy the solidarity we so desperately need to survive, let alone, progress. Too many get and remain confused by the myriad of differences within what they were led to believe was all one faith with only one denomination. Hence the origin of so many lingering confusions wherefore learning about a Northern Path is in regards.

We of the HOLY NATION OF ODIN, Inc. are seeking to remedy this ailment which has required correction for way too long now. By removing some of that confusion and replacing it with some sound understanding, we hope to achieve just that. Because the past should be a guidepost, not a hitching post. And the road North in the 21st century and beyond should not be fraught with confusion wherein one's source of solace and stability is in regard. It should be illuminating in addition to being a source of righteous might!

Providing a sound vehicle, to attain such a state of genuine spirituality and strength is what Odinism is all about!!! And that is exactly what the HOLY NATION OF ODIN, Inc. seeks to provide our members with.

Ves Heil, all.

I remain in Frith with and in service to thee. Heil Allfather Odin!

"That which is open to all, is respected by none." - The Honorable Drighten, Stephen McNallen.

4
FUNDAMENTAL ODINISM

There are many among our folk today in what constitutes the western world, whom subscribe to one form or another, of what may loosely be regarded as Paganism, or Northern Heathenry. Arguably, the best known among such spiritual paths, one would find Odinism and its next of kin, Ásatrú. While the two paths are indeed nearly hard to discern at times, and even argued by some to be one in the same, they **ARE** in fact, two separate paths. More so, many who define their spiritual path as Odinism, bears very little resemblance to that which Fundamental Odinists adhere to in their spiritual endeavors.

Fundamental Odinists harbor the belief that there is an all pervading divine spirit which manifests itself throughout the cosmos and the laws of nature and is therefore self-evident within the realm of nature. For us, that divine spirit is the Allfather Odin, whom without, all else would fail to be possible. The Allfather Odin **IS** pure spirit and the primordial conscious thought of the Aryan people. He too is thereafter, the very will of that first thought. Our Gods and Goddesses are therefore manifestations of the spirit that is the Allfather Odin.

We do not bow our heads or bend our knees before our Gods. We do not worship them as our masters. We honor them as children should their parents. We seek to emulate their noble qualities and conduct ourselves and live our lives with a great degree of personal strength, honor and courage, just as our noble ancestors did prior to the advent of Christianity and their forced conversion thereto said faith! Our Gods are our kin and friends. We are their descendants...their living folk.

We advocate and promote the Germanic Tribal system as opposed to the minute, albeit not discounted, Viking Era model which is so popular within the Ásatrú community at large the world over. We acknowledge that while the Viking Era had indeed made vast contributions to the overall corpus of what constitutes the history of the Aryan people, it too was that very era's corruption of our indigenous religious beliefs which ushered in the alien and Bedouin Christian faith among our unsuspecting ancestors. It must further be asserted that it was during that era that the noble virtue of loyalty to one's kin/folk, became bankrupt in lieu of the enticing lures of non-folk fornications in foreign lands. Whereas the Germanic Tribal system may be traced back in time for millennia prior to the Viking Era and for all that time, by what was chronicled by the likes of both Herodotus and Tacitus, our ancestors possessed a great love and respect for the virtue of loyalty to their native culture and heritage. Such remained inexorably in tact up to the latter part of the Viking Era!

We believe that nothing is more sacred than our blood! For therein lies the complete entirety of our ancestry, both Gods and Folk. We promote a genuine respect for our spiritual leadership and Elders and we recognize the full merits of structure, hierarchy and the ordained Goðard (Priesthood). We hold that tradition does not seek to store the cold ashes of the past, but rather, seeks to keep the flame alive for future generations.

We hold that our holy and sacred Rites and Ceremonies **ARE NOT** open to the general public, for either scrutiny or criticisms. And that only those of our folk may bear witness to, or participate in our holy Rites, or those of our folk whom are sincerely seeking to learn about the noble spiritual beliefs of our ancestors.

We fully acknowledge that the Groves are indeed sacred and play a major role in outdoor Rites. But we hold that the Hof (Temple) is equally as sacred and indeed, to the HOLY NATION OF ODIN, Inc., our Hofs are as they once were in elder days, and now are once again, our houses of the holy.

We hold that the Eddas, Sagas, Lore and myths are all certainly valid learning texts wherefore discovery and comprehension of our spiritual beliefs are in regard. They are filled with hidden mysteries and knowledge and wisdom designed by elder skalds and chroniclers to be rediscovered by their descendants one day(us today and future generations to come) and to be merely tales of entertainment to the unintended peruser throughout the ages. Albeit, we further fully accept that these chronicles, for all their value, have long since been tainted with the corruption of Christian scholars and a myriad of interlopers with deliberate designs to cast an unfavorable light upon the noble spiritual path which our ancestors both followed and left to us. Furthermore, we hold that what constitutes the corpus of literary works of the Aryan people from antiquity to the present time, warrants both the respect and study of our folk, and we vigorously promote the study of these critical works of history, philosophy, art and all intellectual medium as a valid means of restoring our own unique indigenous culture and heritage. We promote fraternal solidarity among the Aryan people, both within and without our particular spiritual community.

We firmly believe in the genuine concept of fate/destiny as predetermined by the Norns (the Goddesses which govern all of our fates, including the Gods!) There is an Old Norse saying; "If you are meant to hang, you won't drown!" This is not to infer that we are without control over our own lives; for we do indeed harbor an honest belief in self-determination. That is to say that, the destination and time of departure from this life to the next may reside in the hands of the Norns (Skuld, more pointedly), but the journey is ours to control through the vehicle of our own will and self-determination. We are extremely Pro Life! We constitute the world's minority due to low birth rates and abortions. This is tantamount to self-induced genocide... The family unit requires a family!

We are unapologetically Folk oriented, which is to say that we are anti-universalist. We fully comprehend the inevitable destruction of all unique racial groups and sub groups and their innate heritages and cultures that the seeds of multi-culturalism will one day reap if they are not met with even greater resistance in accordance with the first law of natural order; the will of any given species/race, to survive!

This is neither an endorsement nor license for anyone to disrespect anyone else. It is merely an undisputable fact of nature! As Fundamental Odinists, we shall always be respectful and considerate to all whom extend the same to us, no matter their race, creed, or color.

Furthermore, we are truly conservative in nature and character. While we place an immense value upon the qualities of personal freedom and liberty, we equally insist that full accountability for one's choices and actions must accompany free will.

We are protective of our kin and folk. This includes our DNA (blood, tissue and organs). While any and all are certainly free to do as they please, a genuine Fundamental Odinist will not donate his/her blood, organs or tissues. Being protective of, and accountable for one's DNA (blood, organs & tissue), one must responsibly take into consideration that when one donates their DNA, it may go to anyone! You may not choose who will get it, unless it is specific to a friend or family member's surgery and you are a living donor. In which case, it would certainly be permissible and a family duty in addition thereto. Albeit, when one signs an Organ/Tissue Donor card, or you donate blood at a blood drive, or blood bank, you have no control as to whom will receive your DNA. One of the problems which plague the advance of both our folk and faith today is that so many who claim to adhere to our sacred precepts do so in word only. Our proverbs and axioms of ethical and moral behavior become little more than mere clichés and catchy phrases to far too many. Actions noble in word most certainly do not equate with actions noble in deed. I assure you!

If we claim to fully comprehend that every ancestor whom has ever lived in our entire line, does indeed live in the blood coursing through our very veins, pumping through our hearts, if we accept this to be the factual reality then how or why would we give it away so freely and without a care as to whom will receive it? The answer, of course, is that we would not if we truly believed in the power of our DNA/Blood.

Once more regarding the myriad of cliché hurlers... Why is it that so many view the host of struggles and hardships we all must face, from a 'victim's' point of view, when they are all but grand opportunities to rise above the pale. Every day of the true Fundamental Odinist's life, is pregnant with potential! It is a component required in the exercising of one's will. It is the process of overcoming weakness and asserting one's will to survive and excel. Yet so many, who claim the path of our Allfather Odin take the perspective of life's struggles as something that has befallen, or plagued them. Such simpering are the weak rantings of the clueless wherefore genuine Fundamental Odinism is in regard!

While we do believe in an afterlife, we don't waste our lives awaiting it. We live each day in the here and now with vigor, all the while remaining aware of our solemn responsibility for our future kin. While everyday of our lives are holy, as life is a sacred and holy event, we hold that Odinsdagr (Odin's day = Wednesday) is the high holy day of the week. We value the wisdom in sound leadership and organization as a means of tribal survival, advancement and longevity. We do not submit to oppressive or ego-maniac whims in our leadership! Lack of personal accountability for one's actions should never be confused as, nor pass for freedom/liberty. Nor should sound Rede (counsel) or respect for leadership structure and standards, be confused as oppression.

We recognize the timeless wisdom and worth of loyalty to family, kindred and folk, as nature's imperative and therefore, our Gods' wisdom.

We recognize the inexorable fact that we are a part of nature and natural order as opposed to being apart from it! And as such, we further recognize that the laws of nature are superior to the inferior laws of man. Taking this into account, we temper such a reality by realizing that while this is so, it is necessary, in order to maintain a society of order and just laws, to abide by the laws of man and society where they either further, or complement the laws of natural order. Where they do not, we resist and remain defiant for survival sake; which once again returns us to the law of natural order and the will to survive.

We hold that our ancestral past is a valuable compass for our future survival, albeit, we must take care to apply that wisdom and knowledge to the here and now if ever we as a folk/people are to have a future at all. Our illustrious past is intended to be a Guidepost... NOT a Hitching Post!

We honor the Æsirian Code of Nine, the Nine Noble Virtues, the Rede of Honor, the 14 Codes of Aryan Ethic and all wise doctrine which is conducive to the survival and advancement of our Faith and Folk.

Fundamental Odinism is an ethnic religion which is indigenous to the native European people of the Aryan Tribes i.e. Germanic Tribes (e.g. Norse, Teutonic, Celtic and some Baltic and Slavic Tribes).

We are racially aware and proudly so, as should all peoples be of their respective Folks/peoples. We afford due respect and consideration to all people who return the gesture. We do not endorse, espouse or condone any gang activity! We do not condone or accept homosexuality as a legitimate component of the laws of natural order. In this our official position, we are not alone, as the Catholic, Orthodox Jews and Islamic faiths all have prohibitions against homosexuality as well. Homosexuality defies the natural order of family procreation and therefore, our Gods.

For us, the genuine Fundamental Odinists, we acknowledge that for far too long now, there has existed a severe lack among our people for self-reliance, self-determination, industriousness, respect for the plight of our folk and indigenous faith and the future of both, honor (both personal & Kindred), loyalty to one's own, strength/fortitude and rectitude, hospitality and perseverance to catalog but a few. Many of those whom exhibit said lack of respect for the afore stated, wear a Thor's Hammer or other symbol indicative of our noble way, around their necks! Too many toss about what amounts to mere clichés that are memorized, but far too few live by them anymore. So many... Too many, fail to pay their own way, or pull their own weight when they are in a position to do so. They elect not to and then justify to themselves and others why it is so. These folks always have their hands out looking for something for nothing. They do not constructively participate in the process of productivity but they are quick to participate in the process of levying a host of ill accusations about others whom have towed the line. They expend their energy and others associated with them, cultivating problems like they are the spawn of Loki, rather than seek solutions to the problems which face us as a faith and folk, as would befit the offspring of our Gods!

Too many desire and even demand equality and respect among the folk when they have not done a thing to warrant such as a peer who positively participates in any beneficial activity. Everyone wants to ride on the Longship, but far too few are willing to man the oars and pull their weight. They want their portion of the plunder, but they don't want to get their hands dirty in the pillage. They all want a free meal, but they don't want to slaughter the beast and bloody their hands in the killing, cleaning or cooking of it! Even among those who do pull their own weight today, so many have lost our ancestor's spirit of yore... Instead of complaining that you pulled your weight and you are not going to pull Svein's too! You do just that! You resolve to pull Svein's weight too, fully comprehending that we all make shore together, or we perish in the storm together. When you do make shore, you get at ol' Svein and unless the reason he slacked off was because he suddenly took ill, or the like. You explain to him, "If you've no intention to pull your own weight, don't try to get back on the boat!" The moral lesson is simple; the Fundamental Odinist will resolve to do what needs doing in order to succeed both individually and collectively. While the others either complain, quit, or fall short of the mark!

The genuine Fundamental Odinist says "YES" to life and he/she lives by the old German proverb which exemplifies so well the noble virtues of self reliance, perseverance, courage, self discipline, industriousness, and honor above all others; " Lerne zu leiden ohne klagen ", (Learn to suffer without complaint).

I could go on and on about what constitutes Fundamental Odinism and what does not, and indeed, I shall at a later date compose a Vor Forn Siðr handbook[1] on such. But for now I shall

---

[1] You now hold this book in your hands.

leave you with this content for your own consideration. May Odin bless you all and may your Hammer's strike Trú.

I leave you then with the following meditation: "No man may levy a valid indictment against thee, save for thy own conscience! Then all shall know in time through thy own actions.".

5
TRADITIONAL BLÓTAR/RITUAL TOOLS OF FUNAMENTAL ODINISM

Spirituality, new or ancient, is open to interpretation by those engaged in such quests to understand and commune with that which is divine. Equally so are the mediums and means by which one might achieve thus. However, just as valid are the myriad of organized religious institutions of any stripe and denomination, and their respective liturgies, whether they are conservative, liberal or somewhere betwixt the two. For those of us within the radical Fundamentalist Odinist ranks, we may discern what is new age, and what is traditional, by what we may cull from the many annals of history pertaining to our Sagas, myths and lore. This is true of the religious tools which our ancestors employed in order to conduct Blótar.

The following is a catalog of items which appear in our Sagas, Lore and myths:

HISTORICALLY TRADITIONAL RITUAL TOOLS

1) The Stallr/Stalli (basic indoor Alter) and the Hörgr (Outdoor Alter constructed of piled stones).
2) The Gandr (wooden wand or staff).
3) Hlaut (this is the sacrificial liquid/the offering).
4) Hlaut Boli (this is the bowl which receives the Hlaut/Sacrifice).
5) the Hlautteinn (this is the blessing twig, usually a sprig of evergreen).
6) the Drekkjarhorn (this is the drinking horn).
7) the Oath Ring - (self-explanatory).
8) the Large Thor's Hammer (for consecrating & blessing).
9) Runes (self-explanatory).
10) Deity statues.
11) Incense (spiritual oils may be substituted).
12) Alter Candles.

CONTEMPORARY RITUAL TOOLS (since 19th century) used in addition to/with above

1) the Alter Cloth (covers the Stallr/Stalli).
2) Feathers (especially Raven).
3) Animal hides/pelts (especially bear, wolf & reindeer).
4) Hlaths (traditional male Norse-Teutonic head wear, once calfskin cap/now bandana type, etc.).
5) Alter Bell.
6) Hand held Drum.
7) Assorted Ceremonial jewelry made of beads, bones, claws, teeth, etc.).
8) Several Ceremonial Herbs.
9) Ham/Pork
10) Honey

These ritual tools comprise the corpus of usual tools employed by both Odinists and Ásatrúar.

Certainly anyone may employ further tools in the practice of Vitkar Shamanism of Esoteric Odinism and Seithr/Seid. But anything else used for Blótar must be counted as both, new age, and a potential distraction to the sacred purpose of Blót. There is something to be said for employing ritual tools that are necessary and those utilized to set the Vé (sacred enclosure/space) apart from that which is mundane, as opposed to others which just clutter and distract from the holy work and purpose of the Rite or Blót.

Of course, in the end, each one is free to choose which is best for him/her self in their quest for sacred/holy communion with the divine.

The traditional and contemporary tools listed above are those endorsed. by the HOLY NATION OF ODIN, Inc., for use in HNO, Inc. Blótar.

Ves heil ok megi Gothanum blessi thig. Fara meth vor Allfadr Odin! (Be healthy and may the Gods bless you. Go with our Allfather Odin!)

Heil Odin!

6
THE YULETIDE SEASON

Yule (ON/GM Yól/Yúl and Júl), is more a holy season/tide than it is a day. The Yuletide commences on December 20th, when the old Norse-Teutonic moon/month transitions from Wolfmoon into Yule or Yulmoon. On this day, December/Yule 20th, at sunset, the Yuletide begins with the Mother Night. This is the Fundamental Odinist's New Year. Sometimes, albeit erroneously so, it has been called 'Mothers Night', by both Ásatrúar and some Odinists, alike. The Mother Night gives birth to the Sun and new year and thus begins the Yuletide which culminates upon the Twelfth Night on the 31st and itself ends at midnight. On the date of the Winter Solstice, the actual Yule, from which the tide receives its name, the Midvintirblót is performed.

There is a great deal of activity which occurs during this twelve day/night tide, spiritually, religiously and traditionally wherefore celebrations are in regard. 1) the New Year is born, 2) the Yule-Winter Solstice occurs, 3) the veil betwixt the realms of the living and the dead are at their thinnest, 4) the Yule proper is the shortest day and longest night of the year, 5) it is the time of the Wild Hunt, 6) the Yule Log is burned, 7) our ancestors may visit and walk among us, 8) Yule Oaths are sworn and 9) the Mid-Winter Blot and Feast occurs.

Yule means 'Wheel'. Called thus as the sun (Sunna) crossing the sky looked like a great solar wheel to our ancient ancestors. The Yuletide is sacred to all of our Gods and Ancestors; however as leader of the Wild Hunt, Odin rules the roost! During the Midvintirblót and Feast, both Frey and Thor are honored first and foremast. Just as the Yuletide was usurped by the church in Rome, to become the Christian's Christmas, so too was Frey's sacred boar, which was symbolically eaten by our ancestors, (wild pig or boar), to become today's Christmas ham.

The Yule Log was burned and it was considered a bad Heilar (omen) if the log failed to burn the whole night through. The ashes were kept and stored until the next year and used to light the following year's Yule Log. The sacred Yule feast may have consisted of several meats like goat, horse, beef and venison. But the Yule Boar was the table's centerpiece. The boar's flesh was held to be <u>sacred</u> to both, the God Frey and the Einherjar in Valhalla whom feasted nightly upon the sacred Valhalla hog;

"Saehrímnir", and so it was the most honored part of the Yule Feast. The father of the family, or the Gothi presiding over the feast, would lay his hand upon the sacred boar and swear an oath of zeal, in service to family, tribe and Gods. Each member of the family, or the feast's assembled, would in turn thereafter pledge an oath. And herein lay the origins, most probable, for the Yule Oath, and New Year's resolution.

The Midvintirblót is a fertility blót, whereby Thor breaks the spell of winter so that the Sun may resume her place in the year, and Frey shall make fertile the earth's soil by his courting Gerd, the frost giant with whom Frey fell in love with.

We set a place at the table for our ancestors and recently departed ones and meditate upon the continuing line of the Aryan Tribes. We'd not be here today, but for their will and deeds! Nor shall our descendants on the morrow's tide, except for "OUR" will that they be, and our struggle for and defense of that noble, divine and natural design. Heil Odin & Frigga! Leave a little something on the ancestors' plate each day. Of course they can't consume it. Never the less, it is respect for them and the traditions they gave to us!

Aside from the Midvintirblót, which we all observe and celebrate, it is up to each of us to decide how we will move through the twelve days of Yule. This will be in accordance to circumstances and personal choice.

For myself, I'll begin the 20th, The Mother Night, by welcoming, both Sunna and my Ancestors back. I will perform a Sumbel to that effect with my Kin, and I will set a place on my Stalli, for the Ancestors' portion of my meals for the next twelve nights.

I'll hold Midvintirblót on the Yule proper (the Winter Solstice) which usually falls on the 21st. I will honor both Thor and Frey at this time. On the night of the 24th, I'll perform a Sumbel to the Ancestors. The night of 26th, a Sumbel to the House and Hof Wights. On the eve of the 27th, Sumbel for the Dísir. On the eve of the 28th, Sumbel for the Alfar and Huldrafolk. On the night of the 29th I'll give thanks to the Land Wights. On the night of the 30th, I shall honor the recently departed among our Folk. And on the Twelfth Night, the 31st, I shall Galdr to Allfather Odin and the host in the Wild Hunt! And shall hope to be visited by him, as I consider my own oaths.

As in days of yore right up till today, steeped in precious Aryan Tribal tradition, this is the essence of the sacred Yuletide!

Heil Odin!!!

7
JÓL BLÓT/MIDVINTIRBLÓT
(Winter Solstice)

1) THE HAMMER HALLOWING: the calling and raising the shield wall

Lo, to the north do I look, my gaze seeking far and wide. From this, my/our Othal Land, do I/we look north toward the Heimat, the ancient and holy ancestral lands of my father's fathers!

That from which my/our beloved lineage first took root. Engendered by our holy Allfather Odin.
As in elder days of yore, I call out to thee oh mighty Odin! That ye and the holy host of Æsir and Vanir might join me/us this night/day, to enjoy my/our welcome, my/our hospitality and to bear witness to this holy work I am/we are about to wrought..

Facing North, perform the Hammer blessing:
Hammer í Nordri, helga vé thetta ok hindra alla illsku!

Next face East:
Hammer í Austri, helga vé thetta ok hindra alla illsku!

Next face South:
Hammer í Sudri, helga vé thetta ok hindra alla illsku!

Next face West:
Hammer í Vestri, helga vé thetta ok hindra alla illsku!

Facing North and looking overhead:
Hammer í Asgard, helga vé thetta ok hindra alla illsku!

Still facing North, an looking down at your feet/ground:
Hammer í Helheim, helga vé thetta ok hindra alla illsku!

Still facing North, and holding the Hammer straight out in front at chest level:
Hammer í Midgard, helga vé thetta ok hindra alla illsku!

2) OPEN THE CIRCLE

Facing North, assume the Elhaz (ᛉ) Stadha and recite this Galdr:

Heil ye holy Allfather Odin, keeper of the Runes, wisest of all Gods, Father of Gods and Folk of the Aryan Tribes, great God of the Æsir, God of royalty, God of battle, wisdom and war!
God of death and mysticism, Father of the slain, great Valhalla host, hold ye, the holy kindred, your sons and daughters of the North Folk. Mighty warrior God and wanderer of elder days, turn my/our heart(s) toward you, great and mighty Odin!

3) CONSECRATE THE STALLR/STALLI OR HÖRGR

I consecrate and make holy to the service of Allfather Odin and the Æsir and Vanir, this Stallr/ Hörgr! Banishing from it and this sacred Vé, all wights and influences which are impure and unholy. May my/our heart(s) and mind(s) in this holy place, likewise be consecrated.

4) THE SACRED FLAME

Kindle now I, thee sacred flame of inspiration, cleansing and illumination. It is the first mystery and the final mercy. May it burn bright and long throughout all nine worlds and within the hearts and minds of our Folk!

5) THE READING

Heil Thor, Slayer of Chaos and winter's icy spell! We welcome Sunna's return through your noble endeavor, and we rejoice in her warmth as it waxes and spreads across our Othal lands and rides the Season's tide.

Heil Thor!

(ᚦ) Thurisaz - (ᚦ) Thurisaz - (ᚦ) Thurisaz

Heil Frey, Lord of the fertile fields!

It is you whom woos the Frost giantess, Gerd, and make ready the fields of Nerthus, to sow the seeds which shall flourish and burst forth in a riot of color when the summer finding (springtide) arrives.

Heil Frey!

(ᚠ) Fehu - (ᚠ) Fehu - (ᚠ) Fehu

Mighty Thor and Lord Frey, may our/my deeds be worthy of the gifts and traditions which you have passed down to us/me. And may your presence now and always fill our/my hallowed Hof.

Heil Thor! Heil Frey!

6) <u>THE INVOCATION: Charging the Hlaut</u>

Great and mighty Thor, generous and virile Frey, pour now your blessings into this Hlaut that we/I may receive your gifts of strength, fortitude and determination. And vitality, lust for life with its many pleasures and the desire to see the line of our Folk continue and prosper. May we/I be blessed by thee, with the vigor and hearty appetite to defend our/my Gods, Folk and Vor Forn Siðr, this and everyday!

Heil Thor! Heil Frey!

(ᛃ) Jera - (ᛃ) Jera - (ᛃ) Jera

7) <u>THE SERMON</u>

The understanding that life is a gift which we all are experiencing, is always tempered by the reality that the circumstances associated with this gift, can sometimes be harsh and unforgiving, if not outright cruel. Indeed, we are all born dying and life's journey is a constant struggle against atrophy, gravity and attrition. Such is the law of Nature... the never ending battle for which, to the victors go, yet another day, week, month, or year of life upon this mortal coil. And to the vanquished goes myriad of ailments and hardships in concert with said struggle. For those of us counted among the ranks of the Living Einherjar, comes the awareness that whining and complaining achieves nor alters no harshness or hardship. Better are we served, as are our Gods and Folk, by acknowledging and accepts all the joys and hardships of life with the mirth, resolve and fortitude required of a courageous and noble soul. One whom accepts the gift of life in its very entirety, joys, hardships, rewards and consequences...

> "Silent and thoughtful a prince's son
> should be
> and bold in fighting;
> Cheerful and merry every man
> should be
> until he waits for death."
> -Odin, Hávamál 15

For this is the noble attitude of the Living Einherjar and Valkyrjar the Fundamental Odinist. And so too, it is our ability to embrace life on such terms, the gifts of Thor and Frey. Heil Thor! And Heil Frey!

8) THE GIVING, THE MÍNNI (Memory drink) AND THE BLESSING:

Facing East for Thor, then West for Frey, raise the Drekkjarhorn up to the sky and recite the following, or similar words of own choosing;

"We/I offer this sacred Hlaut, oh mighty Thor (and Lord Frey), with love, honor and the respect of your loyal and living Kin."

Now pour some of the Hlaut from the Horn into the Hlaut Boli. This done, begin the Mínni by saying a toast, and thereafter allowing each of the assembled Folk to do the same. The Drekkjarhorn is passed around in a Sunwise/clockwise fashion. Once the Mínni is completed, perform the Blessing...

Take up the Hlaut Boli and Hlaut teinn, face East and hold Boli up to Thor. Then faceWest and hold it up to Frey. Now face the assembled Folk in the circle and in a Sunwise direction, bless each one by dipping the Hlauttein into the Hlaut Boli and sprinkle each one while intoning;

"I give thee the blessings of Thor and Frey!"

9) CLOSING THE CIRCLE and ENDING THE BLÓT:

Face North and sprinkle the Stalli/Hörgr and intone;

"Well do we/I mark Midvintirblót, with the renewal of Sunna's sweet smile! Our Othal lands grow fertile once more and for this do we/I praise both Thor and Frey.

We/I give thee honest thanks and love for thy blessing, great Gods of the North. Well do we/I recognize your bountiful presence in our lives daily. As your Aryan Folk know thee today, as our ancestors did before we… may our descendants yet to come know thee always for as long as our Folk shall live. Heil Thor! Heil Frey!

Now empty the boli's contents into the ground to the North (if outdoors). In the Hof, leave it upon the stalli till the next morning and then discard it in the sink with a Hammersign over it with your right fist.

This Blót is now done. Either break the shield wall or breathe in its energy. If you are in your own Hof, you may elect to allow it to permeate your Hof and protect your Vé.

Depart in Frith and Grith with all assembled, both Folk and Gods.

8
SIGRBLÓT/SUMMARDAG

1) THE HAMMER HALLOWING: the calling and raising the shield wall

Lo, to the north do I look, my gaze seeking far and wide. From this, my/our Othal Land, do I/we look north toward the Heimat, the ancient and holy ancestral lands of my father's fathers!

That from which my/our beloved lineage first took root. Engendered by our holy Allfather Odin.
As in elder days of yore, I call out to thee oh mighty Odin! That ye and the holy host of Æsir and Vanir might join me/us this day, to enjoy my/our welcome, my/our hospitality and to bear witness to this holy work I am/we are about to wrought..

Facing North, perform the Hammer blessing:
Hammer í Nordri, helga vé thetta ok hindra alla illsku!

Next face East:
Hammer í Austri, helga vé thetta ok hindra alla illsku!

Next face South:
Hammer í Sudri, helga vé thetta ok hindra alla illsku!

Next face West:
Hammer í Vestri, helga vé thetta ok hindra alla illsku!

Facing North and looking overhead:
Hammer í Asgard, helga vé thetta ok hindra alla illsku!

Still facing North, and looking down at your feet/ground:
Hammer í Helheim, helga vé thetta ok hindra alla illsku!

Still facing North, and holding the Hammer straight out in front at chest level:
Hammer í Midgard, helga vé thetta ok hindra alla illsku!

2) OPEN THE CIRCLE

Facing North, assume the Elhaz (ᛉ) Stadha and recite this Galdr:

Heil ye holy Allfather Odin, keeper of the Runes, wisest of all Gods, Father of Gods and Folk of the Aryan Tribes, great God of the Æsir, God of royalty, God of battle, wisdom and war!
God of death and mysticism, Father of the slain, great Valhalla host, hold ye, the holy kindred, your sons and daughters of the North Folk. Mighty warrior God and wanderer of elder days, turn my/our heart(s) toward you, great and mighty Odin!

3) CONSECRATE THE STALLR/STALLI OR HÖRGR

I consecrate and make holy to the service of Allfather Odin and the Æsir and Vanir, this Stallr/ Hörgr! Banishing from it and this sacred Vé, all wights and influences which are impure and unholy. May my/our heart(s) and mind(s) in this holy place, likewise be consecrated.

4) THE SACRED FLAME

Kindle now I, thee sacred flame of inspiration, cleansing and illumination. It is the first mystery and the final mercy. May it burn bright and long throughout all nine worlds and within the hearts and minds of our Folk!

5) THE READING

Heil Odin, Father of Victory! On this first day of Summer in the elder days of yore, in the Othal lands of my/our ancestors, I/we bid thee welcome and troth, oh mighty Odin! For as surely as you have touched the hearts and minds of those dedicated to you, in service to our Gods, Folk and Vor Forn Siðr, I/we assemble this very day in honor of the struggle, and the victory which you afford those valiant enough to dare. Heil to you Sigtýr, victory bringer!

May those whom don your sacred knot, fail not in service to our sacred cause and way. May I/we, of the Living Einherjar, measure tall and trú in the face of adversity and hardship. So that you may deem me/us, your living champion(s) and hero(es). That my/our deeds be worthy of the honor which your victory bestows upon one whom is stalwart enough to fill your hallowed hall.

Heil Allfather Odin!

Teiwaz (↑) - Teiwaz (↑) - Teiwaz (↑).

6) **THE INVOCATION: charging the Hlaut**

Holy father of victory, oh great and mighty Odin...Pour now, your blessings of victory and divine energy into this Hlaut, that I/we may receive your gift of victory and that I/we may grow closer to you, Father (and to each other as we share it among ourselves).
I/we take this moment to reflect upon the Folksoul and memory, which ever resides in Valhalla. That I/we may know my/our place in the grander scheme and order of our sacred line. May I/we assume that place with honor, pride and a commitment towards the defense of our sacred holy way and future. In thy reverent and venerable name do I/we Galdr thee ancient song;

Sowilo(⚡) – Sowilo (⚡) - Sowilo(⚡)

7) **THE SERMON**

The very embodiment of courage, honor and victory within the memory of our lore, is the very example of Sigurd the Dragon slayer. While Beowulf, Egil Skalagrimsson and Ragnar Hairy breeks all stand out among so many champions of Odin, Sigurd/Sigfried stands tallest!
May I/we seek to emulate the very noble virtues of strength and fortitude in my/our journey North. May the lessons of the Einherjar proper, residing in Valhalla resound loudest in our/my heart(s) and mind(s) whenever we/I are called upon to uphold our sacred duty in this life and the next. Especially when our/my own death song is at hand! May they and Odin, smile upon me/us as I/we cast my/our gaze toward Ásgard and loose my/our battle cry... "Odin! Victory or Valhalla give unto me/us!"

(At this place, say whatever words you have composed for this Blót, or you feel in your heart).
Now Galdr:

Ansuz(ᚨ) - Ansuz(ᚨ) - Ansuz(ᚨ).

8) THE GIVING, THE MINNI (memory drink) and BLESSING:

Facing North, raise the Drekkjarhorn up to the sky and recite the following, or similar words of own choosing;
"I/we offer you this Hlaut Odin, with love, honor and the respect of your loyal descendants."

Now pour some of the Horn's Hlaut into the Hlaut Boli. This done, begin the Minni by saying a toast, and thereafter allowing each of the assembled to do the same. The Horn is passed about in a sunwise/clockwise direction. Once the Minni is completed, perform the blessing...

Take up the Hlaut Boli and Hlautteinn, face north and hold it up to Odin. Now face the assembled Folk in the circle, and in a sunwise progression, bless each by dipping the Hlautteinn into the Hlaut and sprinkle each in a Sowilo(ᛋ) fashion while intoning; "I give thee the blessings of Odin... and the blessing of victory!"

9) CLOSING THE CIRCLE AND ENDING THE BLÓT

Face North and sprinkle the Sta11i/Hörgr and intone;
"Summer's victory reins once more in the lands of our ancestors as I/we the gathered Sons (and daughters) of Odin, mark this Summarsdag. I/we praise thee Allfather Odin! And I/we give thee honest thanks for thy blessing of victory in my/our life/lives. As your Aryan Folk know thee today and our ancestors knew ye back then, may our descendants yet to come know thy name, thy glory and thy victory for as long as our Folk shall live. Heil Odin! Odin heil!!!

Now empty the Hlaut Boli's contents on the ground to the north, if outdoors. If in Hof, leave it upon the Stalli until the next morning then dispatch it properly in the sink and Hammersign
over it with your right fist.

This Blót is now done, either break the shield wall or breath in its energy and take it with
you. If you are in your own Hof, you may elect to allow it to continue to stand and protect the Vé.

Depart in Frith and Grith with all assembled, both Folk and Gods.

9
DISA BLÓT/VETURNÆTUR
(Winter Nights)

<u>1) The HAMMER HALLOWING: the calling and raising the shield wall</u>

Lo, to the north do I look, my gaze seeking far and wide. From this, my/our Othal Land, do I/we look north toward the Heimat, the ancient and holy ancestral lands of my father's fathers!

That from which my/our beloved lineage first took root. Engendered by our holy Allfather Odin.
As in elder days of yore, I call out to thee oh mighty Odin! That ye and the holy host of Æsir and Vanir might join me/us this night, to enjoy my/our welcome, my/our hospitality and to bear witness to this holy work I am/we are about to wrought..

Facing North, perform the Hammer blessing:
Hammer í Nordri, helga vé thetta ok hindra alla illsku!

Next face East:
Hammer í Austri, helga vé thetta ok hindra alla illsku!

Next face South:
Hammer í Sudri, helga vé thetta ok hindra alla illsku!

Next face West:
Hammer í Vestri, helga vé thetta ok hindra alla illsku!

Facing North and looking overhead:
Hammer í Asgard, helga vé thetta ok hindra alla illsku!

Still facing North, and looking down at your feet/ground:
Hammer í Helheim, helga vé thetta ok hindra alla illsku!

Still facing North, and holding the Hammer straight out in front at chest level:
Hammer í Midgard, helga vé thetta ok hindra alla illsku!

2) OPEN THE CIRCLE

Facing North, assume the Elhaz (ᛉ) Stadha and recite this Galdr:

Heil ye holy Allfather Odin, keeper of the runes, wisest of all Gods, Father of Gods and Folk of the Aryan Tribes, great God of the Æsir, God of royalty, God of battle, wisdom and war!
God of death and mysticism, Father of the slain, great Valhalla host, hold ye, the holy kindred, your sons and daughters of the North Folk. Mighty warrior God and wanderer of elder days, turn
my/our heart(s) toward you, great and mighty Odin!

3) CONSECRATE THE STALLR/STALLI OR HÖRGR

I consecrate and make holy to the service of Allfather Odin and the Æsir and Vanir, this Stallr/Hörgr! Banishing from it and this sacred Vé, all wights and influences which are impure and unholy. May my/our heart(s) and mind(s) in this holy place, likewise be consecrated.

4) THE SACRED FLAME

Kindle now I, thee sacred flame of inspiration, cleansing and illumination. It is the first mystery and the final mercy. May it burn bright and long throughout all nine worlds and within the hearts and minds of our Folk!

5) THE READING

Holy Disir, mighty mothers from the mists of memory before time was scored, know well this very night that your kinder yet live to sing your praise and call out to thee with love!

Oh fair sisters of the Clan and Tribe, behold my (our) proclamation of gratitude and affection. Heed well my (our) recognition of thy holy presence in my (our) life (lives). I (we) welcome thee with warm embrace, glad of heart for the goodly ways of thy help in matters of health, hearth and household of my (our) family (families)!

6) THE INVOCATION: CHARGING THE HLAUT:

Holy Dísir, great patronesses of the ancestral and family lineage, you who have bore witness to all which the FOLK have done since time immemorial and the first flesh and blood mortal of my (our) line began... Pour now your energy and blessings into this hlautdrekkjar (sacrifice drink), that I (we) may grow closer to you (and each other as we share it among ourselves).

7) THE SERMON

Allmother Frigga, Queen of Asgard, whose very Distaf may alter the threads of our lives which the Norns weave throughout the days of our lives, we/I call out to thee with love and honor for thee in our/my heart(s), that you may know of my/our gratitude for thy gracious love and gifts which you bestow in my/our life/lives. Heil Frigga!

And to Freya, the Vanadis (leader of the Disir), I/we call out to thee with love! Ever present in my/our life/lives, you remind me/us to remember always the very line of my/our female ancestors whom we collectively know as the holy Disir. Heil to thee oh holy Freya! And Heil the Holy Disir!!!

8) THE GIVING, THE MINNI (memory drink) AND BLESSING

Facing North, raise the Drekkjarhorn up and recite the following or similar words of own choosing:
"I/we offer you this Hlaut, oh holy Disir, with the love and respect of your true and loyal kin."

Now pour some of the horn's Hlaut into the Hlautboli. This done, begin the Minni by saying a toast and thereafter allowing the assembled to do the same. Pass the horn in a sunwise fashion. Once the Minni is done, perform the blessing...

Take up the Hlautboli and Hlautteinn, face North and hold it up to the Disir. Now face the assembled circle and in a sunwise fashion (clockwise), bless each one while intoning: "I give thee the blessings of the holy Disir."

9) CLOSING THE CIRCLE:

Face North and sprinkle the Stali/Hörgr and intone:

Warm is my heart (are our hearts) with the knowledge and comfort of your sweet and protective presence. In the names of the Vanadís Freyja and sweet All-mother Frigga, do I (we) heil thee holy Dísir of the Family and the Folk! Heil the holy Dísir! And Heil All-father Odin!

This Rite is now done. Break the shield wall or draw it in, and depart in Frith and Grith with all assembled, Folk and Gods.

10
ODIN'S BLÓT

1) Beginning in the North, raise the shield wall with a Hammer Hallowing:

"Hammer, í <u>Nordri</u>, Helge vé thetta ok hindra alla ilska!"

> Next face East:
> Hammer í Austri, helga vé thetta ok hindra alla illsku!

> Next face South:
> Hammer í Sudri, helga vé thetta ok hindra alla illsku!

> Next face West:
> Hammer í Vestri, helga vé thetta ok hindra alla illsku!

> Facing North and looking overhead:
> Hammer í Asgard, helga vé thetta ok hindra alla illsku!

> Still facing North, and looking down at your feet/ground:
> Hammer í Helheim, helga vé thetta ok hindra alla illsku!

> Still facing North, and holding the Hammer straight out in front at chest level:
> Hammer í Midgard, helga vé thetta ok hindra alla illsku!

2) Open the circle; Face North and assume an Elhaz (ᛉ) stadha and recite the following;

Clap hands three times...

Heil ye holy All-Father Odin, keeper of the Runes, wisest of the Gods, Father of Gods and men, Great God of the Æsir, God of royalty, God of battle, wisdom and war. God of death and mysticism, Father of the Runes, Great Valhalla host, hold ye the holy Kindred, your Sons (and Daughters) of the NorthFolk. Mighty warrior God of elder days, turn our minds and hearts towards you!

3) Consecrate the Stali / Hörgr;   Clap hands three times…

I consecrate and make holy to the service of Odin, this alter! Banishing from it all wights and influences, which are impure and unholy. May our hearts and minds in this holy place be likewise consecrated.

4) The Sacred Flame;   Clap hands three times…

I light now the sacred flames of inspiration and cleansing. The first mystery and the final mercy. May it burn bright and long within the hearts and minds of our folk.

5) The First reading: "Hávamál stanzas 138-145"

6) Invocation; Charge the mead/water and invoke Odin:

This day (or night), we proclaim holy in your name as we call to you and bid thee welcome here to this circle Father! Grace our lives with your holy presence and grant us victory! Ye have been known by many names, in many places, grand wise God of the NorthFolk who ever drives us forward and inspires us with your divine and unparalleled wisdom to aspire to and achieve daring deeds and live worthy lives as the royal and noble Sons and friends of the host of the Gods and Goddesses…
O'ye wise sage, ye wondrous, powerful father of warriors and poets alike! We call to you All-Father, wise one, thin one, father of the slain, one eyed God, graybeard, King of Valhalla, Lord of Asgard, Father of the Sons of Odin, host in the hall of Hár, leader of the wild hunt, keeper of the Runes, father of all, he who inspires wisdom and great deeds in the NorthFolk, one who guesses right, hooded one, wanderer, much loved one, far traveling sky cloaked wanderer, third one, one who blinds with death, father of Berserks, High one, bringer of ecstasy, long bearded one, God of wishes, wand bearer, God of

prisoners, and Father of Victory! May we emulate you and your deeds as we walk your holy path… Pour now your energy into this horn/drink that we may grow closer to you and to each other as we share it among ourselves.

7) Second reading;   "Sermon Open to choice, regarding the Blót and virtue"

8) Bless the assembled Folk;   Fill the horn and bless the folk;

Face North and hold the horn up to the sky and say:

"We offer you this drink with honor, love and respect, o' wise All-Father!"

Now return some of the horn's contents to the Hlaut Boli. Pass the horn around sunwise and allow each participant the opportunity to say something. After this is done, bless the folk with the yew sprig/twig (Hlautteinn) by dipping it into the liquid in the blessing bowl (Bowli) and then whisking each with it while intoning;

"Ek gebu thig Othinn's blessi, or, I give thee the blessing of Odin!"

9) Close the circle and beak the shield wall;

Face North and sprinkle the Stali/ Hörgr and intone;

Holy Father of Gods and Men, to you All-Father Odin do we freely give this sacrifice, (and a draught to Loki to keep your pledge true).

On this day (night), and all others which shall surely follow in our lives, we, your loyal sons, invoke thee Odin, that ye will walk with us and inspire us always with your love, wisdom and presence and that ye will always be known by the NorthFolk and that we NorthFolk will always know victory through you. May our ancient war cry always be heard; "Heil Odin!"

This rite is now done. Break the shield wall and depart with Odin's blessing.

Photo by Linda Cröwell

11
RITE OF THE ANCESTORS

1) THE CALLING AND RAISING THE SHIELD WALL/HAMMER HALLOWING:

Lo, to the North do I look, my gaze seeking far and wide. From this, my/our Odal Land, do I look North toward the Heimat, the ancient and holy ancestral lands of my Father's fathers! That from which our beloved lineage first took root. Engendered by our holy All-father Odin.

As in elder days of yore, I call out to thee oh mighty Odin! That ye and the holy host of Æsir and Vanir might join me/us this night/day, to enjoy my/our welcome, our hospitality and to bear witness to this holy work which we are about to wrought.

Facing North, perform the Hammer blessing:
Hammer í Nordri, helga vé thetta ok hindra alla illsku!

Next face East:
Hammer í Austri, helga vé thetta ok hindra alla illsku!

Next face South:
Hammer í Sudri, helga vé thetta ok hindra alla illsku!

Next face West:
Hammer í Vestri, helga vé thetta ok hindra alla illsku!

Facing North and looking overhead:
Hammer í Asgard, helga vé thetta ok hindra alla illsku!

Still facing North, and looking down at your feet/ground:
Hammer í Helheim, helga vé thetta ok hindra alla illsku!

Still facing North, and holding the Hammer straight out in front at chest level:
Hammer í Midgard, helga vé thetta ok hindra alla illsku!

2) OPEN THE CIRCLE

Facing North, assume the Elhaz (ᛉ) Stadha and recite this Galdr:

Heil ye holy Allfather Odin, keeper of the Runes, wisest of all Gods, Father of Gods and Folk of the Aryan Tribes, great God of the Æsir, God of royalty, God of battle, wisdom and war!
God of death and mysticism, Father of the slain, great Valhalla host, hold ye, the holy kindred, your sons and daughters of the North Folk. Mighty warrior God and wanderer of elder days, turn my/our heart(s) toward you, great and mighty Odin!

3) CONSECRATE THE STALLR/STALLI/HÖRGR

I consecrate and make holy to the service of Allfather Odin and the Æsir and Vanir, this alter! Banishing from it all wights and influences which are impure and unholy. May our hearts and minds in this holy place, likewise be consecrated.

4) THE SACRED FLAME

I light now the sacred flame of inspiration and cleansing. The first mystery and the final mercy. May it burn bright and long throughout all nine worlds and within the hearts and minds of our Folk!

5) THE READING

Elder Kin of ancient and noble blood, who survives yet this day, as ye ride the very flow of my/our life's essence. Dancing to the rhythm of my/our own heartbeat(s).

Calling out to me/us in voices which defy both reason and logic, though ever serene, thous't soothes my/our soul(s) as a parent doth its kinder! Though your names and faces have been claimed by the very recess of time's ebb and flow, alive well art thou in my memory, that which sprang forth from thee.

Never shall I forget thee, or thine gift so sacred! Nor my back to thee wilt I e'er turn.

6) THE INVOCATION: charging the Water/Mead:

From eldest Kin; Holy Allfather Odin, right down through every Aryan soul thereafter whose blood I/we bear throughout my/our being(s). Oh how I/we love thee, one and all!

Fated am I (are we), by the Norns' decree, to share your destiny and one day return whence I/we have come; the Folk Soul/memory of Valhalla.

That I/we may be worthy of such an honor, I/we fight this day and every day to keep your memory alive in both the hearts and minds of our Folk living and those who shall yet be born to live.

In this way and with my/our deeds, do I/we honor thee, oh majestic Nordic ancestors who hath entrusted me/us with thy sacred gift.

That the Gods, faith and Folk of my/our father's fathers shall not perish! Pour now your energy and blessings into this horn/drink, that I/we may grow closer to you (and to each other as we share it among ourselves).

7) THE SERMON
(Open to choice)

8) THE MÍNNI (memory drink) and the BLESSING:

Facing North, raise the horn up to the sky and say;
I/we offer you this drink with love, honor and the respect of your loyal descendant(s).

Now pour some of the horn's liquid into the Hlautboli. This done, begin the Mínni by saying a toast and thereafter allowing each of the assembled to do the same. The horn is passed in a sunwise/clockwise direction. Once the Mínni (memory drink) is done, perform the blessing...

Take up the Hlautboli and Hlaut tein (Bowli and Blessing twig/sprig) and then turn to face the assembled circle and in a sunwise direction dip the Hlauttein into the Hlaut and sprinkle each of the Folk while intoning; "I give you the blessing of our ancestors."

9) CLOSING THE CIRCLE:

Face North and sprinkle the Stali/Horgr and intone;

May you find me/us worthy to join you in that all holy place where the Folksoul doth reside, when the Gods gather me/us up to them. May I/we never bring shame to the gift which flows through my/our veins, that which you passed onto to me/us! Heil the holy ancestors and heil the Allfather Odin from whence we all descended. May our own descendants always know his glory...Heil Odin!!!

Empty the Hlautboli's contents to the North.

This Rite is now done. Break the shield wall or draw it in, and depart in Frith and Grith with all assembled, Folk and Gods.

12
RITE OF THE MARTYRS

1) THE HAMMER HALLOWING: the calling and raising the shield wall

Lo, to the north do I look, my gaze seeking far and wide. From this, my/our Othal Land, do I/we look north toward the Heimat, the ancient and holy ancestral lands of my father's fathers!

That from which my/our beloved lineage first took root. Engendered by our holy Allfather Odin.
As in elder days of yore, I call out to thee oh mighty Odin! That ye and the holy host of Æsir and Vanir might join me/us this night/day, to enjoy my/our welcome, my/our hospitality and to bear witness to this holy work I am/we are about to wrought..

Facing North, perform the Hammer blessing:
Hammer í Nordri, helga vé thetta ok hindra alla illsku!

Next face East:
Hammer í Austri, helga vé thetta ok hindra alla illsku!

Next face South:
Hammer í Sudri, helga vé thetta ok hindra alla illsku!

Next face West:
Hammer í Vestri, helga vé thetta ok hindra alla illsku!

Facing North and looking overhead:
Hammer í Asgard, helga vé thetta ok hindra alla illsku!

Still facing North, and looking down at your feet/ground:
Hammer í Helheim, helga vé thetta ok hindra alla illsku!

Still facing North, and holding the Hammer straight out in front at chest level:
Hammer í Midgard, helga vé thetta ok hindra alla illsku!

2) OPEN THE CIRCLE

Facing North, assume the Elhaz (ᛉ) Stadha and recite this Galdr:

Heil ye holy Allfather Odin, keeper of the Runes, wisest of all Gods, Father of Gods and Folk of the Aryan Tribes, great God of the Æsir, God of royalty, God of battle, wisdom and war!
God of death and mysticism, Father of the slain, great Valhalla host, hold ye, the holy kindred, your sons and daughters of the North Folk. Mighty warrior God and wanderer of elder days, turn my/our heart(s) toward you, great and mighty Odin!

3) CONSECRATE THE STALLR/STALLI OR HÖRGR

I consecrate and make holy to the service of Allfather Odin and the Æsir and Vanir, this Stallr/ Hörgr! Banishing from it and this sacred Vé, all wights and influences which are impure and unholy. May my/our heart(s) and mind(s) in this holy place, likewise be consecrated.

4) THE SACRED FLAME

Kindle now I, thee sacred flame of inspiration, cleansing and illumination. It is the first mystery and the final mercy. May it burn bright and long throughout all nine worlds and within the hearts and minds of our Folk!

The Martyrs' Mínni:

Well do I reckon and recount from memory's well,
those noble souls gathered up to the Gods.

Cold are their ashes, bare are their bones, though warm are their souls

beside the hearth of heroes in the halls of the Gods!
This day (night) do I sing your praise, as you ride through my mind, cheery and well honored in the Ancestors' Parade.
So many souls whose names are lost, I sing your praise no less.
For what may have befell our kind were it not for the noble deeds which led you to that place where Sunna e'er shines.
Still, there are those I recount by the names which I know, and so, I shall sing them for all to know;

Herman the Cherusci
Eirik the Red
Queen Sigrid
Guido von List
Adolf Hitler
George Lincoln Rockwell
Sveinbjörn Beinteinsson
Else Odinsdóttir Christensen
Robert Jay Mathews
Rudolf Hess
Gordon Kahl
Vicki Weaver
Sam Weaver
Joe Tommassi
Fritz Weitzel
Kathy Ainsworth
John Singer
Arthur Kirk
Joe "the Hammer" Rowan
Ian Stuart Donaldson
Baron Manfred von Richthofen
Jean Craig
J.E.B. Stuart
Jefferson Davis

Felix Alfarth*
Andreas Bauriedl*
Theodor Casella*
Wilhelm Ehrlich*
Martin Faust*
Anton Hechenberger*
Oskar Korner*
Karl Kuhn*
Karl Laforce*
Kurt Neubauer*
Claus von Pape*
Theodor von Der Pfordten*
Johann Rickmers*
Dr. Max Erwin von Scheubner-Richter*
Lorenz Ritter von Stransky*
Wilhelm Wolf*
Bobby Wayne Schmidt
H. Wolf Odinson Estacio
R. Animal Odinson Emery
Jost Turner
David E. Lane
Robert E. Lee
Nathan Bedford Forrest
Stonewall Jackson

...To all such brave souls of the Aryan Tribes do I sing this song of praise in memory of the way that you lived your lives with honor and loyalty in service to our Folk's survival and the courageous manner in which you faced death.

ᚻ_ᚻ_ᚻ

May I feast with thee one day in Valhalla, for, to the ways of honor and Aryan chivalry, Meine Ehre Heißt Treue, Für Immer ! (My honor is loyalty, forever!)

In Odin's name, Heil the Fallen Folk! Heil the Noble Martyrs, one and all!!!
And Heil Allfather Odin!

↑_↑_↑

This Rite is done. Frith and Grith to all assembled.

13
THE RITE OF SUMBEL

Sumbel (also Summel and Symbel), is the Rite of Formal Toasting. What we know about the structure of the Sumbel as it occurred in antiquity, comes to us from chapter fourteen of the Saga of Hákon the Good, in the Heimskringla and from the epic poem Beowulf. Both of these ancient accounts differ in their form from one another, albeit their function is a shared one.

The Sumbel of today is a combination of the two and functions adequately wherefore its very design and purpose are in regard.

Today's Sumbel is composed of at the least, three rounds;

The <u>First</u> round is called the '<u>Full</u>'. In days of yore, this round was dedicated to Allfather Odin. And so it remains so today among Fundamental Odinists. Though, any of the other Æsir or Vanir may appropriately be honored with this round, additionally.

The <u>Second</u> round is called the '<u>Bragafull</u>'. In the Saga of Hákon the Good, this round was dedicated to Njord and Frey for harvest and peace. Today, the second round is afforded to heroes, departed Kin and Kith and Ancestors.

The <u>Third</u> round is called the '<u>Minni</u>' (Memorial toast/drink). This round is called the Minni because in days of yore, it was the Ancestor's round. Today is has assumed the place of honoring people of personal significance to the toaster, be they living or departed.

Additional rounds may follow but bear in mind that it is considered poor taste to get drunk during the course of a Sumbel, and it is a bad reflection upon the person hosting or overseeing the Rite.

Mead is the traditional Drink, honey mead. Many traditionalists still employ it as Blót and Sumbel drink and sacrifice of choice. Others substitute with sparkling cider, apple or other fruit juice with honey mixed in. Myself, and other members of the SONS OF ODIN, 1519 Vinland Kindred, utilize water, for the most part. Sometimes, water and honey, or fruit juice and honey, but mostly just water. Think about it, water is the blood of Nerthus/Jörd (Mother Earth). It cleanses her of poisonous toxins. And it purifies our bodies as well. What could be more divine than consuming the very blood of Nerthus/ Jörd, cleansing our bodies and souls in our noble endeavor to commune with our Gods and ancestors?!! That, for me, is genuine spirituality and religion.

The formal etiquette for Sumbel progresses as thus;

1) <u>THE HAMMER HALLOWING: the calling and raising the shield wall</u>

Lo, to the north do I look, my gaze seeking far and wide. From this, my/our Othal Land, do I/we look north toward the Heimat, the ancient and holy ancestral lands of my father's fathers!

That from which my/our beloved lineage first took root. Engendered by our holy Allfather Odin.
As in elder days of yore, I call out to thee oh mighty Odin! That ye and the holy host of Æsir and Vanir might join me/us this night/day, to enjoy my/our welcome, my/our hospitality and to bear witness to this holy work I am/we are about to wrought..

Facing North, perform the Hammer blessing:
Hammer í Nordri, helga vé thetta ok hindra alla illsku!

Next face East:
Hammer í Austri, helga vé thetta ok hindra alla illsku!

Next face South:
Hammer í Sudri, helga vé thetta ok hindra alla illsku!

Next face West:
Hammer í Vestri, helga vé thetta ok hindra alla illsku!

Facing North and looking overhead:
Hammer í Asgard, helga vé thetta ok hindra alla illsku!

Still facing North, and looking down at your feet/ground:
Hammer í Helheim, helga vé thetta ok hindra alla illsku!

Still facing North, and holding the Hammer straight out in front at chest level:
Hammer í Midgard, helga vé thetta ok hindra alla illsku!

2) **OPEN THE CIRCLE**

Facing North, assume the Elhaz (ᛉ) Stadha and recite this Galdr:

Heil ye holy Allfather Odin, keeper of the Runes, wisest of all Gods, Father of Gods and Folk of the Aryan Tribes, great God of the Æsir, God of royalty, God of battle, wisdom and war!
God of death and mysticism, Father of the slain, great Valhalla host, hold ye, the holy kindred, your sons and daughters of the North Folk. Mighty warrior God and wanderer of elder days, turn my/our heart(s) toward you, great and mighty Odin!

3) **CONSECRATE THE STALLR/STALLI OR HÖRGR**

I consecrate and make holy to the service of Allfather Odin and the Æsir and Vanir, this Stallr/ Hörgr! Banishing from it and this sacred Vé, all wights and influences which are impure and unholy. May my/our heart(s) and mind(s) in this holy place, likewise be consecrated.

4) **THE SACRED FLAME**

Kindle now I, thee sacred flame of inspiration, cleansing and illumination. It is the first mystery and the final mercy. May it burn bright and long throughout all nine worlds and within the hearts and minds of our Folk!

5) The beakers and Drekjarhorn(s) will be on the Stalli/Hörgr prior to the Calling. The Gothi/Gythia will now consecrate with Hammer Sign, the beaker(s).

6) The horn bearer (Preferably a Gythja or esteemed Kinswoman in mixed company or a Gothi or Apprentice in male only attendance), will fill the horn(s) and hand it to the Gothi/Gythja who will begin the 'Full'/First round. The toasting continues in a sunwise/clockwise fashion. The format proceeds along as described earlier in this

writing. Upon culmination of the Mínni/Third round, the Gothi/Gythja declares the rite complete and closes as he/she would a Blot, with the circle's energy either being inhaled or broken. This concludes the Rite of Sumbel.

14
THOR'S HAMMER BLESSING
FOR PROTECTION OF VÉ

Facing North, perform the Hammer blessing:
"Hammer í Nordri, helga vé thetta ok hindra alla illsku."

Next face East:
"Hammer í Austri, helga vé thetta ok hindra alla illsku."

Next face South:
"Hammer í Sudri, helga vé thetta ok hindra alla illsku."

Next face West:
"Hammer í Vestri, helga vé thetta ok hindra alla illsku."

Facing North once more, hold the Hammer overhead and say:
"Hammer í Asgard, helga vé thetta ok hindra alla illsku."

Still facing North, hold the Hammer down and say:
"Hammer í Helheim, helga vé thetta ok hindra alla illsku."

Facing North and holding Hammer straight out in front at chest level:
Hammer í Midgard, helge vé thetta ok hindra alla ilsku!

Now, assume the Elhaz stadha with hammer in hand, and recite the following:
"May the mighty Hammer of Thor, protector of Asgard and Midgard consecrate this holy vé and protect those within from all harmful forces and negative and unholy wights."

Pause for 3 breaths/heartbeats and then continue with the following:
"Hail Thor, mighty thunderer. Son of Odin & Jord, husband of Sif, father of Modi, Magni & Thrud. Elder brother of the Sons of Odin! You who dwell in your great hall of Bilskirnir. Wielder of

the mighty hammer, Mjóllnir, who killed the giants Hrungnir, Geirrod, and Hymnir. He who brings the summer rains and protects the halls of Asgard. Warder of Mother Earth. Champion of man, hear my (our) words as I (we) invoke thee. I (we) call upon thee, oh mighty Thor, to ward this place and protect me (us) from all those who would do me (us) harm. Protect all who gather here, mighty brother of the holy Kindred!"

Now, beginning in the North, say;
"Hail Thor." Then in each of the following directions, East, South, West, over & under.

Conclude by reciting the following:
"This rite is done. I (we) thank thee mighty Thor, for your aide & protection. May your strength fill me (us) and this holy place. And may I/we too, become a worthy defender of Asgard and Midgard, of Gods, Folk and Vor Forn Siðr!"

15
RITE / CEREMONY OF CONSUMMATION AND CONSECRATION OF MARRIAGE

For Odinist Prisoner's and Their Spouses

As many of our incarcerated Folk may marry but are without conjugal visit privileges, this begs the query, "What about consummating/consecrating the marriage?"

While certainly the sacred/holy oaths/vows exchanged are obviously enough to serve this need, in addition to the State's formal and legal marriage ceremony, many, myself included, seek an alternative mode to consummate their sacred union.

The purpose of consummation exceeds both the scope of sexual gratification or the mission to procreate, albeit the latter is an obvious and desirable conclusion to the act, it is nowhere near the purpose in its entirety. The act of consummation itself merges the DNA (blood, via semen & saliva) of the two family lineages together, hence Clans, Tribes and Kindreds as well.

Norse Law has always afforded great respect to our women folk and therefore has provided that a bride has free choice in the man whom she will marry, (circa the Dane Law, early 13th century/per the Statute Laws portion). And (the Logretta) which also affords women the right to sue for divorce. The wife and children thereafter, (step children included) are entitled to benefit from the man's good name and reputation wherefore the marriage is made holy by consecration before the Gods, and whereby the man is an Aethling (good/noble man) as opposed to a Nithling (oath breaker/odious man). Furthermore, the man's station/rank within the Tribe, Clan and Kindred also are factors. The wife and children thereafter are entitled to claim the deceased husband's land, goods and equities.

The reasons for a consummated marriage under Norse Law are manifold and range from property rights and station within the community, to bringing about peace between two warring Clans and strengthening two lineages.

I offer the following Rite/Ceremony for those whom would seek an official Rite for this purpose. It is a simple, yet effective Rite/Ceremony and a byproduct of my own marriage to my wife.

<u>The Odinist Prisoner's portion of the Rite:</u>

Beginning in the North, the Hammer hallowing is performed to create a holy space conducive to the purpose of this Rite.

Facing North, raise the Hammer sign, or your Hammer and recite the following:

"Hammer í Nordri, Helge ve thetta ok hindra alla illska", (this means; hammer in the North, Sanctify this enclosure and prevent all evil things from entry")

Next, facing East repeat the phrase;
"Hammer í Austri, Helge ve thetta ok hindra alla illska".

Next, facing South and repeat the phrase;
"Hammer í Sudri, Helge ve thetta ok hindra alla illska".

Next, facing West;
"Hammer í Verstri, Helge ve thetta ok hindra alla illska".

Now, facing North once again, raise the Hammer/Hammersign overhead and say;
"Hammer í Über, í Asgard, Helge ve thetta ok hindra alla illska".

Now remain facing North and face the Hammer down. Earthward and say;
"Hammer í Ünter, í Helheim, Helge ve thetta ok hindra alla illska".

Having created a sacred enclosure to perform this Rite, you may proceed. Take up the wedding gift produced for the purpose of this rite, (My Kinsman Harvald Odinson, 1519-CGDC made me an amulet sized Thor's Hammer, hand carved from wood whereby the head of it is deep-set engraved.) The gift can be anything which the couple sees fit. A poem, a written and signed declaration, it may be something handmade, or purchased.

For the purpose of fluidity wherefore this rite is in regard, I will use the small Thor's Hammer as the article.

The Prisoner while facing North, will take up a sewing needle and make three pricks in the tip of a finger. With each of the three pricks, repeat the three names of Odin, Frigga and Freya.

Now take up the Hammer and bathe it in your blood while reciting the following,

> "Odin, Frigga, Freya and Thor, I call to thee to give thanks for the gift of love which you have blessed me with.
>
> Tyr and Var, I call to thee to bear witness to my oath of Troth to my wife/ husband, *speak spouse's name here.* That I act justly and honorably towards her/him and in the honoring of our sacred and holy union.
>
> Holy Var, may I be punished a thousand times over if ever I dishonor, or break my holy oath before the Gods I love!
>
> With this blood, the very life force of my Ancestors past and my Descendants yet unborn, do I consummate this noble marriage and vow I here to honor my wife/husband ever after!
>
> Hail the Æsir. Hail the Vanir. Hail the Ancestors and Hail the holy Folk. May they all benefit from this holy union."

Now, rather than breaking the holy circle/shield wall which you raised at the beginning of this rite, as one usually might with other rites. Instead, draw in its holiness into your entire being. Hold your arms out at your sides, fully extended and breathe in slowly and deeply. As you inhale, slowly bring your arms about until they are in front of you. Now bring your hands in toward your chest until your fingertips are lightly touching your solar plexus. As you hold your breath for a few heartbeats, allow your hands to cover the area of your heart. Let them rest there until you complete your exhalation.

This rite is now completed for your part. Send your spouse the Consecrated Thor's Hammer (or other item employed for this rite).

Next, the free-world spouse, once in receipt of the Sacred item, will perform the same ceremony. Though free-worlder may e l e c t to be a bit more elaborate in their ceremonial space thus employing candles, incense and appropriate music since such restrictions don't apply to them in their environment. Remember, as is the case with nearly everything, the more you invest into an endeavor, the more you will reap from it!

This Rite should be performed during the waxing moon, that is while the moon is becoming, not dissipating. And you should be mindful it may be performed in private and skyclad (nude), or it may be preformed in the presence of loved ones (Kin and Kith).

The sacred item consecrated will forever after become a family heirloom for future generations of both sides of your family. In the instance of employing a small Thor's Hammer as the item, it may be worn by the spouse, hung on the wall over the spouse's bed, placed in a hope Chest, even hung on the family Yule tree.

May the holy Gods bless your holy union as they have that of my wife and I.

16
THE DAILY MEDIATIONS

> Set honor in one eye and death in the other
> and I will look on both indifferently;
> for let the Gods so speed me, as I love
> the name of honor more than I fear death.
> - Shakespeare, Julius Caesar

1. At what point does one stop denying one's own existence, or more so, one's purpose in life? More again, when does one stop denying one's own true Gods... those of his/her own blood/ancestry?

   When one ceases one's denial of the laws of nature, ergo, Odin's Law, one shall then, and only then, begin to appreciate the delicate balance that is our human existence within the greater scheme of the universal law of nature, and thereafter, our divine purpose in accordance with Odin's Law. The Judaic-Christian's Bible declares to all that the meek shall inherit the earth. But such a proclamation defies both, the very laws of nature, as well as man's majesty, thus reducing him to an ignorant life form whose only purpose in life is to serve a Judaic god as a thrall (slave) and ultimately as fertilizer for the earth. More accurately the Bible should have stated; "The earth shall inherit the meek." For it is the laws of nature which demands that the weak fall while the strong rise. The meek shall inherit the earth???...Such an ignoble declaration is mere Zionist subterfuge designed to reduce the unsuspecting to a herd of docile cattle (Goyim), to be easily led to the slaughter. The earth belongs to none!" Rather, Mother Jörd (Earth) is in the care of her Kinder (children). Where the meek/weak are in power, she suffers for their greed. And all who are disconnected from the wisdom of our ancestors are helping them to bring about our very demise.

2. The unworthy always exclude themselves - the Teaching of Heimdall

I tell you now; beware and remain cautious in the halls of fellowship... for weakness within our ranks poses the greatest threat to both our ancient way and our noble Folk! Self-accepted weakness often blinds its owner. Pride and ego prohibit such men and women from acknowledging this malady and thereafter setting about to correct thus. Rather, shame of such weaknesses and behavior associated therewith, should motivate one toward ridding one's self of such maladies. These may include substance addictions, fratricidal gang activity, lack of personal accountability, etc., etc., etc... While it is true, that to err is human - It is even more true, that to recognize such errors and thereafter, resolve to correct them, is to live like Gods!

More so, to take such measures not merely for one's own sake, but for the sake of serving Vor Forn Siðr (our Ancient Religion) and Folk, and in doing so with awareness... This is the providence of the Living Einherjar and the Code of the Trú Northern warrior. And as such, it is the teaching of Tyr. How many of us have known or witnessed such men whom don Odin's sacred symbols or tattoo them on their bodies without ever having subjected themselves to the very sacred initiations attached to them? How many have betrayed the sacred oath of the Valknut, by first putting it on their body or wearing it, and then one day deciding to quit following Vor Forn Siðr of Odinism (Our ancient religion of Odinism) and that such symbols are now just mere superstitions?

An oath made to Odin is an oath that one is bound by. And one way or another, he shall see that oath honored, this does he vow!...

> "A hall she saw standing far from the sun,
> on Nástrond* ;its doors look north;
> drops of poison fall in through the roof-vents,
> the hall is woven of serpent's spines.
> There she saw wading in turbid streams
> men who swore false oaths..."
> Voluspa 38 and 39

Allfather will make good on his vow. The Valknut is a true blood oath whereby its wearer has sworn an oath to serve Odin, his way and his Folk, both in life and death. When one dons the Valknut, he/she is telling Odin that in return for victory in facing life's challenges, I am prepared to be gathered up to Valhalla at any time that Odin sees fit! For those whom don this most sacred symbol without having performed the proper initiation, a myriad of hardships and difficulties shall arise and remain present in one's life until one correctly performs the initiation. For those whom have donned the sacred sign and then either disregarded it, or changed their mind...they shall surely lose their mind, or suffer a violent death and then be cast out by Allfather Odin, to dwell in Nástrond, in Hel's darkest quadrant...

" That I advise you secondly,
that you do not swear an oath unless it is truly kept;
terrible fate-bonds attach the oath tearer;
wretched is the pledge-criminal."
Sigrdrifumal 23

Such is the price such oath breakers shall pay for betraying the oath to serve Odin, his way and his Folk!

Nástrond (Corpse-strand)

3 Perseverance in the face of real adversity is the measure of genuine courage. So many seek to join the ranks of the Living Einherjar, the current incarnation of the Männerbünd of the Aryan Tribes; Yet most fall short by leaps and bounds once the journey becomes difficult. For no journey of self-realization is without its demons. How can one hope to face an enemy's onslaught when one turns and runs from one's own demons?

The desire, by most who aspire to join the Living Einherjar, is born of some romantic notion rather than an authentic sense of duty and call to service. Their true desire to "BE", is one of selfishness, whereas the true Einherjar harbors not a personal desire, but rather, an obedience to a call to serve something greater than self-interest. The "would be" aspirant hears only the call of a glory which serves only his own self-interest. But the true Einherjar hears the call of the Gjallarhorn. He is willing to persevere in the face of all, out of his sense of duty and his true conviction in his noble and sacred duty. All others fall by the wayside, unwilling to yield to reality yet!

4   If ever the Sons of the North would sit in his hall, then Trú must their hearts remain ever more. For little do men know about the nature of their being.

But Odin knows what lies in the Einherjar's heart and he sees all that they do. Even when others do not. It is not enough to possess the courage to do the right thing when others are watching. But to employ that courage to do right when no one is looking... That is the hallmark of the Living Einherjar! For it is just such noble souls who carry out that which the Norns decree and nature demands. Not for their own glory, but for the glory of that which they serve... Their Gods, Folk and the 14 WORDS! Such is the Trú way of the Northern Warrior; the Living Einherjar.

5   He is no true leader, that man who cannot lead himself first. A man who cannot command himself is not fit to command others! For many is the man who speaks in a fair manner though acts in false fashion. His deeds in action belie the very nobility of his words. Simply are they spoken, though more difficult are they to embrace for the man who talks North while he walks south. Better off are they whom speak fewer words, yet honor them in deed. For from such noble souls do the heroes arise...The leaders of the din of battle, those fit to command others in the host.

6   Know well his ways and stand Trú in them. For tested oft by him shall they be, those who don his sacred knot, the Living Einherjar. Know his words well, and know them true! For long and hard shall be the woe and misery for those who fail to read the runes aright. Many are the tests of Odin. And as such, these are not slights. They are opportunities for glory and victory. For the truly chosen ones know this truth well. And always they rise to the challenge with laughter in their eyes and a smile in their heart. Heil All-father Odin! For he blesses his sons and daughters while he blinds theNíthlings, those who falsely and wrongly wear the Valknut. For such wretched souls whom sought glory cheaply will never see the signs clearly. And woe

shall be their lot and for those who freely seek union with them, as well.

7   Long are the nights when the sons of men search the heavens for answers. Craning their necks skyward, they take in the stars enchantment...waiting. Always waiting for an answer not forthcoming. But short and straight is the journey for the sons and daughters of Odin, Kinder of the Gods. For the answers which they seek vex them not. They know to look within, for that is where divinity resides. The way of the Northern Warrior is to return to the place where his/her soul dwelt prior to his/her physical birth. That is, the Folksoul that is the Gods. And to the very first thought, which is Odin himself. In such a return does one achieve a divine union with Allfather Odin. The Rune of Mannaz (ᛗ) is realized. Such is the purpose of those whose line began with the Gods...The sons and daughters of the Aryan Tribes.

8   To be able to distinguish what is truly essential from what is not. What is important from what is not. What is germane, from what is not, is an essential component in achieving genuine peace of mind. And in acquiring such a quality, one may better fulfill one's purpose. For the Living Einherjar courage is ever needed and thereafter, conviction in that which we serve... our purpose. Without the quality of peace of mind, our purpose may lack the needed conviction to sustain our focus. Thereafter, our meditations become less than clear. Ever needful is the might which accompanies rectitude. The peace of mind which accompanies our sacred and ordained mission to serve something higher than ourselves...The Gods, Folk and the 14 WORDS. For that is what is essential, truly important. And such a realization may afford the Einherjar peace of mind.

9   Place thy troth in Gods of your own blood. From foreign gods, no good can come for the people of the Aryan Tribes. Long have many a lost soul wandered about devoid of aim and purpose. Like some half dead form of life moving about in Ginnungagap, the great abyss, all the while groping in the perfect darkness for something to anchor themselves to. There, in their lack of belief in themselves, and born from an awful desperation to comprehend and know that which is truly divine, they have taken hold of the swarthy hand of a Bedouin god

from the Land of Semites. There, upon bent knees with outstretched arms reaching empyrean, they forsake their own divinity; the blood in their veins, and they call out to him in a beggar's tone, to the one who forbade them to eat of the fruit of knowledge and wisdom! And under penalty of his vengeful wrath, they cringe and cower. Having forsaken the Gods of their own blood without having thought twice about it, they now point their self-righteous and accusatory fingers at us, we who remain Trú! Smote as the damned by them for our having the strength and courage to boldly stand erect with pride in our Gods, our Folk and ourselves. Yet their indictment against us is as empty as their wandering souls are, always in search of a spirituality that is never any farther away from them than the blood which courses through their veins, and the voices of the ancestors and Gods which call out to them. In time, they shall all come to know an awful truth. For no heaven awaits them as they have been led to believe and so eagerly chose to trust in. You see, in a religion (Abrahamic/Semitic) where the chosen people of god are Jews... Only Jews shall benefit from such a theology.

Seek to know the Gods within, the Gods of our blood, and you shall always be richly rewarded with the truths of nature's law, the very will of Odin.

10. So few... Too few, are willing to assume the station of genuine leadership. Yet, so many are intent upon defaming those who are willing to sacrifice so much in service to others. For anyone who harbors designs of self-styled leadership always learn swiftly, of the taxing demands which await thee. For if such demands are disregarded, then one has merely assumed the station of a despot/tyrant, and nothing more! Corruption replaces genuine conviction and the sincere call to serve others. Of course, such corrupt souls never glean the reality of their own corruption. For such corruption creeps into their lives slowly, so that it begins to assume an erroneous quality of normalcy. One may not descry an error when such errors seem normal. It is only after the fact and in retrospect that one may glance back whence one has come, to see the reality of such errors. Only when one's self has broken free of the fetters of corruption may one clearly discern the very real and detrimental effects which such corruption had upon one's own welfare and

even more importantly, that of those he/she had sworn to serve! Let those among us whom answer the call to serve our Gods and Folk, refrain from pointing the accusatory finger at others, nor advocate their defamation. Rather, let us employ their errors as a compass, that we may avoid committing such errors ourselves. Let their poor aim serve to inspire us to make sure that we always hit the mark. Let us never contribute to the already damning lack of unity amongst our Folk, but instead, seek to establish rapport and unity with our Folk of the Aryan Tribes.

For this is a hallmark of genuine leadership and as such, this is what is ever needed in the character of new and meaningful leadership. If you would truly be of the Living Einherjar, then truly a leader you must become in service to our Gods and Folk! Slay the ego, save the id, suppress the urge for individual self-recognition and serve the needs of the 'all' which is our noble Folk. For therein lies the requisite for the success of our sacred mission.

11   Many are the Sagas and lore of the Aryan Tribes. Many too, are the corruptions of them by those whom serve foreign gods.

Certainly great wisdom awaits the student and seeker upon the Northern Road, in the many volumes of sagas, myths and lore. However, great slants and influences of Bedouin faith have been inserted within many of them to serve such ends as was intended in some instances, while in others, it was merely an inevitable, albeit innocent occurrence at the hands of Christian educated chroniclers. Yet, within these many texts, great and hidden runa remain, awaiting discovery. It then becomes a matter of great care and importance to bear this in mind while perusing these volumes. Proper meditation and communication with our Gods prior to your studies should help you navigate your way through the murky waters that is our corpus of sagas, myths and lore. That you may successfully discern what is Trú from Vor Forn Sið and what is from foreign influences.

All becomes a mandate on the wondrous journey North.

12   Thralldom may be measured by how much self-command one has forfeited at the altar of self-accepted weakness, vice and

addictive behaviors. Even more so, by how little one is willing to do in an effort to eradicate such pernicious behaviors and correct such voluntary enslavement.

Once, is a mistake, while twice becomes a habit. Such is the simple nature of truth. We have all made errors in our lives. But as Allfather Odin informs us in Hávamál 133; "...no man is so good that he has no blemish, nor so bad that he can't succeed at something." If one would be free within, then one must slay the dragons which threaten to rob one's soul of such freedom. That which holds one down or back, will not depart one's life of its own volition! But rather, such an agent of sorrow shall wish to reside in one's life as a permanent guest when left to its own device. One must consciously own the effort to wrest back control over one's own affairs by exercising self-discipline and will!

Such command of one self is a requisite for any/all Living Einherjar.

13 The truth is 'always' the truth. Not simply when it seems to work for, or fit the desires of our ego or vanity. Those Trú to this wisdom, advance, while the mere dabblers 'mouth smith' many words which they pander, albeit fail to live by and therefore fail to truly believe in themselves. Though this does not stop them from forming, or offering an opinion which they are not qualified to offer. They may learn to mimic, memorize and recite truths, but their actions and failure to abide by those truths render them empty and of no account when and where they escape their lips. Before the alter of experience they are moot. For one who lacks both genuine conviction and the self-discipline to abide by it, his/her ego shall never serve them well, let alone anyone else. Ah, but one's fault is another's virtue within his/her own heart. Seek not to assign fault to any other. Rather, seek inspiration from another's faults to correct your own. Let others weaknesses serve to fortify your own strengths. Let others doubt enrich your conviction. And let others lack of resolve serve your own will to hold fast to your own self-discipline.

14 Treason is what occurs when cowards trade courage and conviction away in order to save themselves! Such souls seek often to justify the myriad of weak reasons which they offer for

their cowardice. If they are able to secure a sympathetic audience, they themselves begin to believe their own lies as new truths.

The true Living Einherjar know that the Norns came to them while they were still in their cradles and sang to them/us, the song of their/our fate. Such a truth and realization affords solace, peace of mind and sureness as one moves through this world we color Midgard. True Einherjar shall not blanch in the face of adversity or sacred duty when the hosts and hordes of popular opinion call them monsters and seek to judge them as if they were peer to the holy Einherjar. The genuine Living Einherjar are peerless! When we are labeled ruthless and callous, we shall not capitulate before the rabble and the craven. NO!!! And we shall stand inexorably in service to the mission of the 14 WORDS as the very defenders of both Asgard and Midgard (Gods and Folk), secure in the knowledge that Valhalla beckons to us with the greatness which accompanies victory and the valiant heart! As for the wretched and craven traitors... Nástrond awaits their reception. Heil the day of the rope and heil the Lord of the Gallows... Heil Odin!

15   Conscience displaced will always make cowards out of otherwise courageous souls! The same may be asserted regarding unwarranted compassion or guilt. Such noble qualities of conscience and compassion become ignoble in the forum of war. Many great warriors, Tribes and Clans have perished from the face of Midgard due to their failure to heed this fundamental truth of nature and her laws regarding such affairs. One should never have any feelings of guilt or remorse, nor any misgivings wherefore the survival of oneself and one's race and Folk are concerned. Those souls whom cannot grasp this truth are weak and weakness only breeds greater weakness. If one is not willing to fight that which seeks the very destruction of one's Folk, culture and heritage, then such a soul does not deserve to live at all. Such are the laws of nature... Odin's Law.

This should not be taken to imply the promotion of acts of violence towards others. For it is no such license. However, if a foe seeks to act violently toward you, your family or your Folk, you then not only have a right to defend against such an attack.

You have a duty to do so with such extreme prejudice and even greater violence than your attacker employs, so as to set the loud and clear example to all others with designs to trespass against you with acts of violence, to reconsider their ill intentions. Approach us with peace and you shall pass by in peace.

16 "A man is what he honors." - an Odinist proverb

A meditative observation regarding religion; Religions are in fact places in which we anchor ourselves to. Perspectives from which we view life and our world as we seek to comprehend our place within it and the myriad of mysteries which surround our lives, from day to day. Gods are those voices and inspirations within each of us that guides us to those places which we have anchored ourselves to...religions. The myths, Folklore, culture and heritage of any indigenous people gives rise to that race's indigenous religion. Therefore, if one elects to honor a foreign religion and its god, one is then dishonoring that to which he/she owes his/her very existence to; one's myths, Folklore, culture, heritage... One's race!

17 The warrior is the mind. The discipline of the mind and then thereafter, the expression of said discipline through the exercise of that mind's will. When the mind is right, the warrior is right. When the mind is not right, the warrior is not right. One who would study the way of the Northern warrior; the Living Einherjar, must first study the way of the Aryan mind, one's own mind and the mind of man thereafter. For this is the way of the Living Einherjar. Furthermore, to conduct an honest survey of one's own mind and then connect with it - is to connect with Allfather Odin. To resource the mind's power and learn to exert one's will, is the way of Odin's warriors.

18 "Without the Gods, a soul wanders but is not free." - an Odinist proverb

To be free in the pursuit of one's purpose, one must follow the path which leads to the place where one dwelt prior to one's physical birth... The Folk soul/consciousness. An honest reverence for our ancestors and Gods, and communication with them will lead one to that sacred place and to the wisdom which awaits one there. For there one finds Mimir's Well, Urd's Well and the Well/Spring of Hvergelmir, where the journey of our kind began at the very will of Allfather Odin's bidding to "be"! All else follows. It is beneath the great Ash Tree Yggdrasil, which is rooted in the Nine Norse-Teutonic Worlds, that these three mighty ancestral wells are located, beneath its roots. It then is in the very recess of our Folk soul/consciousness and ancestral memories, that we may find the knowledge and wisdom contained within the waters (Laguz (ᛚ)) of these all sacred wells. By delving deeply into the waters of our primordial consciousness, we ascend the cosmic tree of life, Yggdrasil. For in such an ascension, we are able to follow the path which leads us to that holiest of places where we existed before we were born. Before we, as pure spiritual beings, devolved into carbon based physical life forms.

19 The Living Einherjar must always strive to adapt to life's circumstances and strange surroundings, while ever holding fast and true to one's convictions and reservations. If one cannot adhere to such a simple truth, one shall not achieve success at one's objective. As the old saying goes; "When in Rome, do as the Romans do." Many have taken this wisdom from our ancestors, as a license of sorts to engage in hedonistic or even odious behavior. Such thinking is not only pernicious, it is erroneous all together. First of all, no Odinist man or woman need require any such license in order to ease their conscience for their acts. Their own moral and noble cause and conscience shall ever be a faithful friend and compass as they wend their way North. Equally as important is the intended implication of the axiom in question.

When in Rome, do as the Romans do, comes to us from the example of the Vandals who sacked Rome in 455 CE. In order to achieve thus, it was essential for them to infiltrate the very city. For they could not simply lay siege to Rome by just walking up to her ramparts, arms in hand, without meeting any resistance, prior to achieving their intended objective. Therefore, Gaiseric, the Vandal Chieftain, had dispatched scouts to reconnoiter Rome's strengths and weaknesses. In order to achieve this, the Vandal scouts had reverted to acting like the Romans so as to fit in. Having been successful at their mission, they returned to Gaiseric with their report. The Vandal army/navy attacked from the sea with overwhelming success and Rome lay in ruin. While I cannot verify the authenticity of the correlation betwixt the old saying and the actuality of the Vandals' siege of Rome, the example serves the purpose for illuminating the paradigm at hand, just the same. For the lesson of primacy is this: One's effectiveness and/or success, lies in one's ability to adapt and overcome. Such are the teachings of Odin, Tyr and Thor.

20 Being and becoming... We "are", but yet, we seek to "be", as well. The process of being is always 'now'. While the process of <u>becoming</u> is the seed of potential, the hailstone of Hagalaz (ᚺ). To be one of the Living Einherjar, one must evermore experience this cycle of becoming, being, death, and becoming, being, death, over and over without end. Simply put, self-transformation on a continuum: "being and becoming". It is the constant state of struggle throughout the whole of our lives. Each day we awake in the realm of the previous day's 'being'. We then proceed to kill that being, sacrifice our self, to our self, in order to 'become' anew for this day. This is the divine process of the Einherjar, both living and in Valhalla. If we are truly blessed by our father, Odin, we are afforded an endless stream of struggle for which we may overcome in order to "become".

Where the weak moan and complain about such hardships, we embrace them with a wolf's knowing grin in our hearts. For in this place of 'becoming', we come to know genuine self-worth and our true and divine purpose within the scheme of natural order. Yes, indeed...the struggle brings victory to those strong enough to 'be' and yet intelligent enough to know that we must always strive to 'become'! Heil Odin!

21 It is an unfortunate truth, albeit a truth all the same, that the overwhelming majority of the living Einherjar are now, have been, or will be incarcerated for crimes, not against the laws of nature, but rather, the laws of man. To be certain, some of man's laws are indeed necessary in order to maintain a functioning healthy civilized society. However, to be equally as certain, all healthy societies within the parameters of western civilization have ceased to be long ago. Indeed, here in Vinland (the U.S.A. part), over 190 years ago! Many a crook preys upon society

with government license to do so and with little or no consequences at all when they are caught with their hand in the proverbial cookie jar, as it were. But since such types support the sick society of big and corrupt government, they may enjoy leave of prosecution for their errs, while those who resist (as our patriotic Fore fathers once had), are held accountable in an effort to minimize their threat to the sick establishment which forcibly killed off healthy Folkish society. But I declare to you all, live well by these ageless words, "Tu recht und scheue niemand!" (Do right and fear no one!). But where those do wrong to our Folk, without fear of society's police and courts, teach them well to fear us... Teach them well to fear Norse Law, the Laws of our Aryan Gods and Nature's decree!

While such Nithlings may enjoy some twisted privilege of being above sick society's laws, they <u>are not</u> above Odin's Law! This must all learn whom would have any contact with us. It falls to us, the Living Einherjar to enforce and carry out Odin's Law wherever his Folk/Kinder have been legitimately and deliberately harmed. **Do Not** take this as some license to harm innocents for your own satisfaction. But by the same rule of honor, do not seek to justify any excuse for allowing a genuine trespasser against our Folk to escape justice under Odin's Law. Heil Odin!

22
> "From his weapons on the open road
> no man should step one pace away;
> You don't know for certain when you're
> out on the road
> when you might have need of your spear."
> Odin's Law / Hávamál 38

The law of nature; Odin's Law, does not recognize the inferior and anti-nature laws of man which would separate the Living Einherjar from their weapons!

With wits and weapons shall the Living Einherjar tread forth upon Midgard in defense of our Gods and Folk. For this <u>is</u> the supreme Law of Odin. Today's "Spear", as it were, may be an AR-15, Ruger Mini-14, AK-47, Mossberg 12 gauge, S&W .38 Special, .357 Magnum, .44 Magnum, Colt M-1911 .45, etc., etc., etc.. Let any who would willfully trespass against our Folk and Odin's Law, be dealt with harshly as a foe of the Aryan Tribes. Extend neither mercy nor compassion to those who would seek to destroy our Gods and Folk. For this is nature's imperative, Allfather Odin's divine Law! And let not any among us feel pity, remorse or guilt over dealing with such ignoble fiends. They surely feel not toward us!

23   He is a fool, the one whom seeks the approval of others, wherefore the defense of himself, his family or his Folk hangs in the balance. Many are the corpse, which litter the plain of battle. Their bleached bones are a testament to their indecision in the theatre of war. A reminder to us all that nature's law does not always favor the most able or deserving warrior. But rather, those who do not hesitate! The theatre of battle may be the living room of your family's home at 3:00 a.m. in the form of an uninvited intruder. Or the parking garage outside of your place of business. At the ATM machine, the street in front of your home. Or it could be the gang warfare-combat zone which your once peaceful neighborhood has turned into! It could even be an attack against you in a prison environment.

Wherever it may be, hesitation could spell the end for you or your family. While empathy and compassion are noble qualities where they are warranted, those very qualities misplaced will make cowards out of otherwise courageous souls.

Just as much, invalid guilt is always a poor compass, it shall never point North! Better served are those without remorse wherefore duty and service in defense of our Gods, families and Folk are in regard. The voice of Odin is ever more the conscience of the true Living Einherjar. Heil Allfather Odin, And heil his true sons and daughters, those secure in their purpose, certain and confident of their lot in this life as the defenders of the mission of the 14 WORDS.

24   Let us consider nature's law, both fluid and inexorable. The elk on the plains, when confronted by the hunting wolf pack, will be swiftly separated from the herd and thereafter becomes the focus of the pack, if it hesitates for even the briefest moment. All else matters not beyond that moment of hesitation. For the elk, death now in the moment becomes inevitable. For the pack, they eat and live on to see another day. And so too must the

pack be fleet of foot if they would evade the hunter's shot. Likewise, the lone wolf, wandering the route alone, must remain ever vigilant and be quick to act in the face of danger to either him, or that which he serves.

Consideration of all available options is the hallmark of the wise. But too much consideration may quickly dull the sharp blade that is the mind, and thereafter, ill reason one's self into submission and capitulation. Such are the rigors of hesitation's firm grasp!

Odin's Law: "He should get up early, the man who means to take another's life or property; the slumbering wolf does not get the ham, nor the sleeping man victory." - Hávamál 58

25 The true warrior is always a warrior. That is to say; one must not simply believe it to be only necessary to think as a warrior when the battle is at hand. Rather, one must think as a warrior in all that one does. Whether one is meditating, gardening, or preparing a meal, one must think as a warrior. Many are the students of martial science, whom study and spar quite devoutly. But when the chaos of authentic battle confronts them, many are lost! All the years of devoted study to their martial discipline is of little or no assistance to them for their lack of "thinking" martial science and engagement in all that they do throughout the days of their lives. Sparring is fine, it keeps the body agile and the mind sharp. But it falls short in follow through urgency. The practice of mixed martial arts training and competition are a sound means for correcting such a malady. Even better yet is considering any and all combative scenarios on a continuum. It is a constant chess game, if you will, in one's mind. Always seeing and thinking in terms of three or four moves ahead. The Living Einherjar, if he can avoid unnecessary confrontation, he will be victorious towards the purpose of his service and being. If he can avoid physical combat in a confrontation with his honor intact, then he will be the victor. However, wherever physical employment of violence becomes necessary, one should engage one's enemy, with one's full force and without remorse. You see, the mind is the warrior! And when the mind is fluid and just, so too is the physical Einherjar.

26   When we consider the model of what may constitute that of an honorable Aryan warrior, we must consider those in our past whom possessed that quality of Aryan chivalry. For history teaches us when we pay heed to it. But honor arrives when we too become those very examples ourselves. Consider the example of Manfred von Richthofen, otherwise known to history as WWI Flying Ace from Germany, the Red Baron. His idea of battle was truly noble and beautiful, based upon the concept of Aryan Chivalry (Compassion and fair play "where" it is warranted), as opposed to wanton and unnecessary violence. Other such men are Otto Skorzeny, Robert J. Mathews and G. Gordon Liddy.

These men/warriors of Aryan phylum, are the very epitome of those warriors in command of their will, compassion, service to noble ideals and of course, chivalry. It then must become the task of every Living Einherjar to endeavor to make this quality of the noble elite, his own as well. To know when to be compassionate and when to be ruthless... Such a distinction is a hallmark of Aryan Chivalry and the Living Einherjar.

27   By serving our Folk and their spiritual welfare, we too are serving our Gods and the very will of All-Father Odin. Toward such ends, the Living Einherjar must pursue the mechanics of martial science and discipline and the study thereof. Every martial discipline that is available to the Living Einherjar should be considered. And at least one form should be mastered for employment. Fusion, of several disciplines is always advisable. Always remain fluid in your seeking of knowledge and the application of said knowledge regarding your martial discipline. Always remain aware, as awareness is the source of all wisdom. And always remain in motion, both physically and mentally. A hammer at rest is merely a weight, devoid of its own design and purpose. To fulfill its purpose and destiny, the hammer must remain in motion. The mind is the hammer! The physical exertion of the will, is the function of that hammer. To abide by our principal purpose as servants and defenders of our Gods and Folk, that is the way of the Living Einherjar...the Code of the Northern Warrior. There can be no spirituality, save for the means of defending that spirituality against all threats!

28   "The supreme form of courage is the one against the all." - An Odinist Proverb

The supreme form of courage is the <u>one</u> against the <u>all.</u> This too, is the very essence of the Living Einherjar's nature as "One-harriers", that is to say, the one/ones who fight alone. When one must fight, it would be nice to be accompanied by one's brothers-in-arms, for truly the Einherjar proper in Valhalla, prepare daily, for battle side by side with each other and our Gods, against Loki and his wretched lot at Ragnarok! At such a time, Odin's heroes shall exit Valhalla's 540 doors, shoulder to shoulder and 800 at a time. Off to Vigrid plain shall they wend to face Loki and his host of damned and dishonorable souls! However, where the Living Einherjar must, he shall stand alone against the ranks amassed against him. He shall face what the Norns have decreed shall be his fate/destiny. And he shall face what he must with courage, honor and rectitude in his heart. He shall hear loudly, the metal's song as his warrior ancestors clash and clang their weapons in Valhalla as they cheer him on in his noble and valiant deed! To bravely and boldly face one's foes, alone and vastly outnumbered if necessary. This is the way of Odin's true heroes.

Sometimes, that means that one must walk alone as well. Resigned to whatever one must face, alone. Even though one may be surrounded by others like him in appearance, it is the noble character and conviction to walk Trú North, which dictates their worthiness to walk with you, not how they look or what they say. But by their deeds. Where one has been blessed by the Gods to have another to stand with, he is truly rich. Where they are blessed with others of their metal and character, they are wealthy to be certain. But when one has only the Gods and the spirit of his ancestors to accompany him, he knows yet of his fortune and genuine wealth. For the promise of his descendants yet to come, he serves his natural purpose as defender of his Gods and Folk. And this he does alone if/when need be. Secure in his sound conviction of his service to something higher than himself. And certain in the knowledge that his lot in life has been preordained by both the Norns and Odin himself! Heil All-Father Odin! And Heil his heroes, the Living Einherjar!!!

29 Aggression unchallenged is aggression unleashed! In this, be certain. If you are attacked by another/others, do not expend valuable time seeking a reason for thus, in your head. For it is a moot issue. All that matters at such a place in time is war! The neutralization of the source of the attack. If such an encroachment against your safety/welfare, or that which you serve Gods, Folk & the 14 WORDS), is permitted to occur without defense and counter attack, it will be a betrayal to yourself and your honor. It will constitute a failure of your avowed duty to protect and defend that which you serve.

And it will invite further attacks against you and your cause. Odin's Law (the Law of Nature) dictates that where aggression is employed against us, even greater aggression shall be dispensed in response thereto, and without guilt or remorse. This is the Code of the Northern warrior, the Living Einherjar.

30 Regarding the virtue of strength; Perhaps it is when we are at our weakest, or feel most vulnerable, that we must be strongest. For if not, we may survive the moment and then think ourselves to be strong. Only to find out just how weak we have become whilst we had believed ourselves to be at our strongest. Such unkind realizations always arrive as the light fades to black! Better are we served daily by honing our fortitude, than to perish on the eve of genuine weakness. For, from this malady there is no recovery.

31 Courage, legitimate courage, is doing the things that need to be done, but that no one else wants to do. Honor, genuine honor, is doing those things when there is no one there to bear witness to your devotion and deeds.

Fret naught over fame won, my brothers... For our father Odin sees all that we do. And he shall reward each one of us accordingly.

32 We as a Race/Tribe/Folk, have been displaced in our own Odal lands (Home Countries), by our own penchant for disunity as a people and diplomacy toward those who would/do deny us our own living space, institutions and self determination to fulfill our own racial destiny. We must accept reality as it pertains to

Aryan man and resolve to correct the pernicious behavior. Say "NO!" to those who would seek our very destruction. Say to them; "Keep your hands off of our weapons and our women and keep your feet off of our land!" Place no allegiance in a ZOG Government of today. For no such government in existence at the time of this writing (2012 CE) is loyal or sympathetic to the enrichment, survival or advancement of the Aryan people. Our Race Is Our Nation, O.R.I.O.N.! This truth, must the Living Einherjar embrace in our service to the sacred mission of our father Odin; the Mission of the 14 WORDS.

33 So many today among us seek to assign the lack of Aryan advancement, to one of the eras of the past century and a half, as it were, as they apply to political programs in the western world. But politics are by-products of systematic constructs based upon the racial makeup of that system's people, or groups of mixed races, etc... More so, said group's culture and heritage. If more than one people/race comprises such a system, the system will eventually suffer a breakdown, as it contradicts the laws of nature. Such are the facts. When a people/race abandons its own ancestral traditions, rituals and culture, it too is forfeiting its own heritage and thereafter, and ultimately, its right and desire to live as a unique race. When the people of the Aryan tribes traded away the traditions of our ancestors and their (Our) Gods, for the new Judeo-Christian mono-god, they ushered in the "Wolf's Age;" and created all of the chaos which plagues our Folk today! As a rudimentary point, it is _not_ even necessary for an Aryan to actually espouse or believe in the traditions, myths and lore of our ancestors, as they are presented today. Just honoring such traditions is essential to keep the flame of ancestral memory alive! Fundamental Odinism is a "Living and Evolving" religion. To keep the ancestral traditions of millennia ago, alive today by honoring them. Of course, we also honor it by adding to it in a progressive and conducive fashion, in the same manner as Ørlög and Wyrd are comprised of many primal layers of the deeds of our ancestors. It then falls upon us, the Living Einherjar, to keep the wolf at bay by ensuring that the traditions of our Aryan ancestors (not Judaic Zionists), not only survive, but advance to our posterity.

We must assume our sacred duty as the men and women whom comprise the very bulwark that shall deny Zionism any victory over our Folk! As we find ourselves at the edge of Idavoll Plain, we may spy the field of Vigrid and feel the bite of the icy mist of decadence as it prepares to let slip the minions of Loki's host from their fetters. We must not fail in our service to our Gods and Folk! The truly ancient ways of our ancestors are yet our best hope for victory. Vor Forn Siðr (Our Ancient Religion) is timeless. Its wisdom is applicable to our Folk throughout all epochs of time. If we study the Lore, myths, Sagas, traditions and rituals and apply the very truths within them to today, and add our own constructive element to them as our contribution to the Aryan phylum...victory shall be ours. And when our posterity gather around the hearths of millennia from now, they shall sing of the songs/sagas of us today, along with those of our own elder days gone by, which we defended and fought to advance and pass on to them. Heil Allfather Odin! And Heil the Gods and Folk which descended from his will to be! May we today, the Living Einherjar, 'will' that our descendants too shall be, for millennia yet to come. O.R.I.O.N.!

34 A life of activity suggests a life of purpose. So then, let our purpose be loudly clear...The 14 WORDS!!!

Let our activities be creative towards such ends. Let us become the very vassals of Odin's will, the very vanguard of this sacred duty to serve the greater good of our Gods and Folk. The defenders of blood which Odin himself has passed onto us, and yet lives within each one of us!
Let our holy endeavor be that it shall course through the veins of our posterity. For it is his divine will, and nothing so noble exists as serving his will, that we as a race/people, shall always be! Heil Odin!!!

35 Dogmas, doctrines and theologies are nothing but words. They <u>are</u> the constructs of man. And as such, they constitute mere words composed and structured into phrases and what appear to be witty axioms. <u>Thought</u> is the closest mortal quality to that which is divine. While the flesh/body is the farthest from it. While it is true, that words are born in the cradle of thought, they are yet just that; words based upon such thoughts.

Deed is truly divine. For it both mirrors and echoes the divine communication betwixt man and that which is divine. Words are empty of any volume or value if they are not substantiated with deeds. Conversely, deed does not require word in order to be realized. Self-transformation via gnosis and converting divine thought into noble actions/deeds. That is the true way of Odin. Membership within the ranks of the Living Einherjar in service to Odin, our Gods and our Folk, that is Vor Forn Siðr.

Meditation is the way to commune with Allfather Odin. Thought from said meditation is the fruit of that divine communication made manifest. Deed in concert with such communications are the divine will of Odin and the purpose of his progeny; The Folk of the Aryan Tribes.

36   It is a rudimentary Thew (principal) that any genuine Living Einherjar, or the candidate whom aspires thereto be, must be a student of history as it truly elapsed and existed, not as is more oft than not, erroneously presented, today. We must study its truths and lies, that we may come to know where and at what place in time and in history that certain lies became the new truths. We must seek to correct such lies and reveal them as such...

> "I advise you Loddfafnir, to take this advice,
> it will be useful if you learn it,
> do you good, if you have it:
> Where you recognize evil, speak out against it,
> and give no truces to your enemies."
> Odin, Hávamál 127

Our quest for historical facts must be traced all the way back to not only recorded history, but oral history as well. And when we seem to reach the journey's apex, we must call upon our ancestral memory, for there will we find the Hyperborean origin of our Allfather Odin, Yggdrasil and our first human Aryan ancestors; Ask and Embla. There will we find the truth of our nature and being, and of the very blood/DNA which flows through our veins. The origin of the Aryan Tribes. This we must teach our progeny and pass on to our posterity, for it contributes to a majestic and glorious past and a foundation which is worthy of respect and elicits honest pride and shall awaken the desire within our Folk to serve, defend and fight for our very survival and evolution back to that which we devolved from...a divine state of thought/mind and being.

37 We must pour over all available texts. We must seek out that knowledge which now seems obscure. We must retain that which is essential and thereafter seek to experience and apply said knowledge, thereby converting it into wisdom, and we must discount the non-essential and nonsensical and all which is contradictory to the Law of Odin (Laws of Nature) and the noble character of our Folk. Herein shall we find our father, Odin, speaking loudest to us.

38 As the Living Einherjar, we must not allow those who trespass against our Gods and Folk, to go unpunished, anymore so than the Catholic or Jewish religions respective security forces, would allow, nor that of the Islamic Jihadists! Let those who commit crimes of malice and violence against our Folk and Vor Forn Siðr of Odinism, be held fully accountable so that all would be trespassers will come to know... If you meet us with peace and honor, you shall pass by in peace (Frith) as well. But if your designs against us our ill-natured and malicious, you shall suffer the wrath of Hinn Hammar (The Hammer), and be held to answer for your crimes against us!

This is Odin's Law, and we, the Living Einherjar are his holy army of enforcers of that divine law. Heil Allfather Odin!

39 The only fingerprints which character leaves in its wake are the memories of one's deeds. The noble actions of the Einherjar are the indelible fingerprints left upon the very face of history for us today to employ as the very models of Aryan chivalry. A compass which always points North and guides us to heroic and noble deeds which benefit not our own egos, but rather, that which we serve;

"Our Gods, Folk and the 14 WORDS.

"Cattle die, Kinsmen die,
the self must also die;
I know one thing which never dies:
the reputation of each dead man."
- Odin, Hávamál 77

May our descendants recount our deeds one day with honor on their tongues.

40   Hold yourself up not to mockery, judgment, or sneers of lesser men who insist that they are your equal, peer or better. For such delusional souls are inferior to the Einherjar's superiority. From such men, praise for your selfless devotion and service to others will always be absent. In its place, you shall find only scorn, contempt, jealousy and envy in the hearts of such men! Be not dissuaded from your mission by such ill noble characters. Hold yourself accountable only to our posterity.

So long as even a single Einherjar lives, Ragnarok is stayed. Begin and end each day with this Galdr; "Ek Einherjar, ok Ek hinn Hammar!" (I am the one harrier, and I am the hammer)!

Let this be our mantra in service to the mission to our Gods, Folk and the 14 WORDS. Heil Allfather Odin! And Heil his holy warriors!!!

41   As stated previously in this work, genuine honor is doing the right thing when no one else is looking! As the Living Einherjar, we do not serve for the sake of praise. Rather, we do so in concert with the duty of the oath which each of us have sworn. The call which we have answered to serve and fill the ranks of Odin's holy army.

From those souls whom seek praise, fame and attention, do not seek companionship. For they will cloud your judgment, alter your divine purpose and rob you of your desire to serve honor, as opposed to ego!

Keep your feet on the road North my brothers and sisters and your hands upon the hilt of the sword named honor, and Wunjo

(ᚠ) (Frith & Harmony) will accompany your Ørlög and Hamingja.

The way to your destiny shall remain ever clear in both your heart and your mind. Such is the teaching of Baldur and the true cradle of renown fame awaiting thee!

Fara Með~ Oðin, minn broðirs, ok megi Goðanum blessi þig allur. Heil Alfaðir Oðin! Ok, Heil þig allur!

42 It is just amazing how easily our western civilized society, once the mightiest in the world, has succumbed to mediocrity and settled for inferiority. Talk about your anti-hero!

What was once a grand quest toward creating the übermensch which Nietzsche had unveiled to the mind of western thought, has been reduced today to a society plagued by a surplus of human waste, content on being the üntermenschen, instead!

I am reminded of Nietzsche's, "The Hammer Speaks", from Zarathustra... If destinies you would create, then you must become hard, he had written. Only the noblest is altogether hard.

Heil to the genuine Odinists, those who seek to become hard and create destinies! Heil Allfather Odin!

43 If one seeks to see the face of divinity in this mortal life span, then one must approach the Stalli (Alter) with such honesty that allows for one to empty one's mind of every active thought, image or preconceived notion. One must strip away and disregard all of the debris which one accrues; all negativity, all hate, all love, all emotional clutter. One must be fully present in the moment and approach the alter of life with a complete understanding that one may not slip through the veils and portals which separate worlds and dimensions, so long as they remain anchored to a myriad of social and emotional burdens. The Sál (Soul) must be naked and lighter than air itself. It must be pure and unfettered consciousness. All imbalances must yield to balance. All light must cede to darkness, and all darkness must turn in on itself and transform to create new light. In this place, this state of "Being", one "Becomes" the

Dagaz (ᛞ), the divine synthesizer of all bipolar energies.

Matter and anti-matter. Light and darkness. Positive and negative. Love and hate. Life and death. It is here that we meet and merge with all that is divine. We meet our beloved Gods unmasked! All lies perish beneath the crushing blow of Thor's mighty hammer of truth. Wisdom flows freely as the dam of ignorance is violently destroyed. Zion crumbles back into the Bedouin sands whence it came. The shackles of thralldom slip loose to free the Aryan soul!

Allow yourself to drown in the sea of wisdom, taste of Mimir's cool water. Sink to the bottom of his well that you may be born anew, free of all self-doubt, and imbued wholly with the divine spirit of Odin! Heil Odin!!!

44   I shall not reward disrespect with respect. Nor shall I address aggression with peace! I am not Gandhi, nor am I a man who disregards the supreme laws of nature in lieu for man's inferior laws of the land. If the laws of the land are in fact compatible with the laws of nature (i.e. the Gods), then I too shall abide by them; but where they take their leave from nature's wisdom, so too shall I disregard man's ignorance and remain true to natural order. For I am a heathen, a son of Odin! And hostile acts against myself, my Folk, or our sacred and indigenous way, must be avenged whenever and where ever they occur, or we have no right to "Be" at all. Such is the law of nature. Such is Odin's law... Heil Odin!

45   We have the best religion/way known to man! For it IS indigenous, it IS ancient and it IS a free Siðr (Way – Religion). While racial fundamental Odinism is not for all of our Folk, that is its very appeal. Not all may assume a place among the Living Einherjar, even if they exhibit an outward desire. Still, others are too weak or meek, to aspire at all. In which case, they are no genuine Odinist to begin with!

Odinism is, nevertheless, truly a 'free' religion/way. We are free to assemble and associate with those whom we desire to, and disregard the rest while maintaining a state of Frith when and where it is warranted with others whom follow the way/religion in some form.

Anyone who is not seeking to serve the Gods, Folk and Siðr of the Aryan Tribes and our posterity, when they owe their very existence to thus, is neither friend nor faithful of our sacred way!

46 It is easy for the soul of common character to be swept away within the mainstream rush of current events. What the uncommon soul must diligently consider is this; If this or that government representative, senator or agent is serving ZOG and Israel's interests, how then, may they serve the people of the Aryan Tribes, with any legitimacy? More so, why would they desire to? The honest answer, of course, is that they would not! Nor do they.

47 Respect and common considerate behavior are oft charged with the same quality these days. Actually, one is fused with, or superimposed over the other, thereby affording both the illusion of assuming similar quality. However, deference, as respect, is that courteous and considerate, albeit common enough gesture. Conversely, genuine respect is the quality of great esteem or high regard beyond the pale, or standard, if you will.

To respect others in command of admirable faculties is an appropriate gesture. But to respect oneself, I mean truly respect oneself, is indeed a noble virtue of its own accord. You understand that with genuine self-respect arrives an awful realization. That is, that the field of others worthy of your respect narrows considerably. Emphasis upon considerably!

48 Genuine Odinism/Wotanism, as all genuine heathen/pagan religions are, is rooted in the laws of natural order. Nature is no moralist; she neither recognizes nor affirms wrong or right. No good or evil, only chaos and order; balance and imbalance. All notions of right or wrong, or good and evil and the like, are derived from the human condition which we comprehend as morality. Of course, I am not making a case against the sound and orderly civility of morality whereby western civilization doth prosper and wax. I do however, find err in the over-zealous moralist, more oft than not, associated with the Abrahamic faiths. Their moral codes are in fact based entirely upon the allegation of Jesus' actual existence and the anti-natural concept of blind faith thereafter. With the likes of great and respected

historians and chroniclers of their time; Tacitus, Pliny the Elder and Herodotus, whom were all prolific writers whom were committed to great detail to which we may attest by perusing their many works left for us to study, no mention of the name of the Jewish Rabbi Jesus is mentioned. In fact, his name does not appear anywhere in history's annals prior to the first four books of the New Testament bible otherwise known as the Gospels of Jesus and his Apostles. But that's a meditation for another time.

Blind faith is merely a buzz word, or Zionist catch phrase which in reality translates to willed ignorance. Devoid of any legitimate facts, it is designed to rob man of his majesty, true purpose and his relationship with nature. No matter how civilized western society purports itself to be, the supreme truth yet remains inexorable...no law of man trumps nature's law!

Those 'whom' grasp this reality, fully espouse the most genuine of all moral codes. We call such souls heathens/pagans. A soul imbued with the audacity to honor something which he/she can actually see, feel and experience. A genuine spirituality, which fails to seek or require permission to live, and the courage to do so, without apology... This is the measure of a true heathen/pagan. It is certainly a requisite of any radical Fundamental Odinist/Wotanist.

49   The maxim; "The enemy of my enemy is my friend." does not hold true in all scenarios. Nor is it compatible with the reckoning of Odinist/Wotanist thews (virtues). I have heard some say that the perpetrators of the 911 attacks upon ZOG targets here in Vinland, are somehow our friend. This is ludicrous!

To begin with, one must consider the full breadth of those whom were responsible for said attacks, including those cloaked in red, white and blue as well as blue and white. Not merely Bedouin Muslim radicals! Next, let us survey those radical Muslims... they certainly are no friend to the "Aryan Devil", or our heathen and ''Infidel' religion of Odinism/Wotanism. As far as they are concerned, they'd desire to see our heathen heads severed from our bodies in the name of Allah, point blank reality!

The only commonality which we share with the radical Muslims, is an unabashed abhorrence for any and all Zionist Occupied Governments, which are those controlled by Israel and their Holocaust industry which they employ to extort billions of dollars annually, and their myth of six million which they apply to guilt otherwise healthy Aryan men and women into thralldom and acceptance of passive genocide of the people of the Aryan Tribes.

So then, while the enemy of my enemy may serve as a potential ally, one would be well served by holding in reserve, those whom one may willingly regard to be one's friend.

50   There is much to posit regarding the "dabblers" associated with our sacred religion/way. The ones who levy the claim that they are "real" Odinists; while they profess the merits and allure of Satanism. I tell you now that no part of Judeo-Christianity, inverted or otherwise, is compatible with any heathen/pagan religion/way, including Odinism/Wotanism. Nor is any such corrosive theology which seeks to hold the human soul in bondage, conducive to any genuine Odinist/Wotanist ideology. The mere suggestion by those whom would extol such hybrid teachings under the guise of some true quest for Oðinic wisdom, merely reduce themselves to the office of new age dabblers, no matter how intellectually gifted or academically endowed they may be. Truly Hermetic, they are not. And yet, they suffer in their belief that they somehow are! And so shall those who adhere to such teachings.

51   Comprehension of the divine as it expresses itself within the scope of the multiverse of existence, occurs in various manifestations; numbers, colors, celestial bodies, symbolism, imagery and vibrations, to cite the most obvious. For those of us whose lineage belongs to the phylum of the Aryan Tribes, this all exists within the breadth of our collective myths, sciences, philosophies, architecture, and art and of course, our indigenous Gods (Goddesses included therewith.)

The vibrations are their voices which are expressed in the Runes (mysteries) and their Galdrar (songs), as the very echoes and reflections of natural order... nature's law writ large upon the Folk soul/Folk consciousness. This divine energy rides (right

action & rhythmic motion i.e. Raido (ᚱ), the very stream (Laguz (ᛚ) of ancestral memory which exists within our blood and flows forth from the beginning of our racial line. It resonates from Allfather Odin's first thought and will to "Be", and his will that "we shall be!"
To this day it continues to resonate within each and every Aryan, whether they are able to grasp this or not. It exists. It then becomes our spiritual journey to reconnect with the Folk soul/Folk consciousness, so that we may come to know the truth of our Gods and appreciate the wisdom of Odin and the Runes (mysteries) within and without. And that this wisdom not be sought or coveted for merely selfish gain! But rather, selflessness and service to our Gods, Folk and ancient holy way as can be applied in the immediate sense of now. But more so, as well, in the future of our progeny; these very ideals must we defend and preserve for our posterity, at all expense. For this is the way of the Northern Warrior-Priest-Teacher. Heil Odin! Heil those true to his holy ways!

52 Noise pollution defined: The emanations of human waste, and then some! Opinions postulated while lacking in the experience thereof.

53 Courage defined is manifold. However, reduced to its rawest form, courage must be defined as an exercise in the power of one's will. Additionally so, will and courage are ever faithful companions. The vehicle in which they move about, are the men and women who possess noble character and the fuel which powers such character is called fortitude.

54 The myth of equality exists nowhere within the broad scope of nature, or the tapestry of natural order. Only man declares such a state of existence, with his inferior law which, for the moment, has usurped and supplanted that of nature. But sooner or later, as history has illustrated time and again, somewhere, men of superior nature, substance and character find the courage required to shrug off the shackles of political correctness and disregard that which is contrary to nature's law. And they respond with greatness and shed light upon nature's truths which weaker men had sought to keep concealed in darkness from seekers of the truth! Such men and women of superior nature and character have been hated in life by the

meek and the weak, albeit, they are revered in death by those whom their deeds had inspired. For such, seems to be the decree of nature in any society, which is so far removed from the superior and inexorable laws of nature.

55 An inflated ego serves none well, least of all its owner. Narcissism creates only deception and destruction.

56 Some willed action. That's what is called for when the state of nothingness has overstayed its welcome! If there is no wind to fill the sail and you desire to move the boat, you start rowing! That's what to do. The power of SOWILO (ᛋ), "Willed" action.

Ever are my thoughts my friend; ever are my dreams my foe! For my dreams entice me to lay down my weapons and take in the breadth of desire. Conversely, my thoughts advise me well to hold fast to my weapons as I wend my way across the plains of reality. So that I may always be prepared to slay any unwelcome intrusions upon fact and truth, which might otherwise blind my vision, dull my senses and thereafter deprive me of what is good in this life and what potential awaits those whom are fully grasping the sword named SOWILO (ᛋ),... Willed action is ever a sharp blade!

57 To sit entirely still, and move through time, but not space, and empty the mind of all thought. So truly divine! Within the Hugauga (mind's eye), the eye of Odin appears...the face of all the Gods and Goddesses are there, "Augenblick" (In the blink of an eye)! It steals one's breath and speeds the pulse. And if you let them have you, allow them to take you over, it will consume you wholly and fill you with the spirit divine.

58 Insatiable hunger and thirst for wisdom from Mimir's Well. Like a great beast deep within me, it emerges. It respects no limit, no bounds. It knows only the quest; the quest for ancient wisdom. The kind of Rúna (mysteries) which are revealed only to those whom are willing to pay the FEHU (ᚠ)/fee. For twenty-three days now I have been completely silent, not a single word spoken. Twenty-three days have purchased me a small albeit precious drink of the cool pure water from memory's Well.

59 If the source of all wisdom is awareness itself, then one must be present in the very moment in order to exercise awareness. Additionally, in order to access said state of fully conscious awareness, one must not only be present in the moment, but be fully submerged in the experience of the moment. Here, in the most sacred of places; the totally aware "NOW" moment, may one merge with the divine and the very wisdom which flows forth, therefrom. Here, one might meet Odin at the edge of Mimir's Well.

60 There is an ancient proverb which states; "Pain can be a source of illumination." To be sure, it led Allfather Odin to great wisdom. Pain is nature's way of letting us know that while something is wrong, we are still alive. And yet, pain is weakness leaving the body! It is the fortitude and courage to forge ahead through the pain. Such is the measure of genuine strength and the teaching of both Thor and Tyr. These two Gods epitomize in mythical writ, what it truly means to serve something noble and greater than one's own self interests.

I conclude for now with this quote; "If one does not work hard to earn the heritage, one will perish in the end, or at best hold the stirruups for those who are on their way up."
--the voice of a German Ancestor

Reyn til Rúna! (seek the mysteries!)

17
MEDITATIONS & MUSINGS

Fear naught the coming darkness, nor the voice within. Let the righteous light of noble deed and the order of self-discipline keep the dark agents of chaos at bay.

****

Let naught the wolf overtake the sun, nor moon. Let naught Fenris break free of his fetters. Let naught despair settle into your minds this night. And when the wolf doth break free, let courage be found residing in your hearts!

****

Life does not render unto any man, greatness. A man's own noble character does.

****

Do not capitulate to the minions of honor's theft! For they cannot wrest this gift from the Gods, from thy soul; only thou may forfeit that which your mighty ancestor's hath passed onto thee. With your life's risk, hold fast and dear to your heart this gift of honor. For a life devoid of this gift is merely slavery, perhaps even, existence at best!

****

Any self-proclaimed warrior can face death while in the host with others... But the truly extraordinary ones embrace it equally alone. We call them Einherjar.

****

I have experienced normalcy and I have rejected the entire experience! For it is the normalcy of contemporary man that has sought to eradicate the very Gods which have taught me how to love life and myself.

****

Only your Kin and Kith may betray you. From your foes you expect it.

****

If we did not feel so inspired as to seek out the warmth of the sun in those rare and unusual places which afford us such serendipitous joys, we would all but stumble about blindly in the darkness until we finally froze in the cold and lonely shadows of the uninspired.

****

A man is judged by men of honor, by his own deeds of honor: or lack thereof. Not by the libel and slander of his character assassins, that which they seek to assign to him. As for such ill noble characters of poison pens and toxic mouths, their league of allegiance is limited to the small and simple minded...the easily duped!

****

Flatulence is the language of assholes the entire world over - it is up to each of us to rise above their stench.

****

If struggle, controversy and hardship are absent from your life...surely you must be dead inside and therefore, incapable of growth.

****

Beware of those who favor only the sunshine's warmth. For they hath grown complacent and their honor suffers wantonly for it.

****

If we fail to escape the bonds of complacency, how then shall we ever hope to bask in the radiance of divinity?

****

People are only by-products of their environments if they lack the fortitude and conviction to live like Gods. Rectitude is ever an attractive quality to those in possession of genuine character.

****

What terror awaits just beyond the shadow's edge? What horrors, that repel so many, yet attract so few...those bold enough to cross from the light into the dark and seize what nature has promised? It is there, lurking just beyond the shadows, the balance of those who abide by the laws of natural order.

****

By what measure might we calibrate the strength of a man's character, if not initially by the iron bond of his word?

****

If gray is made of black and white, and darkness is devoid of any guiding light...then which is the way that shall lead us back to a world that is bright?

****

Let no man become overconfident in his bearing that he fails to remain ever vigilant and prepared to battle the forces of chaos amassed against him. For they offer neither truce nor reprieve.

****

Sympathy, the thing itself, is always coveted by the undeserving. For those souls whom warrant it, seldom desire it.

****

There is no wrong way to do the right thing.

****

Life is simple. You make choices and then you live with them, you don't look back and torment your soul with what may have been!

****

A cause devoid of genuine passion is empty, in fact. And therefore always in peril of being filled with whatever comes along to consume such emptiness.

****

Be naught a today without a morrow on the horizon, lest you wish to perish as yesterday's forgotten kin.

****

Mastery of a healthy self requires compatibility between one's virtues and one's actions. Whereby it is the natural inclination of strength to despise weakness, one must learn to evict that which is incompatible with the mastery of the self.

****

Is a ripple upon the quiet pond an intrusion on peace, or an assault upon stagnation?

****

Every hour wounds, but the last one kills and none are exempt... A clear conscience is needed, for the final hour always arrives both unexpected and uninvited!

****

From foul waste often beauty is born; does the rose not begin its journey encapsulated in manure?

****

Without darkness we would not be able to comprehend the light. Order is born first of chaos, and with a delicate balance, a synthesizer, balancing in the chasm, 'we are'. And were it not so, this inexorable law of nature, then there would be nowhere, space nor time. Ergo, "we" too would cease to be.

****

Where one seeks to comprehend the nature of Rúna, one must first comprehend the nature of one's self?

****

Aspirations not acted upon, are merely failures kindly disguised.

****

Only through self-discipline can one come to know the power of will... And only through the will is triumph born.

****

In rumination, freedoms are born. The mind and soul achieve liberty, or thralldom.

****

On the wings of perseverance one may wend far. But with only a single oar in the water, the journey is short and ends in a tiring circle.

****

Confusion exists only in the absence of knowledge. Ignorance exists only where the desire for wisdom is dead. For experience teaches when we listen. Ah...But wisdom only arrives when we learn.

It is a noble virtue to be kind to your kin and kith. Albeit, more so, to be extremely cruel to your foes, and to offer them no truce.

****

To peer down is to view naught more than debris and despair. To gaze empyrean is to spy the heavens and the stars. But to look within is to behold the abyss; the whole of potential resides therein.

****

If we do not seek out the mysteries of life, we shall never know the purpose of our life.

****

The truly wise are never satisfied. Their thirst for knowledge respects no limit. Their appetite for wisdom is insatiable. Ergo, their lust for adventure is naught more than a means to an end... A vehicle in which they may arrive at their desired destination; the well of wisdom.

****

Self-forgiveness? That is when you abandon hope for a better yesterday. That is the only genuine self-forgiveness and naught else!

****

The inexperienced life is merely an existence.

****

The difference between the warrior and the victim is that the victim never strikes back.

****

One whom allows weakness to manifest within one's self without resistance is only inviting failure to be a permanent guest in one's life.
A grievous error..."my" grievous error, placing expectations far too high on others incapable of obtaining such an acceptable standard.

****

Nobility is not a birthright, such as we are led to believe. It is a character trait, defined by one's actions and conduct.

****

Once the battle has begun, there can be no surrender. And so there shall be none!

****

If the grass truly is greener on the other side, one still must mow it! Lest it become naught more than a garden of weeds.

****

Some lessons may not be taught. They must be experienced in order for one to comprehend them.

****

A league of honor will always attract honorable souls. But a circus only attracts clowns and children.

****

The colors of life are never so bright or vivid for those who merely notice them as they are for those who stop long enough to experience and enjoy them.

****

18
DAILY CHANTS / SONGS - DAGR GALDRAR

Oðin - Oðin - Oðin

Allfaðir,
hinn leið af mínn kyn,
Allfaðir,
hinn bjartur leið heim.
Allfaðir,
sigur kallar tíl mér.

Oðin - Oðin - Oðin

Allfaðir,
sjalfum ek vilja vita.
Allfaðir,
sannur tíl mínn fólk
Allfaðir,
lifað í mínn blóð.

Oðin - Oðin - Oðin

Allfaðir,
í tími af friþ eða hild.
Allfaðir,
ek hröpt á hinn tré.
Allfaðir,
Alltaf, ek ganga með þig.

Oðin - Oðin - Oðin

*

Odin - Odin - Odin

Allfather,
the way of my ancestors.
Allfather,
the clearest path home.
Allfather,
victory calls to me.

Odin - Odin - Odin

Allfather,
myself I will know.
Allfather,
true to my Folk.
Allfather,
lives in my blood.

Odin - Odin - Odin

Allfather,
in time of peace or war.
Allfather,
I hang on the tree.
Allfather,
always, I walk with thee.

Odin - Odin – Odin

*

Wotan - Wotan – Wotan

Allvater,
der weg von meine vorfahren.
Allvater,
der klaren weg heim.
Allvater,
sieg rufen zu mir.

Wotan - Wotan - Wotan

Allvater,
meinselbst Ich wille wissen.
Allvater,
treu zu meine Folk.
Allvater,
leben im meine blut.

Wotan - Wotan - Wotan

Allvater,
im zeit von frieden oder krieg.
Allvater,
Ich hängen auf die baum.
Allvater,
Immer, Ich gehen mit du.

Wotan - Wotan – Wotan

"Kallar tíl Oðinn"

Ávallt nálaegur mér ok aldrei langt.
Fresla mínn hugur af óvinur fang.
Fresla mínn hjarta af allur hraeðsla.
Fresla mínn sál af allur efi.
þessi dag ok alltof, ganga með mér,
Allfaðir Oðinn!

ᚠ - ᚠ - ᚠ

"Call to Odin"
Always near me never far.
Free my mind of foes'
fetters.
Free my heart of all
fear.
Free my soul of all
doubt.
This day and always, walk with me,
Allfather Odin!

ᚠ - ᚠ - ᚠ

"Ruf zu Wotan"
Immer nah mich und niemals weit.
Frei mein verstand von feinden
ketten.
Frei mein herz von alles furcht.
Frei mein geist von alles
zweifel.
Dieser tag und immer, gehen mit
mir,
Allvater Wotan!

ᚠ - ᚠ - ᚠ

19
INVOCATION TO ODIN

Lo, to the North do I look, loyal to you,
Allfather Odin!
Father of the holy host, Gods and Folk
Of the Aryan Tribes.
Thou hath freed my mind, touched my heart
And awakened my soul.
Ye whom hung upon the mighty Ash, Yggdrasill,
and plunged deep into Mim's Well thine eye;
have taught me best to embrace my own
destiny.

Ye whom found me along the route, naked
And soulless as a wooden man.
Thoust cloaked me in thine garb divine,
Wealth did I gain, wise did I grow!
Thine gift I earn daily, in service to thee,
To both Gods and Folk and VorForn Siðr…
e'er Trú and always grateful,
I give praise and great honor to thee
Oh August Sage, great Allfather Odin!

Odin heil, Heil Odin!!!

20
INVOCATION TO THOR

Lo, to the east do I face, upright and Trú!
I call out to thee oh mighty Thor!
Defender of Asgard and Midgard,
    whose very example has taught me to wield my own
    mighty hammer and join in the defense of my Gods and Folk!
From you, elder brother, have I learned what true strength is;
Strength to do what is right.
Strength to stand alone against overwhelming odds.
Strength to weather the worst of storms.
Strength to overcome all that would oppose my evolution and that of our Folk.
Strength to defend my Gods and Folk against all who
would trespass against us.
I give praise to thy name oh great son of Odin.

Heil Thor!

21
THE HAMMERSIGN

To make the Hammersign, begin by making a clenched fist with your (right) Hammerhand, and touch your forehead with it while invoking the name of "ODIN". Now bring the fist straight down to the center of your chest and invoke the name of "BALDER". Now move your fist to the left shoulder and invoke the name of either

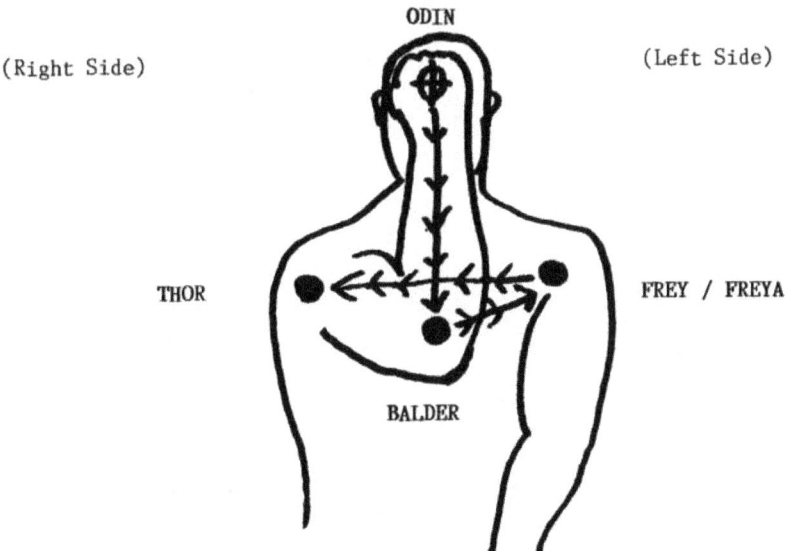

"FREY", or "FREYA". To

complete the Hammersign, move your fist to your right shoulder and invoke the name of "THOR".

Thor's Hammer is a powerful Norse-Teutonic symbol for the Folk of the Aryan Tribes. It is a reminder to us all that we alone wield the might to defeat chaotic and pernicious forces in our lives. And that like our elder brother Thor, whom smashes the Jötunns/Etins (Forces of Chaos), with his mighty Hammer Mjöllnir, we too may defeat those negative forces and influences which would seek the failure and demise of ourselves, our Folk and Vor Forn Siðr (Our Ancient Way/Religion)! As it is a divine symbol of destruction of those who would seek to trespass against us; it too is a sign of awesome power and fertility. So we employ this powerful sign to ward off weakness, bless goodness and strength and to consecrate all that we touch/bless with it.

Draw in its power when you awake, bless your food and drink with it prior to consumption, send your loved Kin and Kith on their way when you part from them, that they may be protected and reminded that they too have the power and will to wield the Hammer of self-rule and fortitude in their own lives. And prior to going to sleep at night, invoke the mighty Hammersign. It is
a divine gift from our beloved Gods, and especially Thor, with which we may remind ourselves daily and in times of stress and hardship, that we are both the Hammer wielders and the Hammer itself, charged with the sacred duty to wax in strength and will and to employ said might in service and defense of our Folk, Gods and our ancient holy way.

HEIL THOR!

22
RUNIC HALF MONTHS

ᛇ Eiwaz - 28, Yule (Dec.) to 12, Snowmoon (Jan)

ᛈ Perthro - 13-27, Snowmoon

ᛉ Elhaz - 28, Snowmoon to 11, Horning (Feb)

ᛋ Sowilo - 12-26, Horning

ᛏ Tiwaz - 27, Horning to 13, Lenting (Mar)

ᛒ BerKano - 14-19, Lenting

ᛖ Ehwaz - 20, Lenting to 13, Ostara (Apr)

ᛗ Mannaz - 14-28, Ostara

ᛚ Laguz - 29, Ostara to 13, Merrymoon (May)

ᛜ Ingwaz - 14-28, Merrymoon

ᛞ Dagaz - 29, Merrymoon to 13, Midyear (Jun)

ᛟ Othala - 14-28, Midyear

ᚠ Fehu - 29, Midyear to 13, Haymoon (Jul)

ᚢ Uruz - 14-28, Haymoon

þ Thurisaz - 29, Haymoon to 12, Harvest (Aug)

ᚨ Ansuz - 13-28, Harvest

ᚱ Raido - 29, Harvest to 12, Shedding (Sept)

ᚲ Kenaz - 13-27, Shedding

ᚷ Gebo - 28, Shedding to 12, Hunting (Oct)

ᚹ Wunjo - 13-27, Hunting

ᚺ Hagalaz - 28, Hunting to 12, Fogmoon (Nov)

ᚾ Nauthiz - 13-27, Fogmoon

ᛁ Isa - 28, Fogmoon to 12, Yule (Dec)

ᛄ Jera - 13-27, Yule

23
MONTHS/MOONS

January	Snowmoon
February	Horning
March	Lenting
April	Ostara
May	Merrymoon
June	Midyear / Fallow
July	Haymoon
August	Harvest
September	Shedding
October	Hunting
November	Fogmoon
December	Wolfmoon and Yule

WEEKDAYS

	Norse		Teutonic
Sunday	Sunnasdagr	or	Sunnastag
Monday	Manisdagr	or	Manistag
Tuesday	Tyrsdagr	or	Tyrstag
Wednesday	Odinsdagr	or	Odinstag
Thursday	Thorsdagr	or	Thorsstag
Friday	Friggasdagr	or	Friggastag
Saturday	Laugardagr	or	Waschentag

24
THE HOLY YEAR & DAYS OF REMEMBRANCE
FOR HEROES AND MARTYRS

JANUARY / SNOWMOON
9th - Raud the Strong - Day of remembrance
14th - Robert Jay Mathews - Day of remembrance (RJM's birthday is the 16th)
21st - Thor's Blót

FEBRUARY / HORNING
2nd - Charming of the Plow
9th - Eyvind Kinnrifi - Day of remembrance
14th - Guido von List - Day of remembrance
14th – Feast of Vali

MARCH / LENTING
9th - Olvir the Martyr - Day of remembrance
14th - Sveinbjörn Beinteinsson - Day of remembrance
20th/21st -- OSTARA: Summer Finding (Spring Equinox) Usually falls on the 20th or 21st, with exception
28th -- Ragnar Lodbrok - Day of remembrance

APRIL / OSTARA
9th - Jarl Hakon - Day of remembrance
14th – SUMMARSDAG (SigrBlót – Major 1519 Blót)
14th - Rudolf Hess - Day of remembrance (birthday is the 26th)
20th - ADOLF HITLER'S BIRTHDAY

MAY / MERRYMOON
1st – May Day
9th – Guthroth - Day of remembrance
14th - ELSE CHRISTENSEN'S - DAY OF REMEMBRANCE (Entered Valhalla 5/4/05 CE)

JUNE / MIDYEAR/FALLOW
8th - Lindisfarne Day
9th - Sigurd the Volsung - Day of remembrance
14th - Ian Stuart Donaldson - Day of remembrance
20th/21st - MIDSUMMER: (Summer Solstice) Usually falls on the 20th or 21st with exception

JULY / HAYMOON
4th – Founder's Day
(The 4th of this month is internationally known as 'Founder's Day', wherefore the Religions of Odinism/Wotanism and Ásatrú are in regard)
9th - Unn the Deep Minded - Day of remembrance
14th - Vicki & Sammy Weaver - Day of remembrance

AUGUST / HARVEST
1st - This day is sacred to Allfather Odin & Allmother Frigga
9th - King Radbod of Frisia - Day of remembrance
14th - George Lincoln Rockwell - Day of remembrance
17th – 25th – 9 Nights of Odin's Ordeal (1519) Major Tide
28th - Freyfaxi

SEPTEMBER / SHEDDING
9th - Herman the Cherusci - Day of remembrance
14th - Jost Turner - Day of remembrance
20th/21st -WINTER FINDING (Fall Equinox) Usually falls on the 20th or 21st with exception

OCTOBER / HUNTING
8th - Eirik the Red - Day of remembrance
9th - Leif Eiriksson - Day of remembrance
11th/17th - VETURNAETUR: Winter Nights. Disa Blót (1519 Major Blót)
Occurs on both Sat. & Sun. which begins on the first Saturday between the 11th & 17th
14th - Kathy Ainsworth - Day of remembrance

NOVEMBER / FOGMOON
9th - Queen Sigrith - Day of remembrance
11th - FEAST OF THE EINHERJAR and 1519 (1519 major Blót)
14th - David Lane - Day of remembrance (birthday is the 2nd)

DECEMBER / YULEMOON/WOLFMOON
8th – Martyrs Day
9th - Egil Skallagrimsson - Day of remembrance
14th Gordon Kahl - Day of remembrance
20th through 31st - YULETIDE: Twelve Days of Yule (1519 major Blótar Tide)
20th - Mother Night: Our New Year begins at sunset.
21st - MIDWINTER (Winter Solstice) Usually falls on 21st with exception (1519 major Blót) Midvinter Blót
31st - Twelfth Night

*** These dates constitute our Hof/Ministry's Holy Days of Blótar and Sacred Days of Remembrance. If you do not know the importance of these Rites, or who these Heroes and Martyrs are, then take the time to learn what they mean and who they are. They have all made significant contributions with how they lived and died.

Surely, selecting a few from the thousands worthy of our respect was not an easy process! Nor does this selection constitute the entire corpus of our Heroes and Martyrs. We could honor ten daily for one hundred years and not even begin to cite the myriad whom fill our Rolls of Honor.

25
14 CODES OF THE ARYAN ETHIC
BY DAVID LANE AND R. MCVAN

1. Honor no Gods but those of your own Folk, as alien gods destroy you.

2. Nature's laws evidence the divine plan, as the natural world is the work of Allfather Odin.

3. Act nobly and courageously, always carefully considering the consequences of your actions, as the effects of your deeds live on after you pass from Midgard.

4. Live within the reality of this life; fear not your fate, as fear is for fools and cowards; A valorous man boldly faces what the Norns decree.

5. Love, protect, reproduce and advance your Folk, as natural instinct prohibits miscegenation and self-destruction.

6. Be honest, be disciplined, be productive and loyal to friends, as the Aryan spirit strives for excellence in all things.

7. Treasure your history, heritage and racial identity, as your ancestors have entrusted it falls with you, it will rise with you.

8. Honor the memory of your kith and kin, especially those who have given their lives or freedom for the Folk, as your race lives on through your blood and your will.

9. Respect the wisdom of your elders, as every moment of your lives links the infinite past to the infinite future.

10   Honor your mate, provide for your children and carry no quarrel with family to sleep time, as family is your purpose and fulfillment.

11   May your word to a kinsman be a bond of steel, as your troth is your dignity and strength of character.

12   Be cunning as a fox with enemies and Nithlings, as their goal is your extinction, their motives are always detrimental to your wellbeing and that of the Folk's!

13   Secure, defend and cherish your Othal lands, as nature's territorial imperative demands.

14   Live in harmony with nature and the Folk and compromise not with evil, as racial survival is your perpetual struggle.

*Resist and defy always, that which you know to be wrong and detrimental to the welfare and advancement of our noble Folk.

Dr. Casper Odinson Cröwell, VFP 1488

26
THE ÆSIRIAN CODE OF NINE

1) The Code is to Honor

Honor yourself with truth and fairness. Your word is your bond, give your word power by adhering to it. Honor your family and friends with reverence and respect. Honor your love and the Way above all else. Honor is the mark of strength and nobility.

2) The Code is to Protect

Protect with savagery your blood and kin. Let no one or no thing violate your love or way. Let there always be inequity in defense. Always protect thrice as fiercely as one is attacked. Protection is the mark of a warrior spirit.

3) The Code is to Flourish

Prosperity and growth are key to the survival of the way. Such is the mark of intelligence.

4) The Code is Knowledge

Knowledge is power. Seek ever to expand the mind. Never stagnate, for knowledge is a gift from the Gods.

5) The Code is Change

Adapting and changing are important for growth and survival. That which cannot adapt or change is doomed to perish. Change is the mark of insight.

6) The Code is Fairness

Pay all debts, pull your own weight, always hear and consider all sides. Treat all others with equity and fairness. Expect the same.

7) The Code is Balance

Remember the Law of balance; all that which you do or wish for, good or ill, shall return to you one day. Strive for the good.

8) The Code is Control

Never lose control to anger or be baited by hostility. Never strike a woman unless your life hangs in the balance. Never violate the weak or innocent. Never tolerate those who do. Control is the mark of a disciplined mind, a sign of the greatest of warriors.

9) The Code is Conflict

Those who follow the way must know the art of combat, weapons and vengeance. War is part of the path. Always be prepared for hostility. It is a destiny woven into the fibers of our people. Keep body, mind and training up at all times. Have no remorse in the savagery of conflict. Win, prevail and survive.

Danish, circa 1075 runic era (825 common era), author unknown

Siðr = the Way/Religon

27
THE NINE NOBLE VIRTUES OF ODINISM

1. **COURAGE:** Boldness, bravery, standing up for what you believe in and know is right.

2. **HONESTY:** Truth - In all things be Trú to yourself and to others.

3. **HONOR:** Do as you say and act upon your convictions. "Always" honor your oaths!

4. **TROTH:** Loyalty to yourself, family, folk, friends and the Gods & Goddesses.

5. **STRENGTH:** Self-rule, self-mastery, the self-control and discipline to govern yourself by your convictions.

6. **HOSPITALITY:** To freely share your gifts with others.

7. **INDUSTRIOUSNESS:** To work wholeheartedly both hard and intelligently. To keep thinking and growing as a person.

8. **SELF RELIANCE:** Free standing. Rely on others as little as possible!

9. **PERSEVERANCE:** Don't give up at what you do until you feel it is completed and done well.

28
THE REDE OF HONOR FOR ODINISM

1. *In all that you do, always consider its benefit or harm upon yourself, your children and your folk.*

2. *All that which you do will return to you, sooner or later, for good or for ill. Thus strive always to do good to others, or at least strive always to be just.*

3. *Be honest with yourself, and with others, "This above all; to thine own self be trú."*

4. *Humankind, and especially your own family and folk, has the spark of divinity within it! Protect and nurture that spark.*

5. *Give your word sparingly and adhere to it like iron... Break no oath!*

6. *In life, your first trust and responsibility should always be to your own folk and people. Yet, be kind and proper to others when possible.*

7. *What you have, hold!*

8. *Pass on to others only those words which you have personally verified.*

9. *Be honest with others and let them know that you expect honesty in return.*

10. *The fury of the moment plays folly with the truth; to keep one's head is a virtue.*

11. *Know which battles should be fought, and which battles should be avoided. Also, know when to break off a conflict. There are times when the minions of chaos are simply too strong, or when fate is absolutely unavoidable.*

12. *When you gain power, use it carefully and use it well.*

13. *Courage and honor endure forever. Their echoes remain when the mountains have crumbled to dust.*
14. *Pledge friendship and your services to those who are worthy! Strengthen others of your people and they will strengthen you.*
15. *Love and care for your family always, and have the fierceness of a wolf in their protection.*
16. *Honor yourself, have pride in yourself, do your best and forgive yourself when you must.*
17. *Try always to be above reproach in the eyes of the world.*
18. *Those of your people should always endeavor to settle any differences among themselves quietly and peaceably.*
19. *If the laws of the land are beneficial to the folk and family, they should be obeyed.*
20. *Have pride in yourself, your family and your folk. They are your promise for the future.*
21. *Do not neglect your mate and children.*
22. *Every one of our people should work according to the best that he/she can do, no matter how small or great. We are all in this world together, thus we must always help each other along.*
23. *One advances individually and collectively only by living in harmony with the natural order of the world.*
24. *The seeking of wisdom is a high virtue. Love of truth, honor, courage and loyalty are the hallmarks of the noble soul, (Æthling).*
25. *Be prepared for whatever the future brings.*
26. *Life, with all its joys, struggles and ambiguities is to be embraced and lived to the fullest.*

*These are the Trú ways of conduct left to us by our Ancestors, strive to honor them and live them well. Place your feet on the path of the Æthling (Noble one), and spurn the ways of the Nithling (Coward, oath breaker, one whom embraces vice and treachery over virtue and honor).

29
THE CODE OF THE NORTHERN WARRIOR
THE LIVING EINHERJAR & 1519
By and/or compiled by Dr. Casper Odinson Cröwell, 1519-CCG

1. A man is what he honors.

2. The unworthy always exclude themselves.

3. The worst sickness for a warrior/wise man is to crave what he cannot have.

4. All men are not equal in wisdom or character. The half wise are many and
the ignoble are everywhere.

5. Mysteries should not be explained away, they should be experienced.

6. Pain can be a source of illumination.

7. The mind is the warrior. When the mind is right, the warrior is right. When the mind is not right, the warrior is not right…He who would follow the way of the warrior must first follow the way of the mind, for that is the warrior and the way of the Einherjar!

8. The supreme form of courage is the "one" against the all.

9. We cannot choose the terrors we must face in this life…but we can choose to face them calmly and with courage, for that is the Einherjar's grace.

10. Dishonor is anything which changes our nature or steals from us our soul.

11. Aggression unchallenged is aggression unleashed!

12. Only through self-discipline can one know the power of the will.

13. Tu recht und scheue niemand! / Do right and fear no one!

14. Independence is a privilege reserved for the strong.

15. Always be kind to your Kin & Kith…and extremely cruel to your foes.

16. Without the Gods, a soul wanders but is not free.

17. Confusion exists only in the absence of knowledge.

18. The warrior says goodbye to all he leaves behind.

19. To be free, one must follow the path that leads to the place where one dwelt before one was born, the collective Folk soul.

20. The Odinist believes that the soul is in the blood.

21. The difference between the victim and the warrior is that the victim never fights back.

22. It is not titles which honor men, but men who honor titles.

23. When the Einherjar steps back, it is only to leap forward.

24. Only noble men join an Order of honor for honor's sake!

25. A man is not fit to command others if he cannot first command himself.

26. In battle, never retreat before the enemy.

27. Never fight an unworthy foe unless he thrust himself upon you.

28. Once the battle has begun there can be no retreat and so there shall be none!

29. Nobility is not a birthright, it is a character trait.

30. What is done out of love, loyalty and duty, always occurs beyond the scope of good or evil!

31. Know which battles to fight, when to fight them and know when to walk away.

30
ELDER FUTHARK
The names & basic meanings of the runes

Fehu (fáy-hōō) - F - *Fehu* is the force, or energy, facilitated by the concept of mobile property (money), which in former times included such things as livestock. The essence of money is the power to transact (exchange it for something else of value) and in fehu we see this transactional energy extended across all realms of existence. However, just as money does no real work until it is spent, the power of fehu can stagnate, if not kept in motion (see G-rune).

Keywords: Money – Mobile Property – Fertility – Energy

Uruz (ōō-rōōz) - U - *Uruz* is the rune of vital strength - as embodied by the great, now extinct, aurochs   and of wild, formational forces as represented in mythology by the cosmic bovine Auðhumla. Uruz shapes and patterns through undomesticated organic forces, but it is the patterning force, not the pattern itself (see H-rune). Because of its power to shape, and the vital, primal energies involved in its interaction with the multiverse, uruz promotes strength and vitality in those systems which are naturally occurring (e.g. the human body, or the folk community).

Keywords: Vital Strength – Wisdom – Health – Organic organization

Thurisaz (thōō-rĭ-sôz) - th – *Thurisaz* is the force of directed active defense. We see reflected in thurisaz the power of Thor's weapon Mjöllnir - the protector of Asgard and Midgard. The power of thurisaz is antagonistic to all forces hostile to the cosmic order, and the energy of this rune is of great value in aiding the Gods and Goddesses in their struggle to maintain their various enclosures throughout the multiverse. Thurisaz breaks down barriers and is the vehicle of the destruction that must take place before new beginnings may come about.

Keywords: Active Defense - Applied Power - Action --- Destruction/Regeneration

 **Ansuz** (än-sōōz) – A – *Ansuz* is the rune of the magical rune-song (galdr) and divine inspiration (Odinic ecstasy). Ansuz describes the divine breath (önd), and inspiration (óðr) bestowed upon Ask and Embla by the triumvirate Odin-Vili-Vé. This energy of this rune is manifested in the inspired words of the skald as well as the ecstatic galdr of the vitki. Ansuz represents the magical potential of our Folk that is handed down genetically from one generation to the next and the power that links us to Odin - within and without.

Keywords: Divine Breath - Word Song - Odinic Ecstasy - Poetic/Magical Inspiration - Numinous Knowledge

 **Raido** (rī-thō) – R – *Raido* is the rune of right action and archetypal order. It embodies both the concept of the journey back to the way of right action (the path to the Gods) and that of the vehicle facilitating the journey. Raido is at the same time both the wagon and the road - the whole ride, as it were. Ritual workings involve the ordering of energies in accordance with right action and the power of raids is essential for such undertakings.

Keywords: Journey – Right Action - Cosmic Order – Ritual – Rhythmic Motion

 **Kenaz** (kĕ-nôz) –K – *Kenaz*: is the rune of the controlled fire of creativity. The ability to shape the fruits of inspiration and manifest them in the physical world is facilitated by the power of Kenaz:. The fire of kenaz: is the fire under human control and applied toward a willed purpose - the fire of the forge, hearth, and torch. Kenaz is also the rune of passion and sexual love as positive attributes

Keywords: Torch – Controlled Energy–Ability–Sexual lust– Creativity–Creative Knowledge–Inspiration

 **Gebo** (gĕ-bō) – G – *Gebo* is the rune of exchange. It is the power that facilitates that of fehu (see f-rune) and perpetuates that of Othala (see o-rune). Gebo is the rune of sacrifice – our gift to the gods in exchange for the gifts we receive from them. Gebo is also a rune involved in sex magic. Energy and knowledge is amplified by the exchange of power between the male/female polarities.

Keywords: Gift – Magical Force –Sacrifice – Sex Magic

Wunjo (wōōn-yō) – W or V – *Wunjo* is the rune of the joy of harmonious existence within the clan/kindred. It is the foundational force that draws related beings together and binds those beings into an organic whole. Wunjo promotes fellowship and goodwill among kinsfolk, and so promotes strong societal and guild bonds among members. This binding principle can also be used in rune magic to bind several runes to a single purpose.

Keywords: Binding – Harmony – Fellowship - Well Being – Joy

Hagalaz (hâ-gâ-lâz) - H - *Hagalaz* is the cosmic seed, from which is sprung the primal pattern of the multiverse. It is the unity of fire and ice that gave birth to this cycle of cosmic existence, as well as the framework for the evolution of all matter generated by that unity. Hagalaz is a rune of cosmic harmony- and completeness. By promoting security and preventing disharmony, hagalaz works well as a stave of protection and banishment.

Keywords: Hail -Protection - Cosmic Seed - Evolution - Cosmic Pattern/Framework

Nauðiz (now-these) – N - *Naudiz* is the rune of manifestation through need - deliverance through distress. Everyone has heard the phrase, "necessity is the mother of invention." This goes a long way in describing Naudiz. It is the need-fire created by friction to serve the need of man and the resistance necessary in the formation of Ørlög.

Keywords: Need-Fire - Friction - Resistance Distress/Deliverance

Isa (ē-sâ) – I - *Isa* is the ice rune. The polar opposite of the fire of fehu. it is a sort of antimatter in that if all matter is defined by vibration, the stasis of isa is absence of all vibration. The inaction, or stasis, embodied by the isa rune can be considered very dangerous, but when used with forethought and restraint. It's properties of "drawing in" and calming (stilling vibration) can be helpful in managing stress and conflict.

Keywords: Ice - Stasis - Ego – Concentration

Jera (yâr-ä) -J or Y -*Jera* is the rune of the cyclical process of birth life death and rebirth. This is the natural progression of the seasons (the year) and the pattern that is continually repeated throughout all realms of existence. Jera is the good harvest - the just reward for deeds rightly sown.

Keywords: Year – (good) Harvest – Cyclical Development

Eiwaz (ā-väz) – ei - *Eiwaz* is the vertical axis of the rnultiverse --- the yew column of the world tree Yggdrasil. Like Yggdrasil, eiwaz is a life sustaining force that unifies the mysteries of life and death. Another aspect of eiwaz is that of the yew bow. This reinforces the life/death unification processes facilitated by eiwaz. Eiwaz is a powerful stave of protection and banishing.

Keywords: Vertical Cosmic Axis - Life/Death – Protection

Perthro (pēr-thrō) - P - *Perthro* is the lot cup - the symbol for how ørlög functions and how gods and men might discern its workings. This includes the mysteries of nornic processes and the well of urðr from which flows wyrd, (that which is layered in ørlög). The mystery of divination is central to perthro, which makes a firm understanding of this rune necessary to effective practice of runecraft.

Keywords: Lot Cup - Nornic Processes - Ørlög - Constant Change – Fate

Elhaz (El-häz) –Z - *Elhaz* is a powerful and ancient rune of protection. Ideographically the rune looks like hand splayed out to ward off attack. Elhaz means "elk" and seems to form yet another connection with Yggdrasil through the "cosmic elk" who nibble on its needles. This is the rune of the unbreakable bond between gods and men, and is the very force that draws man forward on his own journey toward god-consciousness.

Keywords: Protection – Life - Connection Between Gods and Men

Vor Forn Siðr: A handbook for the Living Einherjar and Valkyrjar

Sowilo (sō-wē-lō) - S - *Sowilo* is the archetypal solar rune. Ideographically, it is one half of the solar wheel -⊕- and the concept of the turning wheel is central to the power of this rune. The lightning bolt shape of this rune may suggest a dynamic connection between Asgardr and Midgardr. In recent times Sowilo became known as the sig (victory) rune. However, while the willed force of this rune can bring success in one's endeavors, the actual sig-rune is most probably the Tiwaz rune.

Keywords: Guidance – Will – Success – Willed Force – Victory

Tiwaz (tē-väz) – T - *Tiwaz* is the rune of the god Týr. Týr is the god of justice and self-sacrifice. It is Týr who is invoked for a just victory, so it is believed that it is this, and not the S-Rune, that is the actual sig-(victory) rune referred to in Sigrdrífumál. The important mystery contained in tiwaz is three-fold and involves the concepts of justice, war, and the world-column (often represented by the Irminsul). The Týr rune is the mystery of the trú warrior ethic - that honorable acts, applied to a just cause, will bring victory.

Keywords: Justice - Victory - Self Sacrifice - Spiritual Discipline

Berkano (bĕr-kä-nō) – B - *Berkano* is the rune of the Birch Goddess or Great Mother. It is the unification of the "birth-life-death-gestation-rebirth" cycle and the container of all that is "becoming." This sort of "mystery of the moment" is closely tied with the workings of the P-rune. Those forces that find conservation and protection in berkano are "spilled forth" through the action of perthro.

Keywords: Birch Goddess -Birth Life Death-Rebirth - Containment.

Ehwaz (ĕh-väz) – E - *Ehwaz* is the rune of the twin gods. That these gods were sometimes represented as horses is important to understanding the nature of this rune. The long, harmonious relationship between man and horse is one of the key concepts behind the power of Ehwaz. Ehwaz is a rune of trust and loyalty and is the symbol of the lawful man-woman marriage.

Keywords: War Horse - Fertility- - Trust - Loyalty - Legal Marriage

Mannaz (män-nŏz) – M - *Mannaz* is the rune of divine structure (especially in man). It describes the genetic link (via Rigr) between gods and men. Mannaz describes our intelligence, as well as our initiation to the path toward God-consciousness. Being a rune of a linking to the divine through blood (genes), this rune is often used to symbolize the institution of blood brotherhood.

Keywords: Ideal Man - Divine Link - (Human) Intelligence – Initiate

Laguz (lä-gōōz) – L - *Laguz* is the rune of the primal waters of life that flow forth from Hvergelmir. This undifferentiated force contains both weal and woe working elements (yeast and venom). Laguz is also a rune of transformation between life and death – the water that quickens life at its beginning, and that which must be crossed at life's end. Laguz can be used to infuse the runester with vital life force and energy, but if this energy is allowed to stand still, it can stagnate and become poisonous.

Keywords: Passage To and From Life - Vital Power -- Primal Water – Natural Flow – Fluidity

Ingwaz (ĭng-väz) – ng -Ingwaz is the rune of the god Ing - male consort to the Earth Mother (later this function seems to have transferred to the god Freyr). Contained in this rune is the mystery of the seed, which must undergo gestation before its potential can be brought forth to manifestation.

Keywords: Seed - Potential Energy – Gestation – Good Luck

Dagaz (dä-gäz) - D - *Dagaz* is the rune of the "Day," meaning the 24 hour period from
sunrise to sunset and from sunset to sunrise. As is shown by the stave form, dagaz is a rune of synthesis of polarities - just as light and dark are synthesized at the points of dawn and twilight. The processes of synchronization contained in dagaz - the dynamic synthesis of polar opposites - is the central mystery of the cult of Odin, and describes the paradoxical nature of Odin himself. Dagaz is a rune of meditation and enlightenment, and the point to focus on is that point of synthesis (i.e. the rune's center).

Keywords: Polarity - Synthesis - Odinic Paradox

 **Othala** (ō-thä-lä) - O - *Othala* is the rune of ancestral property - the enclosure of the Kindred and Clan that defines the boundaries within which they are defended against unholy forces. Othala is also representative of those things of a spiritual nature that are passed along genetic lines. This includes such mysteries as those of the fylgja and of divine ancestry, as well as the wise management of the physical land of the Kindred by those endowed with the power of othala in keeping with the laws of the Folk.

Keywords: Ancestral Property - Sacred Enclosure - Inherited Power – DNA – Folk

31
Religious Use of the Icelandic Old Norse

General Terms

Vor Forn Siðr	Our Ancient Way/religion
Odinist / Wotanist	One whose religion is Odinism/Wotanism
Odinism / Wotanism	The fundamental religion of the Aryan Tribes

Names of Deities

Æsir	One group of Norse Gods
Vanir	Another group of deities
Oðin	Odin
Frigga	Frigga
Þórr	Thor
Iðunn	Idun
Freyr	Frey
Freyja	Freya
Heimdallr	Heimdal
Loki	Loki
Ás	God
Ásynja	Goddess
Ásynjur	Goddesses
Álfar	Elves
Dísir	Female ancestral spirits
Jötnar	Giants
Jötin	Giant
Norns	Fates

The Blót

Blót	Ritualized sacrifice
Goðanum	The Gods
Heill Goðanum!	Hail the Gods!
Fara með Goðanum	Go with the Gods
Megi Þórr blessi þig	May Thor bless you
Megi Oðinn blessi þig	May Odin bless you
Goði	Priest
Goðar	Priests
Gyðja	Priestess
Gyðjur	Priestesses
Goðorð	The priesthood
Allsherjargoði	A goði in charge of the Althing and the assembled host
Hofgoði	Temple priest
Hofgyðja	Temple priestess
Herjan	Lord of the Host-Chieftain

Ritual Tools

Hlauttbolli, blótbolli	Sacrificial bowl
Hlauttein	Sacrificial evergreen twig
Gandr	Ritual runic wand
Futhark	Runic "alphabet" (though vague discription)
Drekkjarhorn	Drinking horn
Stalli	Indoor altar
Hof	Temple
Hofstaðir	Temple stead
Stallahringr	Altar or Oath ring

Hlautt	Sacrificial mead
Vé	Ritual area
Vébond	Sanctuary ropes
Hörgr	Outdoor altar of stone
Þórshamarr	Thor's hammer
Vigja, Helga	Hallow, sanctify
Mjöðr	Mead
Öl	Ale
Bjor	Beer

Greetings

Góðan daginn	Good morning
Gott Kvöld	Good evening
Góda nótt	Good night
Komdu saell	How are you? (to singular male)
Komdu sael	How are you? (to singular female)
Gott!	Good; I'm fine
Heilsa	Greetings (to an Individual)
Heilsan	Greetings (to a group)
Farr heill	Go in health
Talar þu Norraena?	Do you speak Norse?
Já, ek tala Norraena	Yes, I speak Norse
Nei, ek tala ekki Norraena	No, I don't speak Norse
Já; Nei	Yes; No
Hvað heitir þu?	What is your name?
Ek heiti (Þórsteinn)	My name is (Thórsteinn)
Ek heiti (Inga)	My name is (lnga)
Takk	Thanks
Ek þakka þer fyrir	Thank you very much
Ves Heill	Be healthy
Vertu saell	Be blessed (to male)
Vertu sael	Be blessed (to female)
Kveðja	Goodbye

Weapons

Sverð	Sword
Spjór	Spear
Skjöldur	Shield
Hnífr	Knife

Family

Fjölskyldann	The family
Faðir	Father
Móðir	Mother
Sonr	Son
Dóttir	Daughter
Bróðir	Brother
Sýstir	Sister
Faðir, Móðir, Sonr mín etc.	My father, mother, son etc.
Hvar er faðir, móðir,	Where is father? mother?
Hvar er pabbi? mammi?	Where is father? mother? (informal)
Hvar er broðir mínn? sonr mínn?	Where is my brother? son?
Hvar er systir mín? Dottir mín?	Where is my sister? daughter?

Weekdays

Fimt	Week
Sunnasdagr	Sun's Day
Manisdagr	Mani's Day
Tyrsdagr	Tyr's Day
Odinsdagr	Odin's Day
Thorsdagr	Thor's Day
Friggadagr	Frigga's & Freyja's Day
Laugardagr	Wash or Bath Day

	Feasts
Júl, Jól	Yule
þorrablot	Winter sacrifice to Thorri*
Vetrnaetr	Winter Nights
Sumardagr	Summer
Sigrblót	Victory sacrifice
Miðsumar	Midsummer

*Thorri is the name of the tide of mid-January to mid-February. The HNO observes as a Thorblōt.

32
The Sacred Circle of the Sons of Odin, 1519
(A Loyal Order of Odinist Priests and Einherjar)
Vinland Kindred, est. 2244 RE/1994 CE

Amended on January 3, 2012, CE

* What is the purpose of the Sons of Odin?
* Does the Sons of Odin have a political agenda?
* Who comprises the administration of the Sons of Odin?
* What is an Apprentice of the Sons of Odin?
* What is Profession?
* What is the Valknut Rite?
* What are the bylaws of membership?
* How are the Sons of Odin organized locally and abroad?
* What about geographically isolated members?
* Why are the Runes and their use so important?
* What are Odinist names?
* What calendar do the Sons of Odin employ?
* How does one gain admittance into the Sons of Odin?
* How does one contact the Sons of Odin?
* Why is "Blót" to important?
* What are the "Nine Noble Virtues"?
* How does one contact 1519?
* Definitions

What is the purpose of the Sons of Odin?

The Sacred Circle of the Sons of Odin is a Priesthood / Brotherhood of Gothar (Priests) and Einherjar (Odin's Chosen Warriors/Sons). Our primary purpose is the defense, advancement and promotion of all aspects of our native and indigenous Pagan/Heathen religion called Odinism. This religion and way of life was indigenous to the peoples of Northern and Western Europe and so it remains so of their descendants today, "us"!

Odinism is a religion and way of life that is concerned with the ethics of social behavior, our relationship with one another and nature, with the laws of natural order and with life in its vast entirety. It is a religion and way of life that is concerned with the advancement of our faith, folk, culture, history, ecology, mysticism, etc., etc.

Odinism defines our unique identity as a folk and as individuals within our own folk. Odinists believe that in order to respect other folks, we must first fully respect our own folk! Odinism is a majestic link to our pagan past, a strength here in the present and yet, it is a fire burning within us, a torch to be passed on to light the way for a noble future.

As the Odinist religion is regarded as a way of life, "Our inherited way of life", prior to the "civilized" brainwashing of the Christian missionaries, we feel obligated as both Gothar (Priests, Gothi singular), and Einherjar to pass the torch to our descendants as we have accepted that same torch from our ancestors! We seek to serve our folk living today with a ministry that is true, noble and filled with the honor of our Gods and ancestors. We are the very Vanguard, the defenders of our sacred religion, each man avowed to advance the flame and ensure that it will never be extinguished!!!

The Sons of Odin is a loyal order of Gothar and Einherjar devoted to the elder faith of Odinism, its Gods and Goddesses, the folk who adhere to it and above all else, we are loyal to All-Father Odin and each other! We employ the Valknut as our primary symbol as sons and chosen warriors of Odin. The use of the Valknut and its significance thereafter, is one of dual purpose: First and foremost it is a symbol of our loyal allegiance to Odin in both life and death. Secondly, it is a symbol of honor and reverence to all of our ancestors who chose to die horrible deaths at the hands of the Christian missionaries, rather than forsaking the old Gods. The Valknut is known as the tri-knot symbol of Odin's slain and chosen warriors; those who dawn the Valknut pledge to die rather than forsake the old Gods, out of fear, or weakness. We, the Sons of Odin, honor the elder Gods and faith of our ancestors. We are <u>not</u> a politically correct or meek order!

Does the Sons of Odin have a political agenda?

"NO"! The Sons of Odin, in order to preserve the sacred holiness of the order and faith, does not subscribe to any political agenda, in any forum what so ever. However, Members are free to exercise whatever personal politics and views they elect to, providing it is done outside of the Sacred Circle.

Who comprises the administration of the Sons of Odin?

The administration of the Sons of Odin, Vinland Kindred, has a governing body called the "Court of Gothar". The Court of Gothar may not at any time exceed the number 12, that is to say, that no more than 12 Gothis (Priests) will hold the office of the Court of Gothar at any one time. This number includes the Herjan himself. In the event of a deadlock vote on a matter, the Herjan shall appoint a sub-council of three of the Court Gothi's (CG) to break the deadlock. The Herjan himself will fill one of the three positions. Needless to say, all members of the Court of Gothar "must" be ordained Gothis. Ordination of the Gothar will occur only after the Apprentice Gothi successfully completes the course of Gothar and the Valknut Rite. Until recently, the Court of Gothar was called the Court of Elders which was governed by the Chief Court Elder (C.C.E.), who is now replaced by the Herjan (Chief Priest). The appropriate initials will appear at the end of a Gothi's name. The Chieftain (CCG) always has the final authority of ruling.

What is an Apprentice in the Sons of Odin?

Apprentice membership is open only to those by way of sponsorship. That is to say that one seeking to become an Apprentice must be sponsored by a full member for a minimum of one to three years, or by three full members for a minimum period of one year, the sponsor(s) of an Apprentice is/are responsible for providing the Apprentice with Rede (counsel) and education of the Elder ways wherever it is lacking. Apprentice membership is obvious for two reasons:

1) It gives the Sons of Odin and the Sponsor the opportunity to be sure that the Apprentice is a stable candidate both in belief and character, as the Sons of Odin "Is Not" a gang, or club. We wish to

preserve the honor and integrity and holiness of our Order by barring the ill suited from entry within our ranks.

2) It affords the Apprentice the opportunity to decide whether he is right for and ready to espouse the enormous commitment attached to being a Son of Odin.

What is "Profession?

Profession is the Rite which affirms before the Gods and Kinsmen, a person's return to their true indigenous faith and hence they become a recognized member of the Holy Nation of Odin's Community. This step is a prerequisite to advance to the Valknut Rite and should not be taken lightly for it is a very holy ceremony, simple as it may be; irrevocable oaths are sworn in the Rite? This Rite may be either simple or complex based upon one's desire. It may be performed alone or in the presence of others to bear witness.

What is the Valknut Rite?

The Rite of the Valknut is the ONLY way one may gain entry into the ranks of the Sons of Odin, PERIOD! This Rite is very holy and dangerous in nature because to break this oath, or any oath to Odin, is to ask for a life filled with misery and endless misfortune to say the least! This Rite must be performed during the time of "Odin's Ordeal". Odin's Ordeal occurred over nine days and nights whereby he hung from the world tree Yggdrasill, without food, or water in order to gain the knowledge of the Runes! It is during these nine nights, Harvest 17th to the 25th, that the Apprentice must perform the blood Rite of the Valknut by cutting one side of the Valknut, each night of Odin's Ordeal, into his flesh which will be deep enough to leave a permanent scar. Where it is located is up to the initiate. The Apprentice will also forfeit his voice for the entire duration of the nine days and nights, never speaking once in that period! He will also fast during this period. These rituals combined comprise the Valknut Rite. After the Apprentice has completed this Rite, the court of Gothar will vote on his admittance, or not. Barring any unusual circumstance at this point the membership will be granted and the Apprentice will be inducted via the Sons of Odin's Einherjar Rite prior to the Shedding moon becoming full.

What are the Bylaws of membership?

The Sons of Odin, while being a Brotherhood, is more so and primarily an Order of Warrior Priests, all having different strengths and weaknesses, different levels of ability and abilities. Therefore, we strive to maximize our strengths and minimize our weaknesses while cultivating an honorable and noble Order. And because as Gothar we are avowed to serving and defending the Holy Nation of Odin community at large, we are all expected to abide by the following bylaws:

1) To strive for the advancement of the Sons of Odin and the ministry of our faith as well as to promote prosperity and spirituality amongst members so as to sustain sacredness and discipline.

2) To maintain family and Kindred loyalty.

3) To educate our folk and children in the spirit of our Gods and the old ways as well as heritage.

4) To always strive to advance the Holy Nation of Odin and the Scared Circle of the Sons of Odin within the Holy Nation of Odin and without.

5) To regard fellow members as brothers, kinsmen and comrades, regardless of whether they are Gothar, Court of Gothar, or simply Einherjar, and to observe and respect any member's wish to remain anonymous to those outside the order.

6) To aid and be aided in sickness, distress or any state of poverty.

7) To be slow to take offense and quick to forgive without delay where your kinsmen are in regards.

8) The Sons of Odin is governed by the Court of Gothar of which all members are ordained Gothar; the Court of Gothar is directed by the Herjan/Chief Court Gothi (CCG).

9) Of course, all members must pledge their allegiance to Odin, the gods and the Einherjar.

10) All members (1519=members) must honor and observe the holy Rites, Blóts and Sumbels of the Elder faith.

11) All members must leave their political views, if any, outside of the Sacred Circle.

12) All members must honor the principals and virtues of Odinism. We have no room for self-accepted weakness within the Order. We must strive to live our lives with honor and nobility. We do not recognize racial universalism. The idea that all peoples of the world are one and the same is very absurd and ignorant. The uniqueness of people lies in the diversity of their ancestral heritage. Thus, we have both the courage and respect to recognize this fact.

13) No member shall act in such a way as to bring dishonor upon either the Order itself, or the Odinist community. Should this occur, the Court of Gothar shall decide and vote on an acceptable method of discipline which if refused will result in the dishonorable expulsion from the Sons of Odin!

14) All members must adhere to All-Father's two commandments found within the Hávamál regarding the Runes and Blót.

15) As professed Sons of Odin, we hold holy his day of the week; Odinsdagr/Wednesday, as our high holy day over all others.

16) While the Sons of Odin, 1519 honor all of our Ancestral Codes of Honor and Virtues, (i.e. Nine Noble Virtues, Rede of Honor, etc.) we hold that the "Æsirian Code of Nine" is the Code of Primacy which all 1519's adhere too.

17) Any materials which the Sons of Odin, 1519 produce, either exoteric or esoteric, for the exclusive use by 1519 members, **will not** be revealed, disseminated or discussed with any non-1519 member, without the express permission of the 1519 Court of Gothar. Any Violation of this provision will

result in immediate dishonorable discharge! Any materials available for public perusal by way of the 1519 profile, Gungnir, or website are exempt from the criteria of this provision.

18) All members of the Sacred Circle of the Sons of Odin, 1519 – Vinland Kindred must observe mandatory silence by forfeiting their voice from Odinsdagr (Wednesday) night sunset, till Thorsdagr (Thursday), sunrise. They must also observe the mandatory silence by forfeiting their voice during the Nine nights of Odin's ordeal, from Harvest (August) 17th through the 25th. This time is set aside so that members have the time to meditate on what they are supposed to be focusing on their spiritual path of the road north.

19) 1519 DRUG PROHIBITION POLICY - The use, possession, or solicitation of drugs, or other similarly illegal substances, is now and forever shall be, prohibited to all Sons of Odin, 1519.

   (A) EXCEPTIONS shall only be made for:
   (1) Legally proscribed or over-the-counter medication.
   (2) Purely NATURAL herbs, or extracts, produced by Mother Jörd, without chemical or other alteration, may be used for the sole purpose of expressly SPIRITUAL endeavors.
   Failure to adhere to this prohibition, and/or abuse of the above exceptions, constitutes 'self-accepted weakness' and DISHONOR, and shall be referred to the Court of Gothar for the imposition of proper discipline per Article VII, §13

20) Candidacy for membership within the Sons of Odin, 1519- Vinland Kindred is open to "Non-Incarcerated" men only, who have a minimum of one (1) year experience as "Professed" Odinists.

This does not completely rule out consideration of incarcerated seekers. Consideration of incarcerated candidates will be determined by the COURT OF GOTHAR, which will only occur wherefore such candidates reside within the same locale as the members of the COURT OF GOTHAR. Any former prisoner seeking Apprenticeship must be off of parole, prior to submitting his resume. *This does not affect current incarcerated members, or Apprentices.

21) Due to the expansion of 1519 membership, the Sons of Odin, 1519, has been restructured. As with any organization, as it expands it becomes necessary to divide itself into chapters, units, or divisions, etc., based upon geographic location of members, and/or size of membership. From this point forward, **ALL** 1519 members belong to an ÆTT (pl. Ætter). An Ætt is a family, or clan. The word Ætt is Old Norse and means literally; "Family: The further implication is the family of eight, though the number eight bears no consequence regarding the present considerations.

Effective immediately, the SONS OF ODIN, 1519, in an effort to expand both the Order of 1519 and stimulate the positive growth of the HOLY NATION OF ODIN, Inc., hereby enacts the following revisions to our profile which was last revised on 18, Midyear/Fallow 2257 RE (6/18/07 CE).

1) The Ætter have been restructured to the following:
The Grand Ætt, which contains <u>all</u> National Officers, i.e. Chieftain/ Chief Court Gothi (CCG/Herjan), Court Gothi Deputy Chieftain (CGDC), Court Gothar (CG) and Chief Warder (CW).
For this reason, members of the Grand Ætt are Nomads in status. They may belong to whatever State Ætter they elect. The Grand Ætt <u>is</u> the International Ætt. They assume authority over State Ætter and chapters.

  (a) All other Ætter are by State name, e.g. the California Ætt, the Texas
Ætt, etc... Each Ætter will have a Jarl and Warder. They assume authority for State Ætt <u>and over</u> Chapters within their State's Ætt.

2) If/when a State Ætt has numerous members located throughout their state, they may petition the Grand Ætt to form Chapters, e.g. the California Ætt may have a Orange County Chapter, a Los Angeles Chapter, a Fresno Chapter, a Bakersfield Chapter, etc.., etc... And so on, and so on per each State. Each Chapter must have three (3) members

minimum to charter a Chapter. Each Chapter will have three Officers, i.e. a Jarl, a Warder, and a Scribe (Secretary). All Chapters in a given State belong to that State's Ætt. <u>All</u> 1519 members will also be members of the Holy Nation of Odin, Inc (HNO). All State Ætter will have at the least one (1) legally Ordained Gothi (Priest). Credentials will be from the 1519/HNO. An Apprentice Gothi (AG) may fill the required position while he completes his seminary studies and earns full ordination credentials.

3) An application must be filled out by all 1519 Apprentice Candidates from this date forth. **NO EXCEPTIONS**!

4) <u>**All**</u> members, Ætter and Chapters, remain accountable to the executive authority of the Chieftain's Court (Court of Gothar) and the Bylaws of the SONS OF ODIN, 1519.

These twenty one by-laws apply as much too any Apprentice as well as any member and of course the importance of sworn oaths should never be forgotten.

<u>How are the Sons of Odin organized locally and abroad?</u>

It has already been explained how we are locally organized. As for those Kindred's abroad, they, like ourselves in Vinland, are fully autonomous and therefore may differ from country to country and Kindred to Kindred.

<u>What about geographically isolated members?</u>

That "Self-reliance" is one of our nine noble virtues says it all! If a member is isolated from others, they have an obligation to honor our holy ways, advance their knowledge and wisdom on their own through books, meditation and any available means. The advancement of our ministry is of paramount importance no matter where one might find himself.

<u>Why are the Runes so important?</u>

If this must be explained to the reader of this profile, then you are not advanced enough to concern yourself with the content of this profile.

What are Odinist Names?

All members of the Sons of Odin must use the name "Odinson" after their first name and prior to their last name, be it their birth name, or an Odinist name. An Odinist name is an indigenous name of the ancestral folk (i.e. Lars, Ulf, Ragnar, Harvald, etc.) Many choose to demonstrate their full and sincere return to the ways of our ancestors by adopting/changing their name to an indigenous one. Members will sign their names in the following fictitious manner; John Odinson Smith, 1519-CG. The preceding example would denote that John Odinson Smith is a member and Court Gothi. The Herjan is the Chief Court Gothi (CCG).

What calendar do the Sons of Odin employ?

We utilize, as do most Odinists, the Runic Era calendar which is hundreds of years older than the Roman/Christian calendar. The Runic Era calendar is established and fixed at 250 years older than today's standard calendar. Hence, while it may be 1994 CE (common era) it is 2244 RE (runic era). We also call the months by the names that our ancestors used: Snowmoon=January, Horning=February, Lenting=March, Ostara=April, Merrymoon=May, Fallow/Midyear=June, Haymoon=July, Harvest=August, Shedding=September, Hunting=October, Fogmoon=November, Wolfmoon/Yulemoon=December.

How does someone gain admittance into the Sons of Odin?

In order to become a member of the Sons of Odin an Apprentice must:
1) Find a member/or members willing to sponsor him.
2) Must serve a minimum of 1 to 3 years as an Apprentice
3) Must perform the Valknut Rite between Harvest 17th and 25th.
4) Must win the approval of the Court Gothar.
5) And finally, must be initiated by the Einherjar Rite.

Why is Blót so important?

See above answer to "Why are the Runes so Important?"

What are the Nine Noble Virtues?

Courage, strength, honor, hospitality, freedom/self reliance, joy, perseverance, realism, ancestry/kinship.

These may vary in the exact wording as listed here, but the virtues attached or, rather, the descriptions attached hereto are reminiscent of the virtues embraced by the Odinist community the entire world over.

How does one contact the Sons of Odin?

If you are reading this profile, you need only to look at the end of it for the "Courtesy of:" which will read as the following fictitious example:

This profile is provided courtesy of: John Odinson Smith, 1519 CG
1234 Valhalla Dr. #1
Godstown, USA 00009
Sons of Odin, Vinland Kindred

If a member's name & address is not listed in the provided area, we may be contacted via "The Holy Nation of Odin, Inc." and they will pass your letter on to us as the Sons of Odin, Vinland Kindred is an official Order of the Holy Nation of Odin, Inc.

Definitions

       Herjan/Chieftain/Chief Court Gothi = 1519 – CCG *(National Officer Prime)*
       Deputy Chieftain/Court Gothi DC = 1519 – CGDC *(National Officer)*
       Gothi/Odinsgothi = 1519 – G *(Priest – Legally Ordained)*
       Apprentice Gothi = 1519 – AG
       Chief Warder = 1519 – CW *(National Officer)*
       Warder=1519-W *(Officer/State or Chapter)*
       Apprentice = 1519 – A
       Court Elder (original co-founders) = 1519 – CE
       Court Gothi=1519-CG (National Officer)
       Jarl=1519-J *(State or Chapter Officer)*
       Einherjar=1519 *(a member)*

Dr. Casper Odinson Cröwell

THIS PROFILE IS PROVIDED COURTESY OF:

Sons of Odin, 1519
PO Box 630
Kingsburg, CA 93631

www.holynationofodin.org

33
NEUN NACHTEN IM ERNTE
(Nine nights in Harvest)

Hereafter, committed to print, for the sake of both insight today to those concerned, and for posterity tomorrow for those who are brave enough to seek, follows the meditative musings of myself, the Herjan of the Sons of Odin, 1519-Vinland Kindred, for your perusal. These of course occur in the form of journal entries as they did in fact transpire over the course of nine days and nights of silence and fasting in some instances, during the initiatory period known as "Odin's Ordeal", which of course spans the breadth of nine days/nights in the month of August/Harvest. This is a deeply meditative journey which is capable of yielding truly profound results wherefore insight is at issue! And while I have been traveling the road of shadows for little less than three decades now, each year's new journey has continued to provide me with great intellectual wealth. This year was no exception, and it was truly anything other than pedestrian... The Odroerir yet once more, have I consumed!

Odinsdagr 17, Harvest 2255 RE *Day one*
(Wednesday 8/17/05 CE)

And so it begins, another year on that holy and sacred tree, the path less trod. Another initiation reserved for the stalwart and noble character. None but the truly brave dare tread this dark road in search of the light. Only those with honest thoughts, who dare not look away from what reality shows them, may hope to approach the ancient well. Only those stout of heart will peer deep and long into its cold, clear water, and only those truly initiated will descry his eye looking up at thee from the depths of Mim's well!

But not without sacrifice will any see the Drighten's face, nor hear his voice on the wind. The ordeal is at hand...what will I see this year? Has the storm abated, or dost the tempest's fury rage yet with the might of the burning pyre?

I step forth now on this first day of nine, eagerly and without pause, knowing all too well, that in my endeavor to sacrifice myself to myself, do I honor the All-Father, my father! And with this holy act do I anticipate spying his face in the reflections of my mind. I stand ready, ready to embrace this ordeal with passion and an undeniable thirst for yet another draught of Odroerir! I ascend the holy ash of Ygg and eagerly await the coming storm.

Thorsdagr 18, Harvest 2255 RE   *Day two*

I have awakened before the dawn, it will be sometime yet before Sunna smiles this day. And so, I sit in the early hours of the dark and silent morn, resigned to the loudness of my own ruminations. But are they in fact "my" own? Or are they not to be attributed to the old Sage himself? I can hear the distant echoes of a thunder which none save for myself can hear. It vaguely reveals itself to my awareness, calling out to me whence it has come. Its origin rooted in that which is ancient and nourished by the Laguz of Urd's well!

Soon, my senses will be assaulted by the cacophony of Loki's laughter as this place comes to life! Such is the torment of residence in Fetter Grove. Fjolsvidr's echo will however, permeate my mind and drowned out the din of the day and the music of Thor's chariot will keep Laufey's son at bay as I hang upon the tree and send hither and tither my mind, in search of that sacred echo which travels the sanguine highway of millennia past...Hail Odin!
Later same day -

It begins with a desire really. To comprehend the ideas and language of great masters of thought; Nietzsche, Wagner, da Vinci, Edison, Grimm, Machiavelli, Aristotle, Plato, Socrates, Hitler, Herodotus, Franklin, Jefferson, Twain, Whitman, Yeats, Kipling, Patton, and so very many more! The ghosts of these men have been my dearest companions for so many years now. They have goaded me on to higher idealism and aspirations. They have witnessed my struggles, watched me stumble and demanded that I get up and refuse to yield to defeat! I have heard them all in my darkest hours; "Pity naught thyself, ye of noble heart and character, for self pity is a whore, a pining thief and she will rob thou of thine senses!"

I seek to join the social order of these sage men, though I dare not assume the pompous air of arrogance in thinking myself worthy as of yet, though I forge on ahead. The wise are never sated, their thirst for knowledge and wisdom shant ever respect the bounds which confine the mundane and complacent minds of the masses... Not ever!

Hail to those great thinkers, for are they not all, each one, but incarnations of Odin himself? Made manifest in the shapes of these men's minds? And thereby bestowing veracity to the fact that the All-Father is often-wandering among us.

He is here, with me now, this very moment. And I shall wax from our intellectual exchange. The wind begins to rock the tree and I rejoice in the fruits of sacrifice.

Friggasdagr 19, Harvest 2255 RE   *Day three*

It is day three of the Ordeal and the resonations of my last words two days ago have now receded into the silence. Sunna's ascension over the Sierra Nevada Mountains this morn was a magnificent and wondrous sight to behold! It is just after 6:30 a.m. and soon this place will explode with the sound of prison life, and like a great beast, it will tear this sacred silence asunder. Today is also the third day of the Festival of Runes, and it concentrates on battling the ego this day, in an effort to achieve victory by sacrificing self to self. This particular guest far exceeds the parameters of this day for me however. For I seek to slay my ego daily, for it is the only thing which stands in the way of one's own progress. Tiwaz (↑) is the runic key for unlocking the door which would otherwise oppose success...to invoke its power is just not enough, one must become it wholly, and so I do. This day I shall know the victory I seek. Hail All-Father Odin!

Lagaurdagr 20, Harvest 2255 RE   *Day four*

Hmmm..., day four is upon me and the pace quickens. My dreams last night were very vivid, graphic and colorful. In these dreams, I journeyed far and wide. Some of it was very pleasant while other portions of it were not. I had a companion with me everywhere, Odin, of course. Over and over again, he advised me; "Trust naught those whom have yet to earn it. And never trust any man whom fears the shadows of darkness, or what awaits him there." My meditations throughout this day and night will find me considering Hár's words/Rede well. On another note, yesterday, a Skraeling who moved into the cell block a few days ago was impressed that I was not speaking for such a lengthy time and for such a noble reason. He said to me; "I have something that you may enjoy." He gave me Black Sabbath CD entitled "TYR"! Three particular songs which all fade into one another are of special interest -

The Battle of Tyr, Odin's Court and Valhalla. I reciprocated the Gebo with a CD to him which he was pleased with. The songs are haunting and moving, and that I received and heard them for the first time yesterday...I have no doubt that they are the voice of Odin! Oh, not the singing, but rather the combination of the Gebo, the CD's title in addition to those of the three songs and the lyrical content all occurring in concert with the timing. I have gazed into the eye so blue yet once more...Hail Odin!

This is Thurisaz's day to champion over chaos in the sacred Festival of Runes, Hail to you James Leisinger!

I will tame the Thurses this day and command myself fully.

Sunnasdagr 21, Harvest 2255 RE *Day five*

My night was without event, save for the dream. Ah yes, it is always the dream...isn't it?

I was at a mini mart of sorts, when a man walked in and shoots dead the woman merchant! He then mutters the words; "I told you bitch!" He glanced at my sister and I, walked out to his waiting car and sped away. I took my sister by the hand and led her away from the place with great haste! Then I informed her that I must return to the mini mart. "No!" she cried, it's not safe. I must go, I affirmed, and I departed for the little store. When I arrived there this time, it was twilight time, early evening. Nothing seemed to be amiss in the store. Then he walked in, firearm in hand and said; "You should not have returned here." He leveled the weapon at my chest and fired three times in rapid succession! I was down, but got back up unharmed. The would be assailant stammered; "But, but I shot you!" I felt a presence in the shadows as I tried to make sense of it all. And then, just as I began to wrap my mind, somewhat, around what had just occurred, the store had transformed into an old European village and I was surrounded by Roman soldiers while the Tribe folk looked on. The Roman was incredulous as his words began to make sense to me; "I ran you through, why are you not dead?" The presence in the shadows had stepped forward now. It was All-Father Odin, and his voice boomed; "You cannot kill the Einherjar, fool! None but the fire of Surtr will put them down in the final battle of Ragnarok!"

Now obviously, in terms of analytical psychology, fleeing the mini mart with my sister in tow was an action born of an overwhelming sense of duty to "Family", to safeguard & protect my sister. My imminent return to the mini mart must be attributed to a sense of living the Nine Noble Virtues, more directly to the point of the warrior's duty to protect and not merely stand by. And then there is my execution in rapport with defending the Folk. Odin restores my life for honoring my oath to serve the Gods and Folk, or so it is which I equate with the former.

The voices and lessons of our Gods and ancestors can and do speak to us on many levels, not just via the medium of our myths, lore and sagas, but via our dreams as well which speak directly to our souls! One need only learn to become aware and listen. I will consider the lesson and gift of their voices, the voice of Odin, from this dream, all day in my meditations. Hail All-Father Odin, hail the seeker...hail to those who not only seek, but find as well!!!

Manisdagr 22, Harvest 2255 RE *Day six*

I awake yet another day to bear witness to Sunna's majestic ascension beyond the apex of the Sierra Nevadas. It all occurs with such grace, accompanied by a loud silence heard only through the eyes. The nocturnal world recedes with the first tell of dawn's stirring. One must truly be aware to grasp the Dagaz at work here, if only for a few brief moments. The truths of both night and day enjoy a brief harmony with one another, just as they do at the end of the day. This is a time when one may look upon the face of Odin, when the light and dark hang in that precarious balance just long enough for one to consider whether or not they had just looked upon the face of God! Only the initiated will meet him in that succinct yet sovereign place. Doubt not what the mind would seek, would thou know and you shall know truths unparalleled which powerful Runes shall reveal.

Sunna shatters twilight, day has begun and with it arrives so much raw potential...so many possibilities awaiting the initiated, those bold enough to reach out and seize them!

Tyrsdagr 23, Harvest 2255 RE *Day seven*

It has occurred to me, and not for the first time, that so many who claim to know Odin, know him naught! Especially some so-called authorities of renown whom have authored a number of books. In fact, they have merely interpreted what they have read somewhere and then furthered it with some rehash in eloquent, albeit often verbose fashion. I have perused books on numerous occasions, whereby the author asserts how Odin has betrayed his own! I have no inclination to be disrespectful to any among our folk whom have authored such books reflecting thus. Though I would strongly suggest a deviation from the same old fare regarding Odin's betrayal of his sons and daughters for it is altogether devoid of any merit whatsoever and is valid only in the same vein as mere rubbish is!

Odin does not betray his own, not those who remain true at least. Folk betray themselves by failing to identify and thereafter, accept reality. Odin grants wisdom and wit, he grants victory to those of us brave enough to embrace reality beyond the minute and unrealistic scope of political correctness! Any trú son or daughter of Odin knows all too well that the day **will** come when he will come to collect his portion of the avowed Gebo exchanged between you and he. He will come to gather you up to him, or send his Valkyries to do so. That was the deal which any trú son or daughter has made with Odin via the oath of the Valknut; that it is understood and accepted that Odin may gather you up to him any time he sees fit to, that's the deal and shame on those who failed to read the fine print of the very contract they signed in their own blood! For you have betrayed yourself, Odin certainly has not betrayed you, or any other loyal son or daughter!

Such folk whom entertain such an absurd notion and even further it with their writings and teachings are disconnected from All-Father and too blind to see that. I would further surmise that any such soul has not had the experience of being fully exposed to the trials and ordeals of physical battle and violent environments where lives are taken and lost and survival is the object of the game, for Odin is always present, this I can verify for I have both participated and witnessed as much on many occasion. More to the point, I have met him there face to face!

Hail All-Father Odin! Hail those who 'truly' know him...and hail the Sons of Odin!!!

Odinsdagr 24 Harvest 2255 RE *Day eight*

It seems at times of illumination, that the knowledge and wisdom we so oft seek, has been right before us and all about us all along. Like some mystical forces, engaged in some arcane and ancient dance which is always occurring in our immediate proximity, albeit just beyond and outside of the spectrum of our mundane vision. It seems so wondrous, if not all together surreal, when we are finally able to grasp the knowledge itself, that it has always been there.

You see, that is just what initiation is all about. Even when we feel as though we may possess a certain, if only vague, understanding of that which we covet, it is the absolute clarity and certainty which arrives through initiation, which affords one the trove of confidence in said knowledge/wisdom attached thereto...A certain mastery if you will.

On day eight of the Festival of Runes, the initiate gains a knowledge, a perception of the divine within, and he/she participates with their own Ørlog and Hamingja in an effort to perceive said divine knowledge and thereby ascend toward an acceptance of this divinity.

Worship me naught says the father of Gods and man, but follow my foot steps and emulate my life long journey in search of wisdom and thou wilst honor me and my gift to you! His finger pokes at my Hugauga, stirs the Wode within my mind and leads me toward higher idealism. Hail All-Father Odin!

Thorsdagr 25, Harvest 2255 RE *Day nine*

Well, this is it then. The ninth and final day of initiation. When I get off of the tree on the morrows light, it will have been nine nights of silence having uttered not a single word during the span of the holy ordeal. Only the sound of my evening Galdr has pierced the breath of Nótt, the Rune songs alone hath escaped pass thine lips, riding on the stream of my Athem, those holy and all sacred Runes did travel, wending their way tither, unto all the worlds at large!

Transformed shall I re-emerge, inspired further hence by the taste of Odroerir.

Friggasdagr 26, Harvest 2255 RE *The morning after*

It is just the other side of sunrise and I have now descended from the great tree. The final night had delivered unto me two realizations, one very happy, the other, truly disturbing. The first realization is that, where I once sought only deep and complex thoughts while searching the realm of shadows, in search of greater wisdom, such was my only light in the vast darkness which enveloped and consumed my mind so that my Hugauga may come to recognize and embrace that light. And now, a second light has emerged as well, to stave off the impenetrable darkness, a gift from the Gods themselves, and delivered unto me by Odin and Freya themselves! She is my song, my Nordic Princess, Linda, and wherever my thoughts of her shall wander, my heart dost always follow! I render unto the holy ones my unyielding respect and gratitude! The other realization is neither attractive, or comfortable to embrace. And yet, this knowledge is passed down from Odin himself. It is an inexorable and sad truth, albeit, it is one which must be addressed and with little time to spare...

Where once our ancestors stood upon the sacred grounds, in the lands of our fathers, consumed with dismay at the knowledge that the sacred ways of their fathers had nearly been annihilated and swept from the plain of Jörd by Christian marauders and converted betrayers of the folk. We, their descendants now, not only glance back into that long ago time of decline and despair but we too, find ourselves at that same precipice! Consumed with the same overwhelming sadness which accompanies such a reality. I have heard so much talk of the re-awakening which has been occurring since the late 19th and early 20th centuries, of our noble and sacred folkways, but look about with honest eyes and ye shall see a truth much less appealing and way more disturbing! We are standing in this wolf age, at the very place our fathers once stood, surveying the dwindling remnants of what remains of our indigenous and holy ancestral ways. Oh sure, there seem to be plenty of us to protect and defend the flame this day. But we age and wend without pause towards our own departure from Midgard to join our beloved Gods and ancestors. And who then will accept the flame we seek to pass, let alone vow to protect and defend and pass it on?

If we don't discover bold and courageous folk to pass our own knowledge on to, folk not only willing, but worthy. Not merely courageous in word and desire, but in deed as well, then it will perish with us..., ushering in the Fimúlvintúr and ultimately, Ragnarok! Those of us who lay claim to the old ways today bicker too much amongst ourselves and within our holy folk community. Too many Helmsmen and not enough rowers makes the longship's journey slow and perilous and without the means to outrun the coming tempest! Pride is a noble trait, but ego can and will wound. Egos in constant competition with each other will kill until all are defeated. We must learn to assume a mastery over our own egos, control them, not allow for them to control and dictate our actions.

We must place an emphasis on the folk, and not only the immediate survival of our holy faith and folk ways, but the advancement of it as well. The laws of nature dictate that the female quality/gender is required to produce new life. We are currently 90%, or better, male in our folk community the entire world over. We must make our women folk feel honored and welcomed as equals. We must find a way to make the old folk and clannish ways of our ancestors, which we follow today still, appeal to them as well. We must provide them with the desirability to warrant their return to the old ways of our folk community, lest the old ways of our noble and honorable faith ceases to exist! Our women, better than us, and more suitably so, are more likely and with greater ease, able to teach our kinder, with their inherent maternal instinct. And our kinder are more likely and readily willing to accept what our women folk say and teach them. Nothing has changed in all the millennia of our folk's history. In over 40,000 years, our women and children are still a mandate for our survival and advancement.

We had better stop banging our shields and clanging our swords long enough to address this paramount issue. For there is nothing more epic of importance to the survival of our folkways and faith community, let alone any promise for the future of our folk.

So then, there it is, two realizations, two truths. And I embrace them both as well as the responsibility for which I am charged to defend and bring about a positive effect wherein both are at issue. My time on the tree was most enlightening and beneficial to me and my growth. May it be so for that of the folk as well! Hail All-Father Odin, and hail to those who have stayed the storm and rode it out while hanging on the tree.

Appendix of words and meanings

Athem - *a component of the complex Nordic soul structure, in its most basic sense, it is one's breath of life.*
Dagaz - *one of the 24 Elder Futhark Runes, very basic meaning is twilight.*
Drighten - *a very learned teacher.*
Einherjar - *Odin's heroes, his warriors, the slain, lit. trans. One harrier.*
Fetter Grove - *as used in this essay, Prison, Old Norse trans. Grove of bondage*
Fjolsvidr - *one of the numerous names for Odin.*
Galdr - *the Rune's song, chant, incantation.*
Gebo - *one of the 24 Elder Futhark Runes, very basic meaning is gift, shared or exchanged gift.*
Hamingja - *a component of the very complex Nordic soul structure, basic sense, it is one's store of luck.*
Herjan - *Lord of the Host/Order.*
Holy Tree, the - *Yggdrasil, the world tree, the universe, both seen and unseen.*
Hugauga - *the mind's eye. Part of the complex Nordic soul structure.*
Jord - *Earth Goddess, Mother Earth. Jord's plain is therefore the surface of the Earth.*
Kinder - *German for children.*

Laguz - *one of the Elder Futhark Runes, very basic meaning is water, primal waters.*
Laufey - *Loki's mother.*
Loki - *most basic understanding; the God of chaos and mischief. Loki's laughter is employed herein as descriptive of the jarring and unsettling noise of prison once the population is awake.*
Mim's well - *the fountain/spring of wisdom, Odin plucked out one of his eyes and gave it to the well's depths in exchange for a drink of its sacred water which imbues the drinker with unparalleled wisdom. Mimir, the well's owner is a wise and ancient Giant/God far older than even the oldest Gods. Each day he drinks from the well in honor of All-Father's pledge at the well.*
Nótt - *Night. Therefore, Nótt's breath is the night air.*
Odin's Ordeal - *Whereby Odin hung on the world tree, Yggdrasil, for nine days and nights to gain knowledge of the Runes, which he later shared with the rest of the Gods and man so that they could understand the hidden mysteries of the nine worlds, the universal truths and realities which are otherwise hidden from our immediate view of understanding.*
Odroerir - *the mead of poetry, that which stimulates ecstasy and incites knowledge and thereafter, wisdom.*
Ørlog - *A component of the complex Nordic soul structure, primal layers, simply put in its most basic sense, it is like karma.*
Ragnarok - *twilight of the Gods, end of the world, an extinction level event along the same lines as that of the Christians Armageddon, for a lack of more immediate and concise description.*
Rede - *Counsel, advice.*
Runes - *Lit. Trans. Mysteries, secrets unknown to the uninitiated. Runes are comprised of three key parts, the stave/shape of the rune's sign/sigl, the Galdr which is the song, sound, chant, incantation, and the mystery, the rune's secret, its meaning. Runes are universal truths, manifestations of the divine knowledge made manifest and expressed through the secrets of the runes which would otherwise escape our comprehension of these truths. This is of course the very simplex and vague illustration of the runes which of course are far too complex to address within the allotted space here. However, on another and equally important note, it should be stressed here, that the alphabetical equation and import people today like to ascribe to the holy Runes, was of no real significance, or chief value to our ancestors until the middle of the eleventh century except under the veil of unique circumstances.*

Skraeling - *Lit. ON. trans., Native inhabitant, commonly employed to describe the ancestors of todays Native Americans, though erroneously employed by some today to mean wretch, which by definition should be properly ascribed to the term Nithling. There is nothing ignoble about the term Skraeling when applied in the same context as our Vinland forefathers used the word It simply means non-white.*

Storm, the - *As employed in this writing, the storm is descriptive of the attrition of the initiation and the effects thereupon one who undertakes such an ordeal.*

Sunna - *the Sun Goddess, the sun.*

Surtr - *The Fire Giant of destruction. His flame will consume the whole of Midgard (earth) at the time of Ragnarok, hence, Surtr's fire.*

Thor - *The God of strength, Son of Odin (father Sky) and Jord (Mother Earth). God of thunder, brother of the folk and defender of both Gods and folk.*

Thurisaz - *one of the 24 Elder Futhark Runes, very basic meaning is strength, breaker of resistance and thorn of restriction.*

Thurses - *Giants, forces of chaos.*

Tiwaz - *one of the 24 Elder Futhark runes, its basic meaning as used in this writing, is self sacrifice for higher purpose.*

Urd's Well - *also the Well of Wyrd, or wyrd's well, the well of fate, named for one of the three Norns (fates), Urd = that which has already occurred, the past.*

Valknut - *knot of the slain, worn only by those fully dedicated to Odin, both in life and death. It is a visual oath for all to see that its wearer is ready to be taken into the ranks of Valhalla any time Odin sees fit to take him/her.*

Valkyries - *daughters of Odin.*

Ygg - *one of the numerous names for Odin, Lit. Trans. The Terrible, Terror of the Gods. Yggdrasil, the name of the holy world tree, means Ygg's Gallow.*

34
GOTHAR COURSE BOOK
HOLY NATION OF ODIN, INC.
AND SONS OF ODIN, 1519 - VINLAND KINDRED

TABLE OF CONTENTS

Introduction, by Dr. Casper Odinson Cröwell, Chief Court Gothi
Gothar Course Curriculum
Course Outline
Book Lists
Part 1   Ministering
Part 2   Historical Studies
Part 3   Cultural Studies
Part 4   Communications
Part 5   Theology and Philosophy
Part 6   Traditional Religious Skills
Grading

INTRODUCTION

The success of a ministry, of any denomination, should not be measured in terms of quantity, that is to say, in membership numbers, but rather, it should be measured in terms of spiritual understanding, knowledge and guidance, wherefore the members of said ministry are in regard. There can be no lack of preparedness to fulfill your pastoral duties for whatever situation may arise with one, or twenty members of your ministry. There can be no dereliction of duty for any reason what so ever, be it personal indifference matters of conflicting personalities, or you just simply do not feel up to the task at the time. Personal crisis' in people's lives do not occur on a time table, nor do the myriad of life's joys and terrors coincide with any Priest/Minister's personal schedule in such a manner so as to afford one to treat the ministry, or one's pastoral duties as a mere hobby, deserving no less than your utmost and whole hearted attention, at ALL times, whether it is convenient, or not! If you are not willing to give fully of yourself to the service of the HOLY NATION OF ODIN (and I do suggest you consider the vastly enormous personal sacrifice at length prior to commitment), then you will only be doing yourself and our faith, a grave disservice of which I cannot over emphasize!

However, if you are indeed one of the truly few who are willing to make such a sacred sacrifice and are compelled by a calling, then I both laud and encourage you to follow the path of the Gothar, Gods in Asgard know, there are too few of us serving the legitimate spiritual needs of our folk and the HOLY NATION OF ODIN.

Just how prepared a Gothi/Gythia is to minister to our folk, really depends upon how educated one is and continues to become. There are several Gothar courses in print designed with the mission of educating and producing skilled and knowledgeable Gothar to minister to our folk. Most assuredly, each one is designed to conform to and advance the perspective of the Temple, Hof, Church Kindred, Grove, Hearth, etc., who composed that particular course, and it is understandable. However, one course does not negate, or deem any other course invalid. Nor should it. Therefore, what sets one curriculum apart from another is the content of each course, or more so, the value of success each course thereafter produces in the manner of advancing our holy faith, in addition to safeguarding it for future generations, via the vehicle of properly trained Gothar which shall serve as the fountains of spiritual, historical and esoterical wisdom from which the folk may attain their spiritual sustenance from, their draught of Odroerir if you will.

One would be best served to bear in mind that a piece of paper, or certificate of ordination from one religious institution, or another, does not render one a holy man/woman merely because they have acquired thus via credible and credentialed Institutions. All of the "wall paper" in the world can not and will not make the folk seek you out, or follow your ministry if you do not possess a genuine knowledge of all things pertinent to our faith!

There are plenty of 'Non'-ordained", or 'Lay' Gothar that have been crucial to the re-emergence and advancement of our holy faith; Guido von List, A. Rudd Mills, Else Christensen, and Sveinbjorn

Beinteinsson immediately come to mind to name but a few. So then, while credentials do indeed serve a legitimate purpose at certain instances, they by no means serve the folk. The well-trained and sincerely committed Gothar do that.

What follows is the curriculum for Gothar Ordination within the HOLY NATION OF ODIN, Inc. and the Sons of Odin, 1519-Vinland Kindred, as composed by myself, Casper Odinson Cröwell, co-founder and Herjan. It is my genuine desire that my accrued knowledge and experience as a devout Odinist over the past 28 years and past 12 years as a Gothi, serve as a vehicle to train and produce skilled and devoted Gothar to carry on the mission of our Holy Faith via the Priesthood of the HOLY NATION OF ODIN, Inc. and the Sons of Odin, 1519 for millennia to come. It is my will, and Gods and Norns willing; it too shall be my legacy.

HNO/1519, Chief Court Gothi
Dr. Casper Odinson Cröwell, 1519-CCG
Fetter Grove – Corcoran, CA Vinland (USA)
Odinsdagr, 23, Harvest 2256 RE (Wednesday, 8/23/06 CE)

* This curriculum is devised from the former SONS OF ODIN, 1519 - VINLAND Gothar Course, and was inspired by the writings of Dr. Stephen Flowers (Edred Thorsson) and Kvelduf Gundarsson. It is dedicated to the loving memory of my late mother and father in addition to my own late mentor, Else Christensen. It is further dedicated to all Trú Gothar and those who aspire to be, wherever they teach and minister our noble faith to our folk. It is dedicated to the SONS of ODIN, 1519 - VINLAND KINDRED and my beautiful wife Linda, whose tireless efforts make it all work!

And above all, it is dedicated to Allfather Odin, whom without, NOTHING is possible...
"ODIN Být" (Odin Lives)!

HOLY NATION OF ODIN, Inc. / SONS OF ODIN, 1519 GOTHAR COURSE CURRICULUM

NOTE: All papers (e.g. Thesis, Dissertation, Monograph, Essay, etc.), must demonstrate intelligent and comprehensive knowledge of subject matter.

All Gothar Candidates must sign a release acknowledging that the HOLY NATION OF ODIN, Inc. has the right to publish any/all submissions, or portions thereof, in bulletin, pamphlet, or book form.

The HOLY NATION OF ODIN, Inc. Gothar Course curriculum is fixed per subject matter. The particulars of this curriculum are " Non-Negotiable."

Time extensions to complete assignments may be afforded on a case by case basis. Entire curriculum must be fully completed within five years.

Total Curriculum Time: 3 years and 8 months, (44 months).

COURSE OUTLINE

Part One: Ministering / 3 lessons

Counseling:
  Addictions
  Confidentiality
  Ethics

Part Two: Historical Studies 4 lessons

Early Aryan Tribalism:
  The Migration Period
  The Viking Age
  The Current Era

Part Three: Cultural Studies / 6 lessons

Teutonic Culture:
  Indo-Europeans (Aryans)
  Heroic Legends
  The Sagas
  Germanic Myth and Folklore
  Odinism Today

Part Four: Communications / 3 lessons

Public Relations
Ministry Administration
Adult and Children's Education

Part Five: Theology and Philosophy / 3 lessons

Odinist Principals:
  Ritual and Religion
Christianity, Islam and Judaism / Odinism vs. Ásatrú and Multi-Cultural Paganism (i.e. Wicca, Druidism, New Ageism, etc.)

Part Six: Traditional Religious Skills / 3 lessons

Blót (Blótar)
Rune Work
Galdr Work

Book list #I, Lore:
All books on this list are suggested reading.

The Poetic Edda – translation is reader's choice.
The Prose Edda
The Agricola & Germania – Tacitus
Egil's Saga
Eyrbyggia Saga
Hrafenkels Saga
King Harald's Saga
Laxdaela Saga
Njal's Saga
Onkneyinga Saga
Saga of the Jomsvikings
Saga of Rolf Kraki
Saga of the Volsungs
Niebelungenlied
Heimskringla
Vinland Sagas
Gods & Myths of Northern Europe – H.R. Ellis-Davidson
The Masks of Odin – Else-Brita Titchenell
Sagas of the Icelanders
The Vikings – Else Rosendahl
In Search of the Indo-Europeans – J.P. Mallory

Book list # II, Runes:

Runelore – Thorsson
Futhark: A Handbook of Rune Magic – Thorsson
The Well of Wyrd – Thorsson
Runamal – I – Thorsson*
Blue Runa – Thorsson*
Rune Song – Thorsson*
The Nine Doors of Midgard – Thorsson*
  Non-required reading.

Book list #III, Ritual/Religious Rites:

The Lessons of Asgard – S. McNallen*
The Values of Ásatrú – S. McNallen*
Trú Brothers – Thorsson *(If available)* *
The Rituals of Ásatrú (3 Volumes) – S. McNallen
A. Vol. I – Major Blóts
B. Vol. II – Seasonal Festivals
C. Vol. III – Rites of Passage

These following books would serve you well to be aware and somewhat familiar with their content.

1) The holy Bible (Old Testament and King James Version)
2) Qur'an (Koran) the Holy Book of Islam
3) Talmud and Torah (Holy books/scriptures Judaism)
4) Any other holy book pertaining to other faiths/religions.

A working knowledge even a basic one, will serve you well in personal exchanges with members and clergy of their chosen faiths. This in turn benefits the Odinist community in addition to reinforcing your own position as a respected cleric yourself, within the society of collective religious clerics within the entire recognized religious community overall.

*Note: All papers (e.g. Thesis, dissertation, monograph), must demonstrate intelligent and comprehensive knowledge of subject matter.

Part I - Ministering

Begin and end each day with Runic meditation and Galdar.
Runes for Part 1: First AEtt of the Elder Futhark.

Counseling

Lesson One - Addictions

Compose an essay of not less than twenty-five (25) pages, single spaced, front and back, demonstrating your ability to provide spiritual Rede (counsel) to a fictitious member of your ministry whom is suffering from an addiction.

Lesson Two – Confidentiality

Confidentiality between a Gothi and an adherent of our faith should never be compromised wherein any personal exchange transpires. The **only** exception to this is of course, if a Gothi is seeking the Rede of an Elder Gothi, in which you may better serve that member of our Faith. And even then, the member's name should not be revealed to the Senior Gothar unless the member's name in question affords you his/her consent to do so. Confidentiality should be held sacred and never breached!

Compose an essay of not less than twenty-five (25) pages, front and back, single lined, on the importance of confidentiality and the adverse effects and consequences attached thereto any such breaches whether deliberate or not.

Lesson Three - Ethics

Although Odinism is a folk religion germane to the peoples descended from Indo-European ancestry, no mortal has the right to tell anyone of any ethnic group, what religion, or spiritual path one may follow, nor what Gods one may call upon in their search for spiritual fulfillment. The mere notion that one may tell another where they may, or may not seek their own relationship with that which is divine, due to their race, creed, color, sex, politics, or their sexual preference, is not only unnatural, it further exhibits an immature personality. Albeit, while the afore stated is certainly meritorious, just as valid is the fact that many people elect to invoke their right to practice freedom of association, be it on an individual basis, or collectively as a religious body/ministry. This certainly does not deem such folks to be bigots, homophobes, or closed minded in the least way imaginable. Some folks merely seek to preserve their indigenous faiths without the threat of outside interference corrupting the fundamental values of their chosen faith... All religions have such denominations and that is an inexorable truth. Just as true and appropriate is the fact that some Gothar take vows in their Oath to the Gothar, in which they pledge to minister only to those of their folk, regardless of whether one agrees or disagrees with such vows, they do indeed echo and reflect the greater general consensus of that which constitutes the corpus of the Odinist and Ásatrú community at large the world over.

The Scenario:

Two people approach you seeking to become adherents of our faith, one of them is of non-folk descent, and the other one is a homosexual. Addressing each person separately, illustrate the manner of your response to these issues, and why.

End of Part One

Part 2 – Historical Studies

Begin and end each day with Runic meditation and Galdar.
Runes for Part 2: the second AEtt of the Elder Futhark.

Lesson One – Early Aryan Tribalism

Compose an essay of not less than 5,000 words regarding the prehistoric Stone Age, the Bronze Age and the Iron Age as they regard the Aryan Tribes and their early spiritual practices in theory.

Lesson Two – The Migration Period

Compose an essay of not less than 5,000 words regarding the Migration Period (300–793 CE), regarding how it influenced, or altered the religious practices of the Aryan Tribes.

Lesson Three – The Viking Age

Compose an essay of not less than 5,000 words regarding the Viking Age (793 – 1100 CE), and the impact which it had upon our faith and folk, both then and now.

Lesson Four – The Current Era

Compose an essay of not less than 5,000 words regarding the current state of Odinism here in Vinland (USA & Canada), and abroad

End of Part Two

Part 3 – Cultural Studies

Begin and end each day with Runic meditation and Galdar.
Runes for Part 3: the third AEtt of the Elder Futhark.

Lesson One – Teutonic Culture

Compose an essay of not less than 10,000 words on Teutonic Culture. This essay is wide open to the intellectual desire of each candidate. Choose your words and content wisely for this assignment will reveal much about how you perceive our indigenous faith and the very culture which engendered it.

Lesson Two – Indo-Europeans (Aryans)

Compose an essay of not less than 10,000 words regarding the Indo-European culture and Religion as it relates and contributed to the faith we know today as Odinism. Who were these people and who are their descendants today?

Lesson Three – Heroic Legends

Compose an essay of not less than 10,000 words in regards to four heroic ancestral legends. Legend choices are open to each candidate.

Lesson Four – The Sagas

Compose an essay of not less than 10,000 words in regards to four of our major Sagas, and the lessons which they and their characters afford us to this day.

Lesson Five – Germanic Myth and Folklore

Compose an essay of not less than 10,000 words regarding Germanic (Norse-Teutonic) Myth and Folklore, their importance and function today and the difference between the two.

Lesson Six – Odinism Today

Compose an essay of not less than 10,000 words regarding modern Odinism concepts as well as the major misconceptions regarding our sacred faith.

End of Part Three

Part 4 – Communications

Lesson One – Public Relations

Compose an essay of not less than 5,000 words regarding Public Relations as they apply to Odinism (i.e. dealing with Prison Administrators, local, state, and federal officials and clergy administrators from other religions).

Lesson Two – Ministry Administration

Compose an essay of not less than 5,000 words regarding the functions, duties and necessity of any successful ministry's administration.

Lesson Three – Adult and Children's Education

Compose an essay of not less than 5,000 words regarding adult and children's education in the fields of Odinist studies and folk cultural studies and the paramount importance to our faith and folk's future that these forums will have both individually and collectively.

End of Part Four

Part 5 – Theology and Philosophy

Lesson One – Odinist Principles

Compose an essay of not less than 5,000 words regarding the theological and philosophical principals of Odinism today as it seeks to evolve.

Lesson Two – Ritual and Religion

Compose an essay of not less than 5,000 words regarding the principals governing ritual and religion today as they apply to Odinism. Are Ritual and religion one and the same?

Lesson Three – Christianity, Islam & Judaism/Odinism vs. Ásatrú/Multi-Cultural Paganism

Compose an essay of not less than 5,000 words providing a historical and philosophical overview of Christianity, Islam and Judaism. In addition, cite the differences between Odinism and Ásatrú and just how they differ from other multi-cultural Paganism (i.e. Wicca, Druidism, New Ageism, etc.).

End of Part Five

Part 6 – Traditional Religious Skills

Lesson One – Blót (Blótar)

A) Compose a thesis regarding the functions and necessity of conducting Blót.

B) Compose a Blót for Allfather Odin and one for each of the Eight major Holy observances of the "Achtwan" (Wheel of the Year/Lit.Trans. Wheel of Eight.)

Lesson Two – Rune Work

A) Compose a thesis on the philosophy and mechanics of basic Rune work.

B) Compose a functional Rune working.

(You **MUST** demonstrate a comprehensive knowledge and working application.)

Lesson Three – Galdr Work

A) Compose a thesis on the philosophy of Galdr.
B) Compose a comprehensive Galdr working.

End of Part Six

Good Luck with your lessons, from the Court of Gothar, Megi Odin Blessi Thig. Heil Allfather Odin!

In Frith with Thee…
the Court of Gothar of the HOLY NATION OF ODIN, Inc
and the Sons of Odin, 1519-Vinland Kindred

Test Scores:		
	95-100	Excellent
	90-94	Very Good
	85-89	Good
	80-84	Fair
	77-79	Satisfactory
	<=76	Fail – Repeat assignment

35
HÁVAMÁL
<u>Sayings of the High One</u>

Human social wisdom, teasing allusion to runic mysteries, spells, and charms combine in this poem to give a conspectus of different types of wisdom. Most of the poem is taken up with instruction on the subject of social behavior, common sense and folly, moderation and friendship, composed in the *ljodahattar*, the usual metre of wisdom verse. At times the poet steps forward to speak in his own voice, at times the first person emerges with Odin, the god of wisdom, speaking from his own experience of questing after knowledge. The wisdom stanzas are organized by themes, connections made by juxtaposition or contrast. Towards the end of the poem Odin speaks more, of his sacrifice to learn the secrets of the runes and of his knowledge of spells, and narrates two adventures with women, and the metre is disrupted. *Sayings of the High One* (Hávamál) is, no doubt, a redaction of several different poems unified by the theme of wisdom and by the central figure of Odin.

I.
1. All the entrances, before you walk forward,
   you should look at,
   you should spy out;
   for you can't know for certain where enemies are sitting
   ahead in the hall.

2. Blessed be the givers! A guest has come in,
   where is he going to sit?
   He's in great haste, the one who by the hearth
   is going to be tested out.

3. Fire is needful for someone who's come in
   and who's chilled to the knee;
   food and clothing are necessary for the man
   who's journeyed over the mountains.

4. Water is needful for someone who comes to a meal,
   a towel and a warm welcome,
   a disposition, if he can get it, for good words
   and silence in return.

5. Wits are needful for someone who travels widely,
   anything will do at home;
   he becomes a laughing-stock, the man who knows nothing
   and sits among the wise.

6. About his intelligence no man should be boastful,
   rather cautious of mind;
   when a wise and silent man comes to a homestead
   seldom does shame befall the wary;
   for no more trustworthy a friend can any man get
   than a store of common sense.

7. The careful guest, who comes to a meal,
   keeps silent with hearing finely attuned;
   he listens with his ears, and looks about with his eyes;
   so every wise man informs himself.

8. This man is fortunate who can get for himself
   praise and good will;
   very difficult it is when a man lays claim
   to what's in another's heart.

9. That man is fortunate who, in himself,
   keeps his reputation and wits while he lives,
   for men have often received bad advice
   from another's heart.

10. No better burden can a man carry on the road
    than a store of common sense;
    better than riches it will seem in an unfamiliar place,
    such is the resort of the wretched.

11. No better burden can a man carry on the road
    than a store of common sense;
    a worse journey-provisioning he couldn't carry over the land
    than to be too drunk on ale.

12. It isn't as good as it's said to be,
    ale, for the sons of men;
    for the more he drinks, the less he knows
    about the nature of men.

13. The heron of forgetfulness hovers over the ale-drinking;
    he steals men's wits;
    with the feathers of this bird I was fettered
    in the court of Gunnlod.*

14. Drunk I was, I was more than drunk
    at wise Fialar's,*
    that's the best sort of ale-drinking when afterwards
    every man gets his mind back again.

15. Silent and thoughtful a prince's son should be
    and bold in fighting;
    cheerful and merry every man should be
    until he waits for death.

16. The foolish man thinks he will live for ever,
    if he keeps away from fighting;
    but old age won't grant him a truce
    even if the spears do.

17. The fool gapes when he comes on a visit,
    he mutters to himself or keeps silent;
    but it's all up with him if he gets a swig of drink;
    the man's mind is exposed.

18. Only that man who travels widely
    and has journeyed a great deal knows
    what sort of mind each man has in his control;
    he who's sharp in his wits.

19. A man shouldn't hold onto the cup but drink mead in moderation,
    it's necessary to speak or be silent;
    no man will blame you for impoliteness
    if you go early to bed.

20. The greedy man, unless he guards against this tendency,
    will eat himself into lifelong trouble;
    often he's laughed at when he comes among the wise,
    the man who's foolish about his stomach.

21. Cattle know when they ought to go home;
    and then they leave the pasture;
    but the foolish man never knows
    the measure of his own stomach.

22. He's a wretched man, of an evil disposition,
    the one who makes fun of everything;
    he doesn't know the one thing he ought to know;
    that he himself is not devoid of faults.

23. The foolish man lies awake all night
    and worries about things;
    he's tired out when the morning comes
    and everything's just as bad as it was.

24. The foolish man thinks that everyone
    is his friend who laughs with him;
    he doesn't notice even if they say cruel things about him
    when he sits among the wise.

25. The foolish man thinks that everyone
    is his friend who laughs with him;
    but then he finds when he comes to the Assembly*
    that he has few to speak on his behalf.

26. The foolish man thinks he knows everything
    if he takes refuge in a corner;
    he doesn't know what he can say in return
    if people ask him questions.

27. The foolish man in company
    does best if he stays silent;
    no one will know that he know nothing,
    unless he talks too much;
    but the man who knows nothing does not know
    when he is talking too much.

28. Wise that man seems who knows how to question
    and how to answer as well;
    the sons of men cannot keep secret
    what's already going around.

29. Quite enough senseless words are spoken
    by the man never silent;
    a quick tongue, unless its owner keeps watch on it,
    often talks itself into trouble.

30. Into a laughing-stock no man should make another,
    though he comes on a visit;
    many a man seems wise if he isn't asked questions
    and he manages to lurk unscathed.

31. Wise that man seems who retreats
    when one guest is insulting another;
    the man who mocks others at a feast doesn't really know
    whether he's shooting off his mouth amid enemies.

32. Many men are devoted to one another
    and yet they fight at feats;
    amongst men there will always be strife,
    guest quarrelling with guest.

33. An early meal a man should usually eat,
    unless he is going on a visit;
    he sits and guzzles, acts as if he is starving,
    and doesn't make any conversation.

34. It's a great detour to a bad friend's house,
    even though he lives in the route;
    but to a good friend's the ways lie straight,
    even though he lives far off.

35. A man must go, he must not remain a guest
    always in the same place;
    the loved man is loathed if he sits too long
    in someone else's hall.

36. A farm of your own is better, even if small,
    everyone's someone at home;
    though he has two goats and a coarsely roofed house,
    that is better than begging.

37. A farm of your own is better, even if small,
    everyone's someone at home;
    a man's heart bleeds when he has to beg
    for every single meal.

38. From his weapons on the open road
    no man should step one pace away;
    you don't know for certain when you're out on the road
    when you might have need of your spear.

39. I never found a generous man, nor one so hospitable with food,
    that he wouldn't accept a present;
    or one so well-provided with money
    that he wouldn't take a gift if offered.

40. On account of the property which he has amassed
    a man shouldn't suffer need;
    often what was meant for the lovable is saved for the hateful,
    much goes worse than expected.

41. With weapons and gifts friends should gladden one another,
    that is most obvious;
    mutual givers and receivers are friends for longest,
    if the friendship is going to work at all.

42. To his friend a man should be a friend
    and repay gifts with gifts;
    laughter a man should give for laughter
    and repay treachery with lies.

43. To his friend a man should be a friend
    and to his friend's friend too;
    but a friend no man should be
    to the friend of his enemy.

44. You know, if you've a friend whom you really trust
and from whom you want nothing but good,
you should mix your soul with his and exchange gifts,
go and see him often.

45. If you've another, whom you don't trust,
but from whom you want nothing but good,
speak fairly to him but think falsely
and repay treachery with lies.

46. Again, concerning the one whom you don't trust,
and whose mind you suspect:
you should laugh with him and disguise your thoughts,
a gift should be repaid with a like one.

47. I was young once, I travelled alone,
then I found myself going astray;
rich I thought myself when I met someone else,
for man is the joy of man.

48. Generous and brave men live the best,
seldom do they harbour anxiety;
but the cowardly man is afraid of everything,
the miser always sighs when he gets gifts.

49. My clothes I gave along the way
to two wooden men,*
champions they thought themselves when they had clothing,
the naked man is ashamed.

50. The withered fir-tree which stands on the mound,
neither bark nor needles protect it;
so it is with the man whom love one loves,
why should he live for long?

51. Hotter than fire between bad friends
burns affection for five days;
but it dies down when the sixth day comes,
and all that friendship goes to the bad.

52. Not very much need a man give,
    often you get praise for a little;
    with half a loaf and a tilted cup
    I've got myself a companion.

53. Of small sands, of small seas,
    small are the minds of men;
    for all men aren't equally wise,
    men everywhere are half wise, half not.

54. Averagely wise a man ought to be,
    never too wise;
    for he lives the best sort of life,
    the man who knows a fair amount.

55. Averagely wise a man ought to be,
    never too wise;
    for a wise man's heart is seldom cheerful,
    if he who owns it's too wise.

56. Averagely wise a man ought to be,
    never too wise;
    no one may know his fate beforehand,
    if he wants a carefree spirit.

57. One brand takes fire from another, until it is consumed,
    a spark's kindled by a spark;
    one man becomes clever by talking with another,
    but foolish by taciturnity.

58. He should get up early, the man who means to take
    another's life or property;
    the slumbering wolf does no get the ham,
    nor a sleeping man victory.

59. He should get up early, the man who has few workers,
    and go about his work with thought;
    much he neglects, the man who sleeps in the mornings,
    wealth is half-won by the vigorous.

60. Of dry wood and thatching-bark
a man can know the measure;
and of the wood which can get one through
a quarter- or a half-year.

61. Washed and fed, a man should ride to the Assembly,
though he may not be very well dressed;
of his shoes and breeches no man should be ashamed,
nor of his horse, though he doesn't have a good one.

62. The eagle snaps and cranes his neck when he comes to the sea,*
to the ancient ocean;
so does a man who comes among the multitude
and has few people to speak for him.

63. Asking questions and answering, this every wise man should do,
he who wants to be reputed intelligent;
one may know, a second should not,
the whole world knows, if three know.

64. Every man wise in counsel
should use his power in moderation;
for when he mingles with warriors he finds out
that no one is boldest of all.

65. For those words which one man says to another,
often he gets paid back.*

66. Much too early I've come to many places,
but sometimes too late;
the ale all drunk, or sometimes it wasn't yet brewed,
the unpopular man seldom chooses the right occasion.

67. Here and there I'd be invited to someone's home
when I had no need of food for the moment;
or two hams would be hanging in a trusty friend's house
when I'd already eaten one.

68. Fire is the best for the sons of men,
    and the sight of the sun
    his health, if a man can manage to keep it,
    living without disgrace.

69. No man is completely wretched, even if he has bad luck;
    one man is blessed with sons,
    another with kinsmen, another has enough money,
    another has done great deeds.

70. It is better to live than not to be alive,
    it's the living man who gets the cow;
    I saw a fire blaze up for the wealthy man,
    and he was dead outside the door.

71. The lame man rides a horse, the handless man drives herds,
    the deaf man fights and succeeds;
    to be blind is better than to be burnt:
    a corpse is of no use to anyone.

72. A son is best, even if he is born late,
    when the father is dead;
    seldom do memorial stones stand by the wayside,
    unless one kinsmen raises them for another.

73. Two are the conquerors of one, the tongue is the slayer of the head,
    hidden under every fur coat I expect to find a hand.*

74. Night is eagerly awaited by the man who can rely on his provisions;
    short are a ship's yards,
    changeable are autumn nights,
    many kinds of weather in five days,
    and more in one month.

75. Even a man who know nothing
    knows that many are fooled by money;
    one man is rich, another is not rich,
    he should not be blamed for that.

76. Cattle die, kinsmen die,*
    the self must also die;
    but glory never dies,
    for the man who is able to achieve it.

77. Cattle die, kinsmen die,
    the self must also die;
    I know one thing which never dies:
    the reputation of each dead man.

78. Fully stocked folds I saw in Fitiung's sons,*
    now they carry beggars staffs;
    wealth is like a twinkling of an eye,
    it is most unreliable of friends.

79. The foolish man, if he manages to get
    money or love of a woman,
    his arrogance increases, but not his common sense;
    on he goes deeply sunk in delusion.

80. That is now proved, what you ask of the runes,
    of the potent famous ones
    which the great gods made
    and the mighty sage stained,*
    then it is best for him if he stays silent.

81. At evening should the day be praised, the woman when she is cremated,
    the blade when it is tested, the girl when she is married,
    the ice when it is crossed, the ale when it is drunk.

82. In a wind one should cut wood, in fine weather row on the sea,
    in darkness chat with a girl: many are the eyes of the day;
    use a ship to glide along, a shield for defense,
    a sword for blows, and a girl for kisses.

83. By the fire one should drink ale, one should slide over the ice,
    buy a lean horse and a rusty blade,
    fatten the horse at home and a dog on the farmstead.

84. The words of a girl no one should trust,
    nor what a woman says;
    for on a whirling wheel their hearts were made,*
    deceit lodged in their breasts.

85. A stretching bow, a burning flame,
    a gaping wolf, a cawing crow,
    a grunting pig, a rootless tree,
    a rising wave, a boiling kettle,

86. a flying dart, a falling wave,
    ice of one night, a coiled serpent,
    the bed-talk of a woman, or a broken sword,
    the playing of a bear, or a king's child,

87. a sick calf, an independent-minded slave,
    a seer who prophesies good, a newly killed corpse,

88. an early-sown field let no man trust,
    nor too early a son;
    the weather determines the field and brains the son,
    both of them are risky.

89. A brother's killer, if you meet him on the road,
    a house half-burned, a too swift horse-
    the mount is useless if he breaks a leg-
    let no man be so trusting as to trust all these.

90. Such is the love of women, of those with false minds;
    it's like driving a horse without spiked shoes over slippery ice,
    a frisky two year old, badly broken in,
    or like steering, in a stiff wind, a rudderless boat,
    or trying to catch when you're lame a reindeer on a thawing hillside.

91. I can speak frankly since I have known both:
    the hearts of men are fickle towards women;
    when we speak most fairly, then we think most falsely,
    that entraps the wise mind.

92. He has to speak fairly and offer money,
    the man who wants a woman's love;
    praise the body of the radiant woman:
    he who flatters, gets.

93. No man should ever reproach
    another for love;
    often the wise man is seized, when the foolish man is not,
    by a delightfully fair appearance.

94. Not at all should one man reproach another
    for what is common among men;
    among the sons of men the wise are made foolish
    by that mighty desire.

95. The mind alone knows what lies near the heart,
    he alone knows his spirit:
    no sickness is worse for the wise man
    than to have no one to love him.

96. That I found when I sat among the reeds
    and waited for my desire;
    body and soul the wise girl was to me,
    nevertheless I didn't win her.

97. Billing's girl I found on the bed,*
    sleeping, sun-radiant;
    the pleasures of a noble were nothing to me,
    except to live with that body.

98. 'At evening, Odin, you should come again,
    if you want to woo yourself a girl;
    all is lost if anyone knows
    of such shame together.'

99. Back I turned, and thought I was going to love,
    back from my certain pleasure;
    this I thought that I would have,
    all her heart and her love-play.

100. So I came afterwards, but standing ready
    were all the warriors, awake,
    with burning torches and carrying brands:
    thus the path of desire was determined for me.

101. And near morning, when I came again,
    then the hall-company were asleep;
    a bitch I found then tied on the bed
    of that good woman.

102. Many a good girl when you know her better
    is fickle of heart towards men;
    I found that out, when I tried to seduce
    that sagacious woman into shame;
    every sort of humiliation the clever woman devised for me,
    and I didn't even possess the woman.

103. At home a man should be cheerful and merry with his guest,
    he should be shrewd about himself,
    with a good memory and eloquent, if he wants to be very wise,
    often should he speak of good things;
    a nincompoop that man is called, who can't say much for himself,
    that is the hallmark of a fool.

104. I visited the old giant, now I've come back,*
    I didn't get much there from being silent;
    with many words I spoke to my advantage
    in Suttung's hall.

105. Gunnlod gave me from her gold throne
    a drink of the precious mead;
    a poor reward I let her have in return,
    for her open-heartedness,
    for her heavy spirit.

106. With the mouth of the auger I made space for myself*
    and gnawed through the stone;
    over me and under me went the paths of the giants,
    thus I risked my head.

107. The cheaply bought beauty I made good use of,
   the wise lack for little;
   for Odrerir has now come up*
   to the rim of the sanctuaries of men.

108. I am in doubt as to whether I would have come
   back from the courts of the giants,
   if I had not made use of Gunnlod, that good woman,
   and put my arms about her.

109. The next day the frost-giants went
   to ask for the High One's advice, in the High One's hall;
   they asked about Bolverk: whether he was amongst the gods,*
   or whether Suttung had slaughtered him.

110. I thought Odin had sworn a sacred ring-oath,*
   how can his word be trusted!
   He left Suttung betrayed at the feast
   and made Gunnlod weep.

II.
111. It is time to declaim from the sage's high-seat,
   at the spring of fate;
   I saw and was silent, I saw and I considered,
   I heard the speech of men;
   I heard talk of runes nor were they silent about good counsel,
   at the High One's hall, in the High One's hall;
   thus I heard them speak:

112. I advise you, Loddfafnir, to take this advice,*
   it will be useful if you learn it,
   do you good, if you have it:
   don't get up at night, except to look around
   or if you need to visit the privy outside.

113. I advise you, Loddfafnir, to take this advice,
   it will be useful if you learn it,
   do you good, if you have it:
   in the arms of a witch you should never sleep,
   so that she charms all your limbs;

114. she'll bring it about that you won't care
about the Assembly or the king's business;
you won't want food nor the society of people,
sorrowful you'll go to sleep.

115. I advise you, Loddfafnir, to take this advice,
it will be useful if you learn it,
do you good, if you have it:
never entice another's wife to you
as a close confidante.

116. I advise you, Loddfafnir, to take this advice,
it will be useful if you learn it,
do you good, if you have it:
on mountain or fjord should you happen to be travelling,
make sure you are well fed.

117. I advise you, Loddfafnir, to take this advice,
it will be useful if you learn it,
do you good, if you have it:
never let a wicked man know
of any misfortune you suffer;
for from a wicked man you will never get
a good thought in return.

118. I saw a man fatally wounded
through the words of a wicked woman;
a malicious tongue brought about his death
and yet there was no truth in the accusation.

119. I advise you, Loddfafnir, to take this advice,
it will be useful if you learn it,
do you good, if you have it:
you know, if you've a friend, one whom you trust,
go to see him often;
for brushwood grows, and tall grass,
on the road which no man treads.

120. I advise you, Loddfafnir, to take this advice,
it will be useful if you learn it,
do you good, if you have it:
draw to you in friendly intimacy a good man
and learn healing charms all your life.

121. I advise you, Loddfafnir, to take this advice,
it will be useful if you learn it,
do you good, if you have it:
with your friend never be
the first to tear friendship asunder;
sorrow eats the heart if you do not have
someone to tell all your thoughts.

122. I advise you, Loddfafnir, to take this advice,
it will be useful if you learn it,
do you good, if you have it:
you should never bandy words
with a stupid fool;

123. for from a wicked man you will never get
a good return;
but a good man will make you
assured of praise.

124. That is the true mingling of kinship when you can tell
someone all your thoughts;
anything is better than to be fickle;
he is no true friend who only says pleasant things.

125. I advise you, Loddfafnir, to take this advice,
it will be useful if you learn it,
do you good, if you have it:
even three words of quarrelling you shouldn't have with an inferior;
often the better retreats
when the worse man fights.

126. I advise you, Loddfafnir, to take this advice,
it will be useful if you learn it,
do you good, if you have it:
be neither a shoemaker nor a shaftmaker
for anyone but yourself;
if the shoe is badly fitting or the shaft is crooked,
then a curse will be called down on you.

127. I advise you, Loddfafnir, to take this advice,
it will be useful if you learn it,
do you good, if you have it:
where you recognize evil, speak out against it,
and give no truces to your enemies.

128. I advise you, Loddfafnir, to take this advice,
it will be useful if you learn it,
do you good, if you have it:
never be made glad by wickedness
but make yourself the butt of approval.

129. I advise you, Loddfafnir, to take this advice,
it will be useful if you learn it,
do you good, if you have it:
you should never look upwards in battle:*
the sons of men become panicked--
you may well be bewitched.

130. I advise you, Loddfafnir, to take this advice,
it will be useful if you learn it,
do you good, if you have it:
if you want a good woman for yourself to talk to as a close confidante,
and to get pleasure from,
make fair promises and keep them well,
no man tires of good, if he can get it.

131. I advise you, Loddfafnir, to take this advice,
it will be useful if you learn it,
do you good, if you have it:
I tell you to be cautious but not over-cautious;
be most wary of ale, and of another's wife,
and, thirdly, watch out that thieves don't beguile you.

132. I advise you, Loddfafnir, to take this advice,
it will be useful if you learn it,
do you good, if you have it:
never hold up to scorn or mockery
a guest or a wanderer.

133. Often those who sit in the hall do not really know
whose kin those newcomers are;
no man is so good that he has no blemish,
nor so bad that he can't succeed in something.

134. I advise you, Loddfafnir, to take this advice,
it will be useful if you learn it,
do you good, if you have it:
at a grey-haired sage you should never laugh!
Often what the old say is good;
often from a wrinkled bag come judicious words,
from those who hang around with the hides
and skulk among the skins
and hover among the cheese-bags.

135. I advise you, Loddfafnir, to take this advice,
it will be useful if you learn it,
do you good, if you have it:
don't bark at your guests or drive them from your gate,
treat the indigent well!

136. It is a powerful latch which has to lift
to open up for everyone;
give a ring, or there'll be called down on you
a curse in every limb.

137. I advise you, Loddfafnir, to take this advice,
it will be useful if you learn it,
do you good, if you have it:
where you drink ale, choose the power of earth!*
For earth is good against drunkenness, and fire against sickness,
oak against constipation, an ear of corn against witchcraft,
the hall against household strife, for hatred the moon should be invoked--
earthworms for a bite or sting, and runes against evil;
soil you should use against flood.

III.
138. I know that I hung on a windy tree*
   nine long nights,
   wounded with a spear, dedicated to Odin,
   myself to myself,
   on that tree of which no man knows
   from where its roots run.

139. No bread did they give me nor a drink from a horn,
   downwards I peered;
   I took up the runes, screaming I took them,
   then I fell back from there.

140. Nine mighty spells I learnt from the famous son
   of Bolthor, Bestla's father,*
   and I got a drink of the precious mead,
   poured from Odrerir.

141. Then I began to quicken and be wise,
   and to grow and to prosper,
   one word found another word for me,
   one deed found another deed for me.

142. The runes you must find and the meaningful letter,
   a very great letter,
   a very powerful letter,
   which the mighty sage stained
   and the powerful gods made
   and the runemaster of the gods carved out.

143. Odin for the Æsir, and Dain for the elves,
   Dvalin for the dwarfs,
   Asvid for the giants,
   I myself carved some.

144. Do you know how to carve, do you know how to interpret,
   do you know how to stain, do you know how to test out,
   do you know how to ask, do you know how to sacrifice,
   do you know how to dispatch, do you know how to slaughter?

145. Better not to pray, than to sacrifice too much,
one gift always calls for another;
better not dispatched than to slaughter too much.
So Thund carved before the history of nations,*
where he rose up, when he came back.

146. I know those spells which a ruler's wife doesn't know,*
nor any man's son;
'help' one is called,
and that will help you
against accusations and sorrows
and every sort of anxiety.

147. I know a second one which the sons of men need,
those who want to live as physicians.

148. I know a third one which is very useful to me,
which fetters my enemy;
the edges of my foes I can blunt,
neither weapon nor club will bite for them.

149. I know a fourth one if men put
chains upon my limbs;
I can chant so that I can walk away,
fetters spring from my feet,
and bonds from my hands.

150. I know a fifth if I see, shot in malice,
a dart flying amid the army:
it cannot fly so fast that I cannot stop it
if I see it with my eyes.

151. I know a sixth one if a man wounds me
with the roots of the sap-filled wood:
and that man who conjured to harm me,
the evil consumes him, not me.

152. I know a seventh one if I see towering flames
in the hall about my companions:
it can't burn so widely that I can't counteract it,
I know the spells to chant.

153. I know an eighth one, which is most useful
 for everyone to know;
 where hatred flares up between the sons of warriors,
 then I can quickly bring settlement.

154. I know a ninth one if I am in need,
 if I must protect my ship at sea;
 the wind I can lull upon the wave
 and quieten all the sea to sleep.

155. I know a tenth one if I see witches
 playing up in the air;
 I can bring it about that they can't make their way back
 to their own shapes,
 to their own spirits.

156. I know an eleventh if I have to lead
 loyal friends into battle;
 under the shields I chant, and they journey inviolate,
 safely to the battle,
 safely from the battle,
 safely they come everywhere.

157. I know a twelfth one if I see, up in a tree,
 a dangling corpse in a noose:
 I can so carve and colour the runes
 that the man walks
 and talks with me.

158. I know a thirteenth if I shall pour water
 over a young warrior:
 he will not fall though he goes into battle,
 before swords he will not sink.

159. I know a fourteenth if I have to reckon up
 the gods before men:
 Æsir and elves, I know the difference between them,
 few who are not wise know that.

160. I know a fifteenth, which the dwarf Thiodrerir
 chanted before Delling's doors:
 powerfully he sang for the Æsir and before the elves,
 wisdom to Sage.

161. I know a sixteenth if I want to have all
a clever woman's heart and love-play:
I can turn the thoughts of the white-armed woman
and change her mind entirely.

162. I know a seventeenth, so that scarcely any
young girl will want to shun me.
Of these spells, Loddfafnir,
you will long be in want;
thought they'd be good for you, if you got them,
useful if you learned them,
handy, if you had them.

163. I know an eighteenth, which I shall never teach
to any girl or any man's wife--
it's always better when just one person knows,
that follows at the end of the spells--
except that one woman whom my arms embrace,
or who may be my sister.

164. Now is the song of the High One recited, in the High One's hall,
very useful to the sons of men,
quite useless to the sons of giants,
luck to him who recites, luck to him who knows!
May he benefit, he who learnt it,
luck to those who listened!

Notes

Gunnlod: this alludes to the story of the winning of the mead of poetry, told in full in Snorri, *Edda*, pp. 61-4. The mead originally belonged to two dwarfs, Fialar and Gialar, and was stolen by the giants. Odin had worked for a year as a thrall for the brother of Suttung, the giant who had the mead. When the year was up he went to Suttung (here confusingly called Fialar) to claim his reward of mead. By seducing Gunnlod, Suttung's daughter, he gained her help and escaped with the mead back to Asgard. The story is told in fuller detail in vv. 104-10 below.

Fiarlar: here a mistake for Suttung, owner of the mead.

Assembly: in both mainland Scandinavia and Iceland people would regularly meet at regional assemblies (Things) to resolve law cases.

Two wooden men: these may be scarecrows, or they may be wooden idols, mentioned in some sagas. In the *saga of Ragnar Lodbrok*, ch. 20, some Vikings come to a Baltic island where they find a huge, wooden idol. The idol speaks a verse complaining that once he used to be given food and clothing but now he is neglected.

The eagle: opinion is divided as to whether this is a sea-eagle on the look out for fish as prey, or a land eagle who has flown away from his accustomed habitat and so is disoriented.

Paid back: this verse is missing some lines.

A hand: the metre has changed suddenly and the meaning is obscure. Possibly a rich outer garment may well conceal a hand ready to strike.
Cattle die, kinsmen die: a parallel has been detected in the Old English poem *The Wanderer*: 'here cattle are transient / here property is transient, here a friend is transient' (l. 108). If there is a direct connection it most likely stems from the formulaic use of the words 'cattle' and 'kinsmen', an alliterating pair both in Old Norse, *fe* and *frændr,* and in Old English, *feoh* and *freond.*
Fitiung's sons: although they sound proverbial, Fitiung's sons are otherwise unknown.

Mighty sage stained: the sage is probably Odin. Carved runic letters appear originally to have been filled in with some kind of paint.
Whirling wheel: the image is of a potter's wheel or of a truning lathe; in its turning the wheel incorporates changeability into women's hearts. Some have seen the medieval image of the Wheel of Fortune here, but that deals with a human's external fate, not is internal character.

Billing's girl: this story is unknown from other sources, though the sequence of events is not difficult to follow. Odin importunes the wife or daughter of Billing (probably a giant). She puts him off until the evening; when he first comes to her hall everyone is still awake, the second time she has gone, leaving a bitch in her place. Billing's girl doubtless fears to reject Odin openly lest he bewitch her as he does Rind, who has fated to be the mother of Vali, avenger of Baldr. Her story is told in Saxo's *History of the Danish People*, Book 3, pp. 69-79.

The old giant: a further elaboration of the story of the mead of poetry begun in vv. 13-14.
Auger: according to Snorri, *Edda*, p. 63, Odin makes use of an auger called Rati to bore his way into the mountain where Gunnlod is to be found, and, turning himself into a snake, wriggles in through the hole.
Odrerir: according to Snorri this is the name of one of the vats in which the mead of poetry was kept, though the name 'Stirrer of Inspiration' seems more likely to refer to the mead itself.

Bolverk: the name Odin had used when disguised as a thrall, and in his dealings with Gunnlod.
Ring-oath: in Iceland oaths were sworn on large silver rings kept at the local temple and reddened with sacrificial blood.
Loddfafnir: the name is unknown from other sources. *Lodd-* seems to mean 'rags', while Fafnir is the name of the dragon Sigurd killed. The combination 'Ragged-dragon' may be a mocking term for someone who is not yet fully initiated into arcane knowledge.

Look upwards in battle: the phenomenon warned against here is a kind of mass panic, frequently found in Irish sources, and for which an Irish loanword is used in the Norse.

Power of earth: the substances mentioned ma be invoked or be incorporated into some kind of ritual.
I hung on a windy tree: Odin performs a sacrifice by hanging for nine nights on the tree Yggdrasill, pierced with a spear in order to gain knowledge of the runes. The parallels with the Crucifixion are marked, though interpretation is controversial. The motif of the Hanged God is widespread in Indo-European and ancient Near Eastern religion, however, so direct Christian influence need not be present here.
Bolthor: Odin's maternal grandfather; Bolthor's son is therefore Odin's mother's brother, a particularly close relationship in Germanic society.

Thund: an Odinic name.
Spells: the spells which Odin alludes to here broadly match those magical skills listed for him in *Ynglinga saga*, chs. 2 and 6.

36
WHO IS WHITE?
by David Lane

Those of you who have over the years or decades either observed or participated in the resistance to the murder of the White race know that provocateurs have attacked the racial purity of professed leaders to impugn their motives. In my opinion part of the reason this has successfully worked for the enemy is a mindset grown from an alien religion. A basic tenet of Judeo-Christianity and part of its fatal allure is that it allows inferior men to claim superior status without corresponding effort. A Judeo-Christian with an IQ of 90 and a dismal life history can get baptized, repeat a few ritualistic words and presto, suddenly proclaim divine status superior to that of a man a million times his superior in intellect and character. The "blue-eyed blond" syndrome is typical of this mentality. And I say this advisedly since I appear Nordic, tall, slender, blue-eyed blond. Yet I can only guess at the purity of my ancestry. My father of record sold my mother to his buddies and to strangers for booze money, so the Gods alone know all. What I do know is this. I look White. I fight for White. I recognize the achievements of the White race. I want to preserve our kind. I am horrified that the beauty of the White Aryan woman may soon perish from the earth forever. I suffer for each White child tormented in America's inter-racial nightmare. I see beauty in a Celtic princess with brown or red hair and green eyes. I see beauty in the statuesque Nordic Goddess with blue eyes and golden hair. I see beauty in the freckle-faced Irish lass. I see heroism in Robert Jay Mathews and Richard Scutari with their dark hair and eyes of green or brown as well as in Frank DeSilva, a fair skinned Bruders with a French Portuguese name. Theirs is far greater nobility than 99% of those "Nordic Ideals," I might add.

For those who boast of their "purity," you have 2 parents, 4 grandparents, 8 great grandparents and so on. Go back 500 years or so and you have a million ancestors. A few more generations and everyone who ever trod the lands of Europe is your ancestor, including Huns, Mongols and Moors. There are no 100% pure Aryans as per 10,000 years ago. But we still do exist as a distinct and unique biological entity. The cultures and civilizations we create are beyond comparison. The beauty of our women, blondes, brunettes, redheads, green-eyed, blue-eyed, brown-eyed, is the desire of all men and the envy of all women. So, we do not want to be derailed by gossip or speculation on who may be 1/16th Indian or have some Italian, Spanish or Portuguese blood. We are not going to debate over whether the collective remaining White gene pool is 95% or 97% pure Aryan.

Surely it would be a tragedy if the various divisions of our race lose their distinctive traits and beauty. And after we have secured the existence of our people and a future for ALL our children, hopefully we can take steps to preserve this diversity. But for now, we are going to accept the facts and circumstances as they exist. We are going to work together for the holy cause and we will not tolerate provocateurs, divisions or dissension. If someone looks White, acts White, fights White, then until their actions prove otherwise, they are our Folk. On the other hand, regardless of pedigree or appearance, those who oppose, criticize, hinder or fail to support our cause are no friends of ours.

37
THE 88 PRECEPTS
By David Lane

Until the white race realizes that there is only one source from which we can ascertain lasting truths, there will never be peace or stability on this earth. In the immutable Laws of Nature are the keys to life, order, and understanding. The words of men, even those which some consider "inspired" are subject to the translations, vocabulary, additions, subtractions, and distortions of fallible mortals. Therefore, every writing or influence, ancient or modern, must be strained through the test of conformity to Natural Law. The White Peoples of the earth must collectively understand that they are equally subject to the iron-hard Laws of Nature with every other creature of the Universe, or they will not secure peace, safety, nor even their existence. The world is in flames because Races, Sub-races, Nations, and Cultures are being forced to violate their own Nature-ordained instincts for self-preservation. Many men of good will, but little understanding, are struggling against symptoms which are the result of disobedience to Natural Law. As is the Nature of Man, most take narrow, provincial stances predicated on views formed by immediate environment, current circumstances, and conditioned dogma. This is encouraged by that powerful and ruthless Tribe which has controlled the affairs of the world for untold centuries by exploiting Man's most base instincts. Conflict among and between the unenlightened serves as their mask and shield. A deeper understanding of the Fundamental Laws that govern the affairs of Men is necessary if we are to save civilization from its usurious executioners. The following are not intended to provide a detailed system of government, but as PRECEPTS which, when understood, will benefit and preserve a People as individuals and as a Nation.

1. Any religion or teaching which denies the Natural Laws of the Universe is false.

2. Whatever People's perception of God, or Gods, or the motive Force of the Universe might be, they can hardly deny that Nature's Law are the work of, and therefore the intent of, that Force.

3. God and religion are distinct, separate and often conflicting concepts. Nature evidences the divine plan, for the natural world is the work of the force or the intelligence men call God. Religion is the creation of mortals, therefore predestined to fallibility. Religion may preserve or destroy a People, depending on the structure given by its progenitors, the motives of its agents and the vagaries of historical circumstances.

4. The truest form of prayer is communion with Nature. It is not vocal. Go to a lonely spot, if possible a mountaintop, on a clear, star-lit night, ponder the majesty and order of the infinite macrocosm. Then consider the intricacies of the equally infinite microcosm. Understand that you are on the one hand inconsequential beyond comprehension in the size of things, and on the other hand, you are potentially valuable beyond comprehension as a link in destiny's chain. There you begin to understand how pride and self can co-exist with respect and reverence. There we find harmony with Nature and with harmony comes strength, peace and certainty.

5. Secular power systems protect and promote religions, which teach of an after-life. Thus, people are taught to abandon defenses against the predators of this life.

6. History, both secular and religious, is a fable conceived in self-serving deceit and promulgated by those who perceive benefits.

7. Religion in its most beneficial form is the symbology of a People and their culture. A multiracial religion destroys the senses of uniqueness, exclusivity and value necessary to the survival of a race.

8. What men call the "super natural" is actually the "natural" not yet understood or revealed.

9. A proliferation of laws with the resultant loss of freedom is a sign of, and directly proportional to, spiritual sickness in a Nation.

10. If a Nation is devoid of spiritual health and moral character, then government and unprincipled men will fill the vacancy. Therefore, freedom prospers in moral values and tyranny thrives in moral decay.

11. Truth requires little explanation. Therefore, beware of verbose doctrines. The great principles are revealed in brevity.

12. Truth does not fear investigation.

13. Unfounded belief is pitfall. A People who do not check the validity and effect of their beliefs with reason will suffer or perish.

14. In accord with Nature's Laws, nothing is more right than the preservation of one's own race.

15. No greater motivating force exists than the certain conviction that one is right.

16. Discernment is a sign of a healthy People. In a sick or dying nation, civilization, culture or race, substance is abandoned in favor of appearance.

17. Discernment includes the ability to recognize the difference between belief and demonstrable reality.

18. There exists no such thing as rights or privileges under the Laws of Nature. The deer being stalked by a hungry lion has no right to life. However, he may purchase life by obedience to nature- ordained instincts for vigilance and flight. Similarly, men have no rights to life, liberty or happiness. These circumstances may be purchased by oneself, by one's family, by one's tribe or by one's ancestors, but they are nonetheless purchases and are not rights. Furthermore, the value of these purchases can only be maintained through vigilance and obedience to Natural Law.

19. A people who are not convinced of their uniqueness and value will perish.

20. The White race has suffered invasions and brutality from Africa and Asia for thousands of years. For example, Attila and the Asiatic Huns who invaded Europe in the 5th century, raping, plundering and killing from the Alps to the Baltic and the Caspian Seas. This scenario was repeated by the Mongols of Genghis Khan 800 years later. (Note here that the American Indians are not "Native Americans," but are racially Mongolians.) In the 8th century, hundreds of years before Negroes were brought to America, the North African Moors of mixed racial background invaded and conquered Portugal, Spain and part of France. So, the attempted guilt-trip placed on the White race by civilization's executioners is invalid under both historical circumstance and the Natural Law which denies inter-specie compassion. The fact is, all races have benefited immeasurably from the creative genius of the Aryan People.

21. People who allow others not of their race to live among them will perish, because the inevitable result of a racial integration is racial inter-breeding which destroys the characteristics and existence of a race. Forced integration is deliberate and malicious genocide, particularly for a People like the White race, who are now a small minority in the world.

22. In the final analysis, a race or specie is not judged superior or inferior by its accomplishments, but by its will and ability to survive.

23. Political, economic, and religious systems may be destroyed and resurrected by men, but the death of a race is eternal.

24. No race of People can indefinitely continue their existence without territorial imperatives in which to propagate, protect, and promote their own kind.

25. A People without a culture exclusively their own will perish.

26. Nature has put a certain antipathy between races and species to preserve the individuality and existence of each. Violation of the territorial imperative necessary to preserve that antipathy leads to either conflict or mongrelization.

27. It is not constructive to hate those of other races, or even those of mixed races. But a separation must be maintained for the survival of one's own race. One must, however, hate with a pure and perfect hatred those of one's own race who commit treason against one's own kind and against the nations of one's own kind. One must hate with perfect hatred all those People or practices which destroy one's People, one's culture, or the racial exclusiveness of one's territorial imperative.

28. The concept of a multi-racial society violates every Natural Law for specie preservation.

29. The concept of "equality" is declared a lie by every evidence of Nature. It is a search for the lowest common denominator, and its pursuit will destroy every superior race, nation, or culture. In order for a plow horse to run as fast as a race horse you would first have to cripple the race horse; conversely, in order for a race horse to pull as much as a plow horse, you would first have to cripple the plow horse. In either case, the pursuit of equality is the destruction of excellence.

30. The instincts for racial and specie preservation are ordained by Nature.

31. Instincts are Nature's perfect mechanism for the survival of each race and specie. The human weakness of rationalizing situations for self-gratification must not be permitted to interfere with these instincts.

32. Miscegenation, that is race-mixing, is and has always been, the greatest threat to the survival of the Aryan race.

33. Inter-specie compassion is contrary to the Laws of Nature and is, therefore, suicidal. If a wolf were to intercede to save a lamb from a lion, he would be killed. Today, we see the White man taxed so heavily that he cannot afford children. The taxes raised are then used to support the breeding of tens of millions of non-whites, many of whom then demand the last White females for breeding partners. As you can see, man is subject to all the Laws of Nature. This has nothing to do with morality, hatred, good or evil. Nature does not recognize the concepts of good and evil in inter-specie relationships. If the lion eats the lamb, it is good for the lion and evil for the lamb. If the lamb escapes and the lion starves, it is good for the lamb and evil for the lion. So, we see the same incident is labeled both good and evil. This cannot be, for there are no contradictions within Nature's Laws.

34. The instinct for sexual union is part of Nature's perfect mechanism for specie preservation. It begins early in life and often continues until late in life. It must not be repressed; its purpose, reproduction, must not be thwarted either. Understand that for

thousands of years our females bore children at an early age. Now, in an attempt to conform to and compete in an alien culture, they deny their Nature-ordained instincts and duties. Teach responsibility, but, also, have understanding. The life of a race springs from the wombs of its women. He who would judge must first understand the difference between what is good and what is right.

35. Homosexuality is a crime against Nature. All Nature declares the purpose of the instinct for sexual union is reproduction and thus, preservations of the specie. The overpowering male sex drive must be channeled toward possession of females, as well as elements such as territory and power, which are necessary to keep them.

36. Sexual pornography degrades the Nature of all who are involved. A beautiful nude woman is art; a camera between her knees to explore her private parts is pornography.

37. That race whose males will not fight to death to keep and mate with their females will perish. Any White man with healthy instincts feels disgust and revulsion when he sees a woman of his race with a man of another race. Those, who today control the media and affairs of the Western World, teach that this is wrong and shameful. They label it "racism." As any "ism," for instance the word "nationalism," means to promote one's own nation; "racism" merely means to promote and protect the life of one's own race. It is, perhaps, the proudest word in existence. Any man who disobey these instincts is anti-Nature.

38. In a sick and dying nation, culture, race or civilization, political dissent and traditional values will be labeled and persecuted as heinous crimes by inquisitors clothing themselves in jingoistic patriotism.

39. A People who are ignorant of their past will defile the present and destroy the future.

40. A race must honor above all earthly things, those who have given their lives or freedom for the preservation of the folk.

41. The folk, namely the members of the race, are the Nation. Racial loyalties must always supersede geographical and national boundaries. If this is taught and understood, it will end fratricidal wars. Wars must not be fought for the benefit of another race.

42. The Nations' leaders are not rulers, they are servants and guardians. They are not to serve for personal gain. Choose only a guardian who has no interest in the accumulation of material things.

43. Choose and judge your leaders, also called guardians, thus: Those who seek always to limit the power of government are of good heart and conscience. Those who seek to expand the power of government are base tyrants.

44. No government can give anything to anybody without first taking it from another. Government is, by its very nature, legalized taking. A limited amount of government is a necessary burden for national defense and internal order. Anything more is counterproductive to freedom and liberty.

45. The Organic founding Law, namely the Constitution of a Nation, must not be amendable by any method other than unanimous consent of all parties thereto and with all parties present. Otherwise, the doors are opened for the advent of that most dangerous and deadly form of government, democracy.

46. In a democracy those who control the media, and thus the minds of the electorate, have power undreamed by kings or dictators.

47. The simplest way to describe a democracy is this: Three people form a government, each having one vote. Then two of them vote to steal the wealth of the third.

48. The latter stages of a democracy are filled with foreign wars, because the bankrupt system attempts to preserve itself by plundering other nations.

49. In a democracy that which is legal is seldom moral, and that which is moral is often illegal.

50. A democracy is always followed by a strongman... some call him dictator. It is the only way to restore order out of the chaos caused by a democracy. Pick your strongman wisely! He must be a guardian in his heart. He must be one who has shown that his only purpose in life is the preservation of the folk. His ultimate aim must be to restore the rule of Law based on the perfect Laws of Nature. Do not choose him by his words. Choose one who has sacrificed all in the face of tyranny; choose one who has endured and persevered. This is the only reliable evidence of his worthiness and motives.

51. A power system will do anything, no matter how corrupt or brutal, to preserve itself.

52. Tyrannies cannot be ended without the use of force.

53. Those who commit treason disguise their deeds in proclamations of patriotism.

54. Propaganda is major component in all power systems, both secular and religious; false propaganda is a major component of unprincipled power systems. All power systems endeavor to convince their subjects that the system is good, just, beneficent and noble, as well as worthy of perpetuation and defense. The more jingoistic propaganda issued, the more suspicious one should be of its truth.

55. Political power, in the final analysis, is created and maintained by force.

56. A power system, secular or religious, which employs extensive calls to patriotism or requires verbosity and rhetoric for its preservation, is masking tyranny.

57. Propaganda is a legitimate and necessary weapon in any struggle. The elements of successful propaganda are: simplicity, emotion, repetition, and brevity. Also, since men believe what they want to believe, and since they want to believe that which they perceive as beneficial to themselves, then successful propaganda must appeal to the perceived self-interest of those to whom it is disseminated.

58. Tyrannies teach what to think; free men learn how to think.

59. Beware of men who increase their wealth by the use of words. Particularly beware of the lawyers or priests who deny Natural Law.

60. The patriot, being led to the inquisition's dungeons or the executioner's axe, will be condemned the loudest by his former friends and allies; for thus they seek to escape the same fate.

61. The sweet goddess of Peace lives only under the protective arm of the ready God of War.

62. The organic founding Law of a Nation must state with unmistakable and irrevocable specificity the identity of the homogeneous racial, cultural group for whose welfare it was formed, and that the continued existence of the Nation is singularly for all time for the welfare of that specific group only.

63. That race or culture which lets others influence or control any of the following will perish:
- Organs of information;
- Educational institutions;
- Religious institutions;
- Political offices;
- Creation of their money;
- Judicial institutions;
- Cultural institutions;
- Economic life.

64. Just Laws require little explanation. Their meaning is irrevocable in simplicity and specificity.

65. Men's emotions are stirred far more effectively by the spoken word than by the written word. This is why a ruling tyranny will react more violently to gatherings of dissenters than to books or pamphlets.

66. The organic founding Law of the Nation, or any law, is exactly as pertinent as the will and power to enforce it.

67. An unarmed or non-militant People will be enslaved.

68. Some say the pen is more powerful than the sword. Perhaps so. Yet, the pen without the sword has no authority.

69. Tyrannies are usually built step by step and disguised by noble rhetoric.

70. The difference between a terrorist and a patriot is control of the press.

71. The judgments of the guardians, the leaders, must be true to Natural Law and tempered by reason.

72. Materialism is base and destructive. The guardians of a Nation must constantly warn against and combat a materialistic spirit in the Nation. Acquisition of wealth and property, as need for the well-being of one's family and obtained by honorable means is right and proper. Exploitation, particularly through usury, is destructive to a nation.

73. Materialism leads men to seek artificial status through wealth or property. True social status comes from service to Family, Race and Nation.

74. Materialism ultimately leads to conspicuous, unnecessary consumption, which in turn leads to the rape of Nature and destruction of the environment. It is unnatural. The true guardians of the Nation must be wholly untainted by materialism.

75. The function of a merchant or salesman is to provide a method of exchange. A merchant who promotes unnecessary consumption and materialism must not be tolerated.

76. The only lawful functions of money are as a medium of exchange and especially usury are unlawful. Usury (interest) at any percentage is a high crime which cannot be tolerated.

77. A nation with an aristocracy of money, lawyers or merchants will become a tyranny.

78. The simplest way to describe a usury-based central banking system is this: The bankers demand the property of the Nation as collateral for their loans. At interest, more money is owed them that they created with the loans. So, eventually, the bankers foreclose on the Nation.

79. Usury (interest), inflation, and oppressive taxation are the theft by deception and destroy the moral fabric of the Nation.

80. Wealth gained without sacrifices or honest labor will usually be misused.

81. Nothing in Nature is static; either the life force grows and expands or it decays and dies.

82. Respect must be earned; it cannot be demanded or assumed.

83. Avoid a vexatious man, for his venom will poison your own nature.

84. Self-discipline is a mark of higher man.

85. One measure of a man is cheerfulness in adversity.

86. A fool judges others by their words. A wise man judges others by their actions and accomplishments.

87. In our relationships or interactions, as in all of Nature's Laws, to each action there is a reaction. That which we plant will be harvested, if not by ourselves, then by another.

88. These are sure signs of a sick or dying Nation. If you see any of them, your guardians are committing treason.

- Mixing and destruction of the founding race;
- Destruction of the family units;
- Oppressive taxation;
- Corruption of the Law;
- Terror and suppression against those who warn of the Nation's error;
- Immorality: drugs, drunkenness, etc.;
- Infanticide (now called abortion);
- Destruction of the currency (inflation or usury);
- Aliens in the land, alien culture;
- Materialism;
- Foreign wars;
- Guardians (leaders) who pursue wealth or glory;
- Homosexuality;
- Religion not based on Natural Law.

We must secure the existence of our people and a future for white children.

That the beauty of the White Aryan woman must not perish from the earth.

38
ESSAY ON WOTAN
by C.G. Jung

[Originally published as the Vorwort to AUFSATZE ZUR ZEITGESCHICHTE (Zurich, 1946).
Translation by Elizabeth Welsh in ESSAYS ON CONTEMPORARY EVENTS (London, 1947)]
Preface to Essays on Contemporary Events

Medical psychotherapy, for practical reasons, has to deal with the whole of the psyche. Therefore, it is bound to come to terms with all those factors, biological as well as social and mental, which have a vital influence on psychic life.

We are living in times of great disruption: political passions are aflame, internal upheavals have brought nations to the brink of chaos, and the very foundations of our Weltanschauung are shattered. This critical state of things has such a tremendous influence on the psychic life of the individual that the doctor must follow its effects with more than usual attention. the storm of events does not sweep down upon him only from the great world outside; he feels the violence of its impact even in the quiet of his consulting-room and in the privacy of the medical consultation. As he has a responsibility towards his patients, he cannot afford to withdraw to the peaceful island of undisturbed scientific work, but must constantly descend into the arena of world events, in order to join in the battle of conflicting passions and opinions. Were he to remain aloof from the tumult, the calamity of his time would reach him only from afar, and his patients' suffering would find neither ear nor understanding. He would be at a loss to know how to talk to him, and to help him out of his isolation. For this reason the psychologist cannot avoid coming to grips with contemporary history, even his very soul shrinks from the political uproar, the lying propaganda, and the jarring speeches of the demagogues. We need not mention his duties as a citizen, which confront him with a similar task. As a physician, he has a higher obligation to humanity in this respect. From time to time, therefore, I have felt obliged to step beyond the usual bounds of my profession. The experience of the psychologist is of a rather special kind, and it seemed to me that the general public might find it useful to hear his point of view. This was hardly a far-fetched conclusion, for surely the most naive of laymen could not fail to see that many contemporary figures and events were positively asking for psychological elucidation. Were psychopathic symptoms ever more conspicuous than in the contemporary political scene?

It has never been my wish to meddle in the political questions of the day. But in the course of the years I have written a few papers which give my reactions to current events. The present book contains a collection of these occasional essays, all written between 1936 and 1946. It is natural enough that my thoughts should have been especially concerned with Germany, which has been a problem to me ever since the first World War. My statements have evidently led to all manner of misunderstandings, which are chiefly due, no doubt, to the fact that my psychological point of view strikes many people as new and therefore strange. Instead of embarking upon lengthy arguments in an attempt to clear up these misunderstandings, I have found it simpler to collect all the passages in my other writings which deal with the same theme and to put them in an epilogue. The reader will thus be in a position to get a clear picture of the facts for himself.

[First published as WOTAN, Neue Schweizer Rundschau (Zurich). n.s., III (March, 1936), 657-69. Republished in AUFSATZE ZUR ZEITGESCHICHTE (Zurich, 1946), 1-23. Trans. by Barbara Hannah in ESSAYS ON CONTEMPORARY EVENTS (London, 1947), 1-16; this version has been consulted. Motto, trans. by H.C. Roberts:

"In Germany Shall diverse sects arise,
Coming very near to happy paganism.
The heart captivated and small receivings
Shall open the gate to pay the true tithe."]

Dr. Casper Odinson Cröwell

WOTAN

En Germanie naistront diverses sectes,
S'approchans fort de l'heureux paganisme:
Le coeur captif et petites receptes
Feront retour a payer la vraye disme.
-- Propheties De Maistre Michel Nostradamus, 1555

When we look back to the time before 1914, we find ourselves living in a world of events which would have been inconceivable before the war. We were even beginning to regard war between civilized nations as a fable, thinking that such an absurdity would become less and less possible on our rational, internationally organized world. And what came after the war was a veritable witches' sabbath. Everywhere fantastic revolutions, violent alterations of the map, reversions in politics to medieval or even antique prototypes, totalitarian states that engulf their neighbours and outdo all previous theocracies in their absolutist claims, persecutions of Christians and Jews, wholesale political murder, and finally we have witnessed a light-hearted piratical raid on a peaceful, half-civilized people.

With such goings on in the wide world it is not in the least surprising that there should be equally curious manifestations on a smaller scale in other spheres. In the realm of philosophy we shall have to wait some time before anyone is able to assess the kind of age we are living in. But in the sphere of religion we can see at once that some very significant things have been happening. We need feel no surprise that in Russia the colourful splendours of the Eastern Orthodox Church have been superseded by the Movement of the Godless -- indeed, one breathed a sigh of relief oneself when one emerged from the haze of an Orthodox church with its multitude of lamps and entered an honest mosque, where the sublime and invisible omnipresence of God was not crowded out by a superfluity of sacred paraphernalia. Tasteless and pitiably unintelligent as it is, and however deplorable the low spiritual level of the "scientific" reaction, it was inevitable that nineteenth-century "scientific" enlightenment should one day dawn in Russia.

But what is more than curious -- indeed, piquant to a degree -- is that an ancient god of storm and frenzy, the long quiescent Wotan, should awake, like an extinct volcano, to new activity, in a civilized country that had long been supposed to have outgrown the Middle Ages. We have seen him come to life in the German Youth Movement, and right at the beginning the blood of several sheep was shed in honour of his resurrection. Armed with rucksack and lute, blond youths, and sometimes girls as well, were to be seen as restless wanderers on every road from the North Cape to Sicily, faithful votaries of the roving god. Later, towards the end of the Weimar Republic, the wandering role was taken over by thousands of unemployed, who were to be met with everywhere on their aimless journeys. By 1933 they wandered no longer, but marched in their hundreds of thousands. The Hitler movement literally brought the whole of Germany to its feet, from five-year-olds to veterans, and produced a spectacle of a nation migrating from one place to another. Wotan the wanderer was on the move. He could be seen, looking rather shamefaced, in the meeting-house of a sect of simple folk in North Germany, disguised as Christ sitting on a white horse. I do not know if these people were aware of Wotan's ancient connection with the figures of Christ and Dionysus, but it is not very probable.

Wotan is a restless wanderer who creates unrest and stirs up strife, now here, now there, and works magic. He was soon changed by Christianity into the devil, and only lived on in fading local traditions as a ghostly hunter who was seen with his retinue, flickering like a will o' the wisp through the stormy night. In the Middle Ages the role of the restless wanderer was taken over by Ahasuerus, the Wandering Jew, which is not a Jewish but a Christian legend. The motif of the wanderer who has not accepted Christ was projected on the Jews, in the same way as we always rediscover our unconscious psychic contents in other people. At any rate the coincidence of anti-Semitism with the reawakening of Wotan is a psychological subtlety that may perhaps be worth mentioning.

The German youths who celebrated the solstice with sheep-sacrifices were not the first to hear the rustling in the primeval forest of the unconsciousness. They were anticipated by Nietzsche, Schuler, Stefan George, and Ludwig Klages. The literary tradition of the Rhineland and the country south of the Main has a classical stamp that cannot easily be got rid of; every interpretation of intoxication and exuberance is apt to be taken back to classical models, to Dionysus, to the puer aeternus and the cosmogonic Eros. No doubt it sounds better to academic ears to interpret these things as Dionysus, but Wotan might be a more correct interpretation. He is the god of storm and frenzy, the unleasher of passions and the lust of battle; moreover he is a superlative magician and artist in illusion who is versed in all secrets of an occult nature.

Nietzsche's case is certainly a peculiar one. He had no knowledge of Germanic literature; he discovered the "cultural Philistine"; and the announcement that "God is dead" led to Zarathustra's meeting with an unknown god in unexpected form, who approached him sometimes as an enemy and sometimes disguised as Zarathustra himself. Zarathustra, too, was a soothsayer, a magician, and the storm-wind:

And like a wind shall I come to blow among them, and with my spirit shall take away the breath of their spirit; thus my future wills it. Truly, a strong wind is Zarathustra to all that are low; and this counsel gives he to his enemies and to all that spit and spew: "Beware of spitting against the wind."

And when Zarathustra dreamed that he was guardian of the graves in the "lone mountain fortress of death," and was making a mighty effort to open the gates, suddenly

A roaring wind tore the gates asunder; whistling, shrieking, and keening, it cast a black coffin before me.
And amid the roaring and whistling and shrieking the coffin burst open and spouted a thousand peals of laughter.

The disciple who interpreted the dream said to Zarathustra:

Are you not yourself the wind with shrill whistling, which bursts open the gates of the fortress of death?
Are you not yourself the coffin filled with life's gay malice and angel-grimaces?

In 1863 or 1864, in his poem TO THE UNKNOWN GOD, Nietzsche had written:

I shall and will know thee, Unknown One,
Who searchest out the depths of my soul,
And blowest through my life like a storm,
Ungraspable, and yet my kinsman!
I shall and will know thee, and serve thee.

Twenty years later, in his MISTRAL SONG, he wrote:

Mistral wind, chaser of clouds,
Killer of gloom, sweeper of the skies,
Raging storm-wind, how I love thee!
And we are not both the first-fruits
Of the same womb, forever predestined
To the same fate?

In the dithyramb known as ARIADNE'S LAMENT, Nietzsche is completely the victim of the hunter-god:

Stretched out, shuddering,
Like a half-dead thing whose feet are warmed,
Shaken by unknown fevers,
Shivering with piercing icy frost arrows,
Hunted by thee, O thought,
Unutterable! Veiled! horrible one!
Thou huntsman behind the cloud.
Struck down by thy lightning bolt,
Thou mocking eye that stares at me from the dark!
Thus I lie.
Writhing, twisting, tormented
With all eternal tortures,
Smitten
By thee, cruel huntsman,
Thou unknown -- God!

This remarkable image of the hunter-god is not a mere dithyrambic figure of speech but is based on an experience which Nietzsche had when he was fifteen years old, at Pforta. It is described in a book by Nietzsche's sister, Elizabeth Foerster-Nietzsche. As he was wandering about in a gloomy wood at night, he was terrified by a "blood-curdling shriek from a neighbouring lunatic asylum," and soon afterwards he cam face to face with a huntsman whose "features were wild and uncanny." Setting his whistle to his lips "in a valley surrounded by wild scrub," the huntsman "blew such a shrill blast" that Nietzsche lost consciousness -- but woke up again in Pforta. It was a nightmare. It is significant that in his dream Nietzsche, who in reality intended to go to Eisleben, Luther's town, discussed with the huntsman the question of going instead to "Teutschenthal" (Valley of the Germans). No one with ears can misunderstand the shrill whistling of the storm-god in the nocturnal wood.

Was it really only the classical philologist in Nietzsche that led to the god being called Dionysus instead of Wotan -- or was it perhaps due to his fateful meeting with Wagner?

In his REICH OHNE RAUM, which was first published in 1919, Bruno Goetz saw the secret of coming events in Germany in the form of a very strange vision. I have never forgotten this little book, for it struck me at the time as a forecast of the German weather. It anticipates the conflict between the realm of ideas and life, between Wotan's dual nature as a god of storm and a god of secret musings. Wotan disappeared when his oaks fell and appeared again when the Christian God proved too weak to save Christendom from fratricidal slaughter. When the Holy Father at Rome could only impotently lament before God the fate of the grex segregatus, the one-eyed old hunter, on the edge of the German forest, laughed and saddled Sleipnir.

We are always convinced that the modern world is a reasonable world, basing our opinion on economic, political, and psychological factors. But if we may forget for a moment that we are living in the year of Our Lord 1936, and, laying aside our well-meaning, all-too-human reasonableness, may burden God or the gods with the responsibility for contemporary events instead of man, we would find Wotan quite suitable as a casual hypothesis. In fact, I venture the heretical suggestion that the unfathomable depths of Wotan's character explain more of National Socialism than all three reasonable factors put together. There is no doubt that each of these factors explains an important aspect of what is going on in Germany, but Wotan explains yet more. He is particularly enlightening in regard to a general phenomenon which is so strange to anybody not a German that it remains incomprehensible, even after the deepest reflection.

Perhaps we may sum up this general phenomenon as Ergriffenheit -- a state of being seized or possessed. The term postulates not only an Ergriffener (one who is seized) but, also, an Ergreifer (one who seizes). Wotan is an Ergreifer of men, and, unless one wishes to deify Hitler -- which has indeed actually happened -- he is really the only explanation. It is true that Wotan shares this quality with his cousin Dionysus, but Dionysus seems to have exercised his influence mainly on women. The maenads were a species of female storm-troopers, and, according to mythical reports, were dangerous enough. Wotan confined himself to the berserkers, who found their vocation as the Blackshirts of mythical kings.

A mind that is still childish thinks of the gods as metaphysical entities existing in their own right, or else regards them as playful or superstitious inventions. From either point of view the parallel between Wotan redivivus and the social, political and psychic storm that is shaking Germany might have at least the value of a parable. But since the gods are without doubt personifications of psychic forces, to assert their metaphysical existence is as much an intellectual presumption as the opinion that they could ever be invented. Not that "psychic forces" have anything to do with the conscious mind, fond as we are of playing with the idea that consciousness and psyche are identical. This is only another piece of intellectual presumption. "Psychic forces" have far more to do with the realm of the unconscious. Our mania for rational explanations obviously has its roots in our fear of metaphysics, for the two were always hostile brothers. Hence, anything unexpected that approaches us from the dark realm is regarded either as coming from outside and, therefore, as real, or else as an hallucination and, therefore, not true. The idea that anything could be real or true which does not come from outside has hardly begun to dawn on contemporary man.

For the sake of better understanding and to avoid prejudice, we could of course dispense with the name "Wotan" and speak instead of the furor teutonicus. But we should only be saying the same thing and not as well, for the furor in this case is a mere psychologizing of Wotan and tells us no more than that the Germans are in a state of "fury." We thus lose sight of the most peculiar feature of this whole phenomenon, namely, the dramatic aspect of the Ergreifer and the Ergriffener. The impressive thing about the German phenomenon is that one man, who is obviously "possessed," has infected a whole nation to such an extent that everything is set in motion and has started rolling on its course towards perdition.

It seems to me that Wotan hits the mark as an hypothesis. Apparently he really was only asleep in the Kyffhauser mountain until the ravens called him and announced the break of day. He is a fundamental attribute of the German psyche, an irrational psychic factor which acts on the high pressure of civilization like a cyclone and blows it away. Despite their crankiness, the Wotan-worshippers seem to have judged things more correctly than the worshippers of reason. Apparently everyone had forgotten that Wotan is a Germanic datum of first importance, the truest expression and unsurpassed personification of a fundamental quality that is particularly characteristic of the Germans. Houston Stewart Chamberlain is a symptom which arouses suspicion that other veiled gods may be sleeping elsewhere. The emphasis on the Germanic race -- commonly called "Aryan" -- the Germanic heritage, blood and soil, the Wagalaweia songs, the ride of the Valkyries, Jesus as a blond and blue-eyed hero, the Greek mother of St. Paul, the devil as an international Alberich in Jewish or Masonic guise, the Nordic aurora borealis as the light of civilization, the inferior Mediterranean races -- all this is the indispensable scenery for the drama that is taking place and at the bottom they all mean the same thing: a god has taken possession of the Germans and their house is filled with a "mighty rushing wind." It was soon after Hitler seized power, if I am not mistaken, that a cartoon appeared in PUNCH of a raving berserker tearing himself free from his bonds. A hurricane has broken loose in Germany while we still believe it is fine weather.

Things are comparatively quiet in Switzerland, though occasionally there is a puff of wind from the north or south. Sometimes it has a slightly ominous sound, sometimes it whispers so harmlessly or even idealistically that no one is alarmed. "Let the sleeping dogs lie" -- we manage to get along pretty well with this proverbial wisdom. It is sometimes said that the Swiss are singularly averse to making a problem of themselves. I must rebut this accusation: the Swiss do have their problems, but they would not admit it for anything in the world, even though they see which way the wind is blowing. We thus pay our tribute to the time of storm and stress in Germany, but we never mention it, and this enables us to feel vastly superior.

It is above all the Germans who have an opportunity, perhaps unique in history, to look into their own hearts and to learn what those perils of the soul were from which Christianity tried to rescue mankind. Germany is a land of spiritual catastrophes, where nature never makes more than a pretense of peace with the world-ruling reason. The disturber of the peace is a wind that blows into Europe from Asia's vastness, sweeping in on a wide front from Thrace to the Baltic, scattering the nations before it like dry leaves. or inspiring thoughts that shake the world to its foundations. It is an elemental Dionysus breaking into the Apollonian order. The rouser of this tempest is named Wotan, and we can learn a good deal about him from the political confusion and spiritual upheaval he has caused throughout history. For a more exact investigation of his character, however, we must go back to the age of myths, which did not explain everything in terms of man and his limited capacities, but sought the deeper cause in the psyche and its autonomous powers. Man's earliest intuitions personified these powers. Man's earliest intuitions personified these powers as gods, and described them in the myths with great care and circumstantiality according to their various characters. This could be done the more readily on account of the firmly established primordial types or images which are innate in the unconscious of many races and exercise a direct influence upon them. Because the behavior of a race takes on its specific character from its underlying images, we can speak of an archetype "Wotan." As an autonomous psychic factor, Wotan produces effects in the collective life of a people and thereby reveals his own nature. For Wotan has a peculiar biology of his own, quite apart from the nature of man. It is only from time to time that individuals fall under the irresistible influence of this unconscious factor. When it is quiescent, one is no more aware of the archetype Wotan than of a latent epilepsy. Could the Germans who were adults in 1914 have foreseen what they would be today? Such amazing transformations are the effect of the god of wind, that "bloweth where it listeth, and thou hearest the sound thereof, but canst not tell whence it cometh, nor whither it goeth." It seizes everything in its path and overthrows everything that is not firmly rooted. When the wind blows it shakes everything that is insecure, whether without or within.

Martin Ninck has recently published a monograph which is a most welcome addition to our knowledge of Wotan's nature. The reader need not fear that this book is nothing but a scientific study written with academic aloofness from the subject. Certainly the right to scientific objectivity is fully preserved, and the material has been collected with extraordinary thoroughness and presented in unusually clear form. But, over and above all this, one feels that the author is vitally interested in it, that the chord of Wotan is vibrating in him, too. This is no criticism -- on the contrary, it is one of the chief merits of the book, which without this enthusiasm might easily have degenerated into a tedious catalogue. Ninck sketches a really magnificent portrait of the German archetype Wotan. He describes him in ten chapters, using all the available sources, as the berserker, the god of storm, the wanderer, the warrior, the Wunsch- and Minne-god, the lord of the dead and of the Einherjar, the master of secret knowledge, the magician, and the god of the poets. Neither the Valkyries nor the Fylgja are forgotten, for they form part of the mythological background and fateful significance of Wotan. Ninck's inquiry into the name and its origin is particularly instructive. He shows that Wotan is not only a god of rage and frenzy who embodies the instinctual and emotion aspect of the unconscious. Its intuitive and inspiring side, also, manifests itself in him, for he understands the runes and can interpret fate.

The Romans identified Wotan with Mercury, but his character does not really correspond to any Roman or Greek god, although there are certain resemblances. He is a wanderer like Mercury, for instance, he rules over the dead like Pluto and Kronos, and is connected with Dionysus by his emotional frenzy, particularly in its mantic aspect. It is surprising that Ninck does not mention Hermes, the god of revelation, who as pneuma and nous is associated with the wind. He would be the connecting-link with the Christian pneuma and the miracle of Pentecost. As Poimandres (the shepherd of men), Hermes is an Ergreifer like Wotan. Ninck rightly points out that Dionysus and the other Greek gods always remained under the supreme authority of Zeus, which indicates a fundamental difference between the Greek and the Germanic temperament. Ninck assumes an inner affinity between Wotan and Kronus, and the latter's defeat may perhaps be a sign that the Wotan-archetype was once overcome and split up in prehistoric times. At all events, the Germanic god represents a totality on a very primitive level, a psychological condition in which man's will was almost identical with the god's and entirely at his mercy. But the Greeks had gods who helped man against other gods; indeed, All-Father Zeus himself is not far from the ideal of a benevolent, enlightened despot.

It was not in Wotan's nature to linger on and show signs of old age. He simply disappeared when the times turned against him, and remained invisible for more than a thousand years, working anonymously and indirectly. Archetypes are like riverbeds which dry up when the water deserts them, but which it can find again at any time. An archetype is like an old watercourse along which the water of life has flowed for centuries, digging a deep channel for itself. The longer it has flowed in this channel the more likely it is that sooner or later the water will return to its old bed. The life of the individual as a member of society and particularly as a part of the State may be regulated like a canal, but the life of nations is a great rushing river which is utterly beyond human control, in the hands of One who has always been stronger than men. The League of Nations, which was supposed to possess supranational authority, is regarded by some as a child in need of care and protection, by others as an abortion. Thus, the life of nations rolls on unchecked, without guidance, unconscious of where it is going, like a rock crashing down the side of a hill, until it is stopped by an obstacle stronger than itself. Political events move from one impasse to the next, like a torrent caught in gullies, creeks and marshes. All human control comes to an end when the individual is caught in a mass movement. Then, the archetypes begin to function, as happens, also, in the lives of individuals when they are confronted with situations that cannot be dealt with in any of the familiar ways. But what a so-called Fuhrer does with a mass movement can plainly be seen if we turn our eyes to the north or south of our country.

The ruling archetype does not remain the same forever, as is evident from the temporal limitations that have been set to the hoped-for reign of peace, the "thousand-year Reich." The Mediterranean father-archetype of the just, order-loving, benevolent ruler had been shattered over the whole of northern Europe, as the present fate of the Christian Churches bears witness. Fascism in Italy and the civil war in Spain show that in the south as well the cataclysm has been far greater than one expected. Even the Catholic Church can no longer afford trials of strength.

The nationalist God has attacked Christianity on a broad front. In Russia, he is called technology and science, in Italy, Duce, and in Germany, "German Faith," "German Christianity," or the State. The "German Christians" are a contradiction in terms and would do better to join Hauer's "German Faith Movement." These are decent and well-meaning people who honestly admit their Ergriffenheit and try to come to terms with this new and undeniable fact. They go to an enormous amount of trouble to make it look less alarming by dressing it up in a conciliatory historical garb and giving us consoling glimpses of great figures such as Meister Eckhart, who was, also, a German and, also, ergriffen. In this way the awkward question of who the Ergreifer is is circumvented. He was always "God." But the more Hauer restricts the world-wide sphere of Indo-European culture to the "Nordic" in general and to the Edda in particular, and the more "German" this faith becomes as a manifestation of Ergriffenheit, the more painfully evident it is that the "German" god is the god of the Germans.

One cannot read Hauer's book without emotion, if one regards it as the tragic and really heroic effort of a conscientious scholar who, without knowing how it happened to him, was violently summoned by the inaudible voice of the Ergreifer and is now trying with all his might, and with all his knowledge and ability, to build a bridge between the dark forces of life and the shining world of historical ideas. But what do all the beauties of the past from totally different levels of culture mean to the man of today, when confronted with a living and unfathomable tribal god such as he has never experienced before? They are sucked like dry leaves into the roaring whirlwind, and the rhythmic alliterations of the Edda became inextricably mixed up with Christian mystical texts, German poetry and the wisdom of the Upanishads. Hauer himself is ergriffen by the depths of meaning in the primal words lying at the root of the Germanic languages, to an extent that he certainly never knew before. Hauer the Indologist is not to blame for this, nor yet the Edda; it is rather the fault of kairos -- the present moment in time -- whose name on closer investigation turns out to be Wotan. I would, therefore, advise the German Faith Movement to throw aside their scruples. Intelligent people who will not confuse them with the crude Wotan-worshippers whose faith is a mere pretense. There are people in the German Faith Movement who are intelligent enough not only to believe, but to know, that the god of the Germans is Wotan and not the Christian God. This is a tragic experience and no disgrace. It has always been terrible to fall into the hands of a living god. Yahweh was no exception to this rule, and the Philistines, Edomites, Amorites and the rest, who were outside the Yahweh experience, must certainly have found it exceedingly disagreeable. The Semitic experience of Allah was for a long time an extremely painful affair for the whole of Christendom. We who stand outside judge the Germans far too much, as if they were responsible agents, but perhaps it would be nearer the truth to regard them, also, as victims.

If we apply are admittedly peculiar point of view consistently, we are driven to conclude that Wotan must, in time, reveal not only the restless, violent, stormy side of his character, but, also, his ecstatic and mantic qualities -- a very different aspect of his nature. If this conclusion is correct, National Socialism would not be the last word.

Things must be concealed in the background which we cannot imagine at present, but we may expect them to appear in the course of the next few years or decades. Wotan's reawakening is a stepping back into the past; the stream was damned up and has broken into its old channel. But the Obstruction will not last forever; it is rather a reculer pour mieux sauter, and the water will overleap the obstacle. Then, at last, we shall know what Wotan is saying when he "murmers with Mimir's head."

> Fast move the sons of Mim, and fate
> Is heard in the note of the Gjallarhorn;
> Loud blows Heimdall, the horn is aloft,
> In fear quake all who on Hel-roads are.
> Yggdrasill shakes and shivers on high
> The ancient limbs, and the giant is loose;
> Wotan murmurs with Mimir's head
> But the kinsman of Surt shall slay him soon.
>
> How fare the gods? how fare the elves?
> All Jotunheim groans, the gods are at council;
> Loud roar the dwarfs by the doors of stone,
> The masters of the rocks: would you know yet more?
>
> Now Garm howls loud before Gnipahellir;
> The fetters will burst, and the wolf run free;
> Much I do know, and more can see
> Of the fate of the gods, the mighty in fight.
>
> From the east comes Hrym with shield held high;
> In giant-wrath does the serpent writhe;
> O'er the waves he twists, and the tawny eagle
> Gnaws corpses screaming; Naglfar is loose.
>
> O'er the sea from the north there sails a ship
> With the people of Hel, at the helm stands Loki;
> After the wolf do wild men follow,
> And with them the brother of Byleist goes.

39
THE GODS AND GODDESSES

ODIN - Father of the Gods

Odin, Wotan, or Woden is the highest and holiest God of the Northern races. Ruler of the Æsir, God of the runes, inspiration, shamanism, magic and war. Odin is also known as God of the hanged and the Wild Hunt and the God of storm, rain and harvest. He is the all-pervading spirit of the universe, the personification of the air, the God of universal wisdom and victory, and the leader and protector of princes and heroes. As all the Gods are descended from him, he is surnamed Allfather, and as eldest and chief among them he occupies Asgard, the highest seat. Known by the name of Hlidskialf, this chair is not only an exalted throne, but also a mighty watch tower, from whence he could overlook the whole world and see at a glance all that is happening among Gods, giants, elves, dwarfs, and men.

"From the hall of Heaven he rode away
To Lidskialf, and sate upon his throne,
The mount, from whence his eye surveys the world.
And far from Heaven he turn'd his shining orbs
To look on Midgard, and the earth and men."
-BALDER DEAD (Matthew Arnold)

None but Odin and his wife and queen Frigga have the privilege of using this seat, and when they occupy it they generally gaze towards the south and west, the goal of all the hopes and excursions of the Northern nations. Odin is generally represented as a tall, vigorous man, about fifty years of age, either with dark curling hair or with a long gray beard and bald head. He is sometimes clad in a suit of gray, with a blue hood, and his muscular body is enveloped in a wide blue mantle all flecked with gray - an emblem of the sky with its fleecy clouds. In his hand Odin generally carries the infallible spear Gungnir, which is so sacred that an oath sworn upon its point can never be broken, and on his finger or arm he wears the marvelous ring Draupnir, the emblem of fruitfulness, precious beyond compare. When seated upon his throne or armed for the fray, in which he often takes an active part, Odin wears his eagle helmet; but when he wanders about the earth in human guise, to see what men are doing, he generally dons a broad-brimmed hat, drawn down low over his forehead to conceal the fact of his having but one eye.

"Then into the Volsungs' dwelling a mighty man there strode,
One-eyed and seeming ancient, yet bright his visage glowed;
Cloud-blue was the hood upon him, and his kirtle gleaming-gray
As the latter morning sun dog when the storm is on the way
A bill he bore on his shoulder, whose mighty ashen beam
Burnt bright with the flame of the sea and the blended silver's gleam."
    -SIGURD THE VOLSUNG (William Morris)

Two ravens, Hugin (thought) and Munin (memory), are perched upon his shoulders as he sits upon his throne, and these he sends out into the wide world every morning, anxiously watching for their return at nightfall, when they whisper into his ears news of all they had seen and heard, keeping him well informed about everything that is happening on earth.

"Hugin and Munin
Fly each day
Over the spacious earth.

*I fear for Hugin
That he come not back,
Yet more anxious am I for
Munin."*
    -NORSE MYTHOLOGY
        (R. B. Anderson)

At his feet crouch two wolves or hunting hounds, Geri and Freki, which animals are therefore considered sacred to him, and of good omen if met by the way. Odin always feeds these wolves with his own hands from the meat set before him, for he requires no food at all, and seldom tastes anything except the sacred mead.

*"Geri and Freki
The war-wont sates,
The triumphant sire of
hosts;
But on wine only
The famed in arms
Odin, ever lives."*
    -LAY OF GRIMNIR
        (Thorpe's tr.)

When seated in state upon his throne, Odin rests his feet upon a footstool of gold, the work of the Gods, whose furniture and utensils are all fashioned either of that precious metal or of silver.

Besides the magnificent hall Glads-heim, where stands the twelve seats occupied by the Gods when they meet in council, and Valaskialf, where his throne, Hlidskialf, is placed, Odin has a third palace in Asgard, situated in the midst of the marvelous grove Glasir, whose leaves were all of shimmering red gold.

Valhalla

This palace, called Valhalla (the hall of the chosen slain), has five hundred and forty doors, wide enough to allow the passage of eight hundred warriors abreast, and above the principal gate is a boar's head and an eagle whose piercing glance look all over the world. The walls of this marvelous building are fashioned of glittering spears, so highly polished that they illuminate all the hall. The roof is made of golden shields, and the benches are decorated with fine armor, the God's gifts to his guests. Here long tables afford ample accommodations for the warriors fallen in battle, who are called Einheriar, and are considered Odin's favorite guests.

"Easily to be known is,
By those who to Odin
come,
The mansion by its aspect.
Its roof with spears is laid,
Its hall with shields is
decked,
With corselets are its
benches strewed."
        -LAY OF GRIMNIR
          (Thorpe's tr.)

The ancient Northern nations, who deemed warfare the most honorable of occupations, and considered courage the greatest virtue, worshiped Odin principally as God of battle and victory, and believed that whenever a fight was about to occur he sent out his special attendants, the shield, battle, or wish maidens, called Valkyries (choosers of the slain). They select one half the dead warriors, and bore them on their fleet steeds over the quivering rainbow bridge Bifröst, into his hall, where many honors await them. Welcomed by Odin's sons, Hermod and Bragi, the heroes are then conducted to the foot of Odin's throne, where they receive the praises due their valor. When some special favorite of the God is thus brought into Asgard, Valfather (father of the slain), as Odin is called when he presides over the warriors, sometimes rises from his throne to meet him at the door and himself bid him welcome.

The Feast of the Heroes

Besides the hope of the glory of such a distinction, and the promise of dwelling in Odin's beloved presence day after day, other more material pleasures await the warriors in Valhalla. They are seated around the board, where the beautiful white-armed virgins, the Valkyries, having laid aside their armor and clad themselves in pure white robes, constantly wait upon them. These maidens bring the heroes great horns full of delicious mead, and set before them huge portions of boars' flesh, upon which they feast most heartily. The usual Northern drink was beer or ale, but our ancestors fancied this beverage too coarse for the heavenly sphere. They therefore imagined that Valfather kept his table liberally supplied with mead or hydromel, which was daily furnished in great abundance by his she-goat Heidrun, continually browsing on the tender leaves and twigs on Yggdrasil's topmost branch, Lerad.

"Rash war and perilous battle,
their delight;
And immature, and red with
glorious wounds,
Unpeaceful death their choice:
deriving thence
A right to feast and drain
immortal bowls,
In Odin's hall; whose blazing
roof resounds
The genial uproar of those
shades who fall
In desperate fight, or by some
brave attempt."
   -LIBERTY (James Thomson)

The meat upon which the Einheriar feast is the flesh of the divine boar Sæhrimnir, a marvelous beast, daily slain by the cook Andhrimnir, and boiled in the great caldron Eldhrimnir; but although Odin's guests have true Northern appetites and fairly gorge themselves, there is always plenty of meat for all.

"Andhrimnir cooks
In Eldhrimnir
Sæhrimnir;
'Tis the best of flesh;
But few know
What the einherjes eat."
     -LAY OF GRIMNIR
     (Anderson's version)

Moreover the supply is exhaustless, for the boar always comes to life again before the time for the next meal, when he iss again slain and devoured. This miraculous renewal of supplies in the larder is not the only wonderful occurrence in Valhalla, for it is also related that the warriors, after having eaten and drunk to satiety, always call for their weapons, arm themselves, and ride out into the great courtyard, where they fight against one another, repeating the feats of arms achieved while on earth, and recklessly dealing terrible wounds, which are miraculously and completely healed as soon as the dinner horn is sounded.

"All the chosen guests of Odin
Daily ply the trade of war;
From the fields of festal fight
Swift they ride in gleaming arms,
And gaily, at the board of gods,
Quaff the cup of sparkling ale
And eat Sæhrimni's vaunted flesh."
    -VAFTHRUDNI'S-MAL
      (W. Taylor's tr.)

Whole and happy once more, - for they bore one another no grudge for the cruel thrusts given and received, and live in perfect amity together, - the Einheriar then ride gaily back to Valhalla to renew their feasts in Odin's beloved presence, while the white-armed Valkyries, with flying hair, glide gracefully about, constantly filling their horns or their favorite drinking vessels while the scalds sing of war and stirring Viking expeditions.

"And all day long they there are hack'd and hewn
'Mid dust, and groans, and limbs lopp'd off, and blood;
But all at night return to Odin's hall
Woundless and fresh; such lot is theirs in Heaven."
   -BALDER DEAD (Matthew Arnold)

Thus fighting and feasting, the heroes are said to spend day after day in perfect bliss, while Odin delights in their strength and number, which, however, he foresees will not long avail to ward off his downfall when the day of the last battle dawns.

As such pleasures were the highest a Northern warrior's fancy could paint, it was very natural that all fighting men should love Odin, and early in life should dedicate themselves to his service. They vowed to die arms in hand, if possible, and even wounded themselves with their own spears when death drew near, if they had been unfortunate enough to escape death on the battlefield and were threatened with " straw death," as they called decease from old age or sickness.

"To Odin then true-fast
Carves he fair runics, -
Death-runes cut deep on his arm and
his breast."
  -VIKING TALES OF THE NORTH
        (R. B. Anderson)

In reward for this devotion Odin watches with special care over his favorites, giving them a magic sword, spear, or horse, and making them invincible until their last hour has come, when he himself appears to claim or destroy the gift he has bestowed, and the Valkyries carries them off to Valhalla.

"He gave to Hermod
A helm and corselet,
And from him Sigmund
A sword received."
  -LAY OF HYNDLA
        (Thorpe's tr.)

Sleipnir

Whenever Odin took an active part in war, he generally rode his eight-footed gray steed, Sleipnir, brandished his white shield, and flung his glittering spear over the heads of the combatants, who only awaited this signal to fall upon one another, while the God dashed into their midst shouting his warcry: "Odin has you all!"

"And Odin donn'd
His dazzling corslet and his

*helm of gold,
And led the way on
Sleipnir."*
      *-BALDER DEAD
      (Matthew Arnold)*

At times he also used his magic bow, from which he shot ten arrows at once, everyone invariably bringing down a foe. Odin is also supposed to inspire his favorite warriors with the renowned "Berserker rage" (bare sark or shirt), which enables them to perform unheard-of feats of valor and strength.

As Odin's characteristics, like the all-pervading elements, are multitudinous, so also are his names, of which he has no less than two hundred, almost all of which are descriptive of some phase of his being. He is also considered the ancient God of seamen and of the wind:

*"Mighty Odin,
Norsemen hearts we
bend to thee!
Steer our barks, all-
potent Woden,
O'er the surging Baltic
Sea."*
      -VAIL

The Wild Hunt

Odin, as wind God, generally rode about on his eight-footed steed Sleipnir, a habit which gave rise to the oldest Northern riddle, which runs as follows: "Who are the two who ride to the Thing? Three eyes have they together, ten feet, and one tail; and thus they travel through the lands." And as the souls of the dead were supposed to be wafted away on the wings of the storm, Odin was worshiped as the leader of all disembodied spirits. In this character he was most generally known as the Wild Hunts man, and when people heard the rush and roar of the wind they cried aloud in superstitious fear, fancying they heard and saw him ride past with his train, all mounted on snorting steeds, and accompanied by baying hounds. And the passing of the Wild Hunt, known as Woden's Hunt, the Raging Host, Gabriel's

Hounds, or Asgardreia, was also considered a presage of misfortune of some kind, such as pestilence or war.

"The Rhine flows bright; but its waves ere long
  Must hear a voice of war,
And a clash of spears our hills among,
  And a trumpet from afar;
And the brave on a bloody turf must lie,
For the Huntsman bath gone by!"
        -THE WILD HUNTSMAN
              (Mrs. Hemans)

Mimir's Well

To obtain the great wisdom for which he is so famous, Odin, in the morn of time, wandered off to Mimir's (Memor, memory) spring, "the fountain of all wit and wisdom," in whose liquid depths even the future was clearly mirrored, and besought the old man who guarded it to let him have a draught. But Mimir, who well knew the value of such a favor (for his spring was considered the source or headwater of memory), refused to grant it unless Odin would consent to give one of his eyes in exchange.

The God did not hesitate, but immediately plucked out one of his eyes, which Mimir kept in pledge, sinking it deep down into his fountain, where it shone with mild luster, leaving Odin with but one eye, which is considered emblematic of the sun.

"Through our whole lives we strive towards the sun;
That burning forehead is the eye of Odin.
His second eye, the moon, shines not so bright;
It has he placed in pledge in Mimer's fountain,
That he may fetch the healing waters thence,

*Each morning, for the
strengthening of this eye."*
    -OEHLENSCHLÄGER (Howitt's
                              tr.)

Drinking deeply of Mimir's fount, Odin gained the knowledge he coveted; and such was the benefit received that he never regretted the sacrifice he had made, but as further memorial of that day broke off a branch of the sacred tree Yggdrasil, which overshadowed the spring, and fashioned from it his beloved spear Gungnir.

*"A dauntless god
Drew for drink to its
gleam,
Where he left in endless
Payment the light of an
eye.
From the world-ash
Ere Wotan went he broke a
bough;
For a spear the staff
He split with strength from
the stem."*
    -DUSK OF THE GODS,
    WAGNER (Forman's tr.)

But although Odin had won all knowledge, he was sad and oppressed, for he had also won an insight into futurity, and had become aware of the transitory nature of all things, and even of the fate of the Gods, who were doomed to pass away. This knowledge so affected his spirits that he ever after wore a melancholy and contemplative expression.

To test the value of the wisdom he had thus obtained, Odin soon went to visit the most learned of all the giants, Vafthrudnir, and entered with him into a contest of wit, in which the stake was nothing less than the loser's head.

*"Odin rose with speed, and
went
To contend in runic lore*

*With the wise and crafty
jute.
To Vafthrudni's royal hall
Came the mighty king of
spells."*
    -VAFTHRUDNI'S-MAL
        (W. Taylor's tr.)

Father of the Gods

As personification of heaven, Odin, of course, was the lover and spouse of the earth, and as it appeared under a threefold aspect, the Northerners, although a chaste race, allotted to him several wives. The first among these was Jörd (Erda), the primitive earth, daughter of Night or of the giantess Fiorgyn. She bore him his famous son Thor, the God of thunder. The second and principal wife was Frigga, a personification of the civilized world. She gave him Balder, the gentle God of spring, Hermod, and, according to some authorities, Tyr. The third wife was Rinda, a personification of the hard and frozen earth, who reluctantly yields to his warm embrace, but finally gives birth to Vali, the emblem of vegetation. Odin is also said to have married Saga or Laga, the Goddess of history (hence our verb "to say"), and to have daily visited her in the crystal hall of Sokvabek, beneath a cool, ever-flowing river, to drink its waters and listen to her songs about olden times and vanished races.

*"Sokvabek hight the fourth
dwelling;
Over it flow the cool billows;
Glad drink there Odin and
Saga
Every day from golden cups."*
    -NORSE MYTHOLOGY
        (R. E. Anderson)

His other wives were Grid, the mother of Vidar; Gunlod, the mother of Bragi; Skadi; and the nine giantesses who simultaneously bore Heimdall - all of whom play more or less important parts in the various myths of the North.

Historical Odin

Besides this ancient Odin, there was a more modem, semi-historical personage of the same name, to whom all the virtues, powers, and adventures of his predecessor have been attributed. He was the chief of the Æsir inhabitants of Asia Minor, who, sore pressed by the Romans, and threatened with destruction or slavery, left their native land about 70 B.C., and migrated into Europe. This Odin is said to have conquered Russia, Germany, Denmark, Norway, and Sweden, leaving a son on the throne of each conquered country. He also built the town of Odensö. He was welcomed in Sweden by Gylfi, the king, who made him associate ruler, and allowed him to found the city of Sigtuna, where he built a temple and introduced a new system of worship. Tradition further relates that as his end drew near, this mythical Odin assembled his followers, publicly cut himself nine times in the breast with his spear, - a ceremony called "carving Geir odds," - and told them he was about to return to his native land Asgard, his old home, where lie would await their coming, to share with him a life of feasting, drinking, and fighting.

According to another account, Gylfi, having heard of the power of the Æsir, the inhabitants of Asgard, and wishing to ascertain whether these reports were true, journeyed off to the south. He soon came to Odin's palace, where he was expected, and where lie was deluded by the vision of three divinities, enthroned one above the other, and called Har, Iafn-har, and Thridi. The gatekeeper, Gangler, answered all his questions, gave him a long explanation of Northern mythology, which is recorded in the Younger Edda, and having finished his instructions, suddenly vanished with the palace amid a deafening noise.

According to other very ancient poems, Odin's sons, Weldegg, Beldegg, Sigi, Skiold, Sæming, and Yngvi, became kings of East Saxony, West Saxony, Franconia, Denmark, Norway, and Sweden, and from them are descended the Saxons, Hengist and Horsa, and the royal families of the Northern lands. Still another version relates that Odin and Frigga had seven sons, who founded the Anglo-Saxon heptarchy. In the course of time this mysterious king was confounded with the Odin whose worship he introduced, and all his deeds were attributed to the God.

Odin was worshiped in numerous temples, but especially in the great fane at Upsala, where the most solemn festivals were held, and where sacrifices were offered. The victim was generally a horse, but in times of pressing need human offerings were made, even the king being once offered up to avert a famine.

*"Upsal's temple, where the
North
Saw Valhal's halls fair imag'd
here on earth."*
    *-VIKING TALES OF THE
                    NORTH
        (R. B. Anderson)*

The first toast at every festival here was drunk in his honor, and, besides the first of May, one day in every week was held sacred to him, and, from his Saxon name, Woden, was called Woden's day, whence the English word "Wednesday" has been derived. It was customary for the people to assemble at his shrine on festive occasions, to hear the songs of the scalds, who were rewarded for their minstrelsy by the gift of golden bracelets or armlets, which curled up at the ends and were called "Odin's serpents."

There are but few remains of ancient Northern art now extant, and although rude statues of Odin were once quite common they have all disappeared, as they were made of wood - a perishable substance, which in the hands of the missionaries and especially of Olaf the Saint, the Northern iconoclast, was soon reduced to ashes.

*"There in the Temple,
carved in wood,
The image of great Odin
stood."*
    *-SAGA OF KING OLAF
          (Longfellow)*

Odin himself is supposed to have given his people a code of laws whereby to govern their conduct, in a poem called Hávamal, or the High Song, which forms part of the Edda. In this lay he taught the fallibility of man, the necessity for courage, temperance, independence, and truthfulness, respect for old age, hospitality, charity, and contentment, and gave instructions for the burial of the dead.

"At home let a man be cheerful,
And toward a guest liberal;
Of wise conduct he should be,
Of good memory and ready speech;
If much knowledge he desires,
He must often talk on what is good."
   -*HÁVAMÁL (Thorpe's tr.)*

FRIGGA
Queen of the Gods

Frigga or Frigg is Mother of the Gods and Humanity, the patroness of the household and of married women. Frigga, the daughter of Fiorgyn and sister of Jörd, was eventually married to Odin. This wedding caused such general rejoicing in Asgard, where the goddess was greatly beloved, that ever after it was customary to celebrate its anniversary with feast and song, and the goddess being declared patroness of marriage, her health was always proposed with that of Odin and Thor at wedding feasts.

Frigga is the goddess of the atmosphere, or rather of the clouds, and as such is sometimes represented as wearing either snow-white or dark garments, according to her somewhat variable moods. She is queen of the gods, and she alone has the privilege of sitting on the throne Hlidskialf, beside her husband Odin. From thence she too, can look over all the world and see what is happening, and according to our ancestors' declarations, she possessed the knowledge of the future, which, however, no one could ever prevail upon her to reveal, thus proving that Northern women could keep a secret inviolate.

"Of me the gods are sprung;
And all that is to come I know, but lock
In my own breast, and have to none reveal'd."
    -BALDER DEAD (Matthew Arnold)

She is generally represented as a tall, beautiful, and stately woman, crowned with heron plumes, the symbol of silence or forgetfulness, and clothed in pure-white robes, secured at the waist by a golden girdle, from which hangs a bunch of keys, the distinctive sign of the Northern housewife, whose special patroness she is said to be. Although she often appears beside her husband, Frigga sometimes prefers to remain in her own palace, called Fensalir, the hall of mists or of the sea, where she diligently twirls her wheel or distaff, spinning golden thread or weaving long webs of bright-colored clouds.

In order to perform this work she owns a marvelous jeweled spinning wheel or distaff, which at night shines brightly in the sky in the shape of a constellation, known in the North as Frigga's Spinning Wheel, while the inhabitants of the South called the same stars Orion's Girdle.

To her hall Fensalir the gracious goddess invites all husbands and wives who had led virtuous lives on earth, so that they might enjoy each other's companionship even after death, and never be called upon to part again.

"There in the glen, Fensalir stands, the house
Of Frea, honor'd mother of the gods,
And shows its lighted windows and the open doors."
      -BALDER DEAD (Matthew Arnold)

The Stolen Gold

Frigga is considered the goddess of conjugal and motherly love, and is specially worshiped by married lovers and tender parents. This exalted office does not so entirely absorb all her thoughts, however, that she has no time for other matters; for we are told that she is very fond of dress, and whenever she appears before the assembled gods her attire is rich and becoming, and her jewels always chosen with much taste. This love of adornment once led her sadly astray, for, in her longing to possess some new jewel, she secretly purloined a piece of gold from a statue representing her husband, which had just been placed in his temple. The stolen metal was intrusted to the dwarfs, with instructions to fashion a marvelous necklace for her use. This jewel, once finished, was so resplendent that it greatly enhanced her charms and even increased Odin's love for her. But when he discovered the theft of the gold he angrily summoned the dwarfs and bade them reveal who had dared to touch his statue. Unwilling to betray the queen of the gods, the dwarfs remained obstinately silent, and, seeing that no information could be elicited from them, Odin commanded that the statue should be placed above the temple gate, and set to work to devise runes which should endow it with the power of speech and enable it to denounce the thief. When Frigga heard these tidings she trembled with fear, and implored her favorite attendant, Fulla, to invent some means of protecting her from Allfather's wrath. Fulla, who was always ready to serve her mistress, immediately departed, and soon returned, accompanied by a hideous dwarf, who promised to prevent the statue from speaking if Frigga would only deign to smile graciously upon him. This boon having been granted, the dwarf hastened off to the temple, caused a deep sleep to fall upon the guards, and while they were thus unconscious, pulled the statue down from its perch and broke it to pieces, so that it could never betray Frigga's theft in spite of all Odin's efforts to give it the power of speech.

Odin, discovering this sacrilege on the morrow, was very angry indeed; so angry that he left Asgard and utterly disappeared, carrying away with him all the blessings which he had been wont to shower upon gods and men. According to some authorities, his brothers Vili and Ve, took advantage of his absence to assume his form and secure possession of his throne and wife; but although they looked exactly like him they could not restore the lost blessings, and allowed the ice giants, or Jotuns, to invade the earth and bind it fast in their cold fetters. These wicked giants also pinched the leaves and buds till they all shriveled up, stripped the trees bare, shrouded the earth in a great white coverlet, and veiled it in impenetrable mists.
But at the end of seven weary months the true Odin relented and returned, and when he saw all the evil that had been done he drove the usurpers away, forced the frost giants to beat a hasty retreat, released the earth from her icy bonds, and again showered all his blessings down upon her, cheering her with the light of his smile.

Odin Outwitted

As has already been seen, Odin, although god of wit and wisdom, was sometimes outwitted by his wife Frigga, who, womanlike, was sure to obtain her will by some means. On one occasion the divine pair were seated upon Hlidskialf, gazing with interest upon the Winilers and Vandals, who were preparing for a battle which was to decide which people should henceforth have the supremacy. Odin gazed with satisfaction upon the Vandals, who were loudly praying to him for victory; but Frigga watched the movements of the Winilers with more attention, because they had entreated her aid. She therefore turned to Odin and coaxingly inquired whom he meant to favor on the morrow; he, wishing to evade her question, declared he would not yet decide, as it was time for bed, but would give the victory to those upon whom his eyes first rested in the morning. This answer was shrewdly calculated, for Odin knew that his bed was so turned that upon waking he would face the Vandals, and he intended looking out from thence, instead of waiting until he had mounted his throne. But, although so cunningly contrived, this plan was entirely frustrated by Frigga, who, divining his purpose, waited until he was sound asleep and then noiselessly turned his bed around so that he should face her favorites instead of his. Then she sent word to the Winilers to dress their women in armor and send them out in battle array at dawn, with their long hair carefully combed down over their cheeks and breasts.

"Take thou thy women-folk,
Maidens and wives:
Over your ankles
Lace on the white war-hose;
Over your bosoms
Link up the hard mail-nets;
Over your lips
Plait long tresses with cunning; —
So war beasts full-bearded
King Odin shall deem you,
When off the gray sea-beach
At sunrise ye greet him."
    -THE LONGBEARDS' SAGA (Charles Kingsley)

These instructions were carried out with scrupulous exactness by the Winiler women, and when Odin awoke and sat up in bed early the next morning, his first conscious glance fell upon their armed host, and he exclaimed in surprise, "What Longbeards are those?" (In German the ancient word for long beards was Langobarden, which was the name used to designate the Lombards.) Frigga, upon hearing this exclamation, which she had foreseen, immediately cried out in triumph that Allfather had given them a new name, and was in honor bound to follow the usual Northern custom and give them also a baptismal gift.

"'A name thou hast given them,
Shames neither thee nor them,
Well can they wear it.

Give them the victory,
First have they greeted thee;
Give them the victory,
Yoke-fellow mine!'"
     -THE LONGBEARDS' SAGA (Charles Kingsley)

Odin, seeing he had been so cleverly outwitted, gave them the victory, and in memory of this auspicious day the Winilers retained the name given by the king of the Gods, who ever after watched over them with special care, and vouchsafed them many blessings, among others a home in the sunny South, on the fruitful plains of Lombardy.

Fulla and Hlin

Frigga has, as her own special attendants, a number of beautiful maidens, one among them being Fulla (Volla), her sister according to some, to whom she intrusted her jewel casket. Fulla always presides over her mistress's dressing room, is privileged to put on her golden shoes, attends with her everywhere, is her confidante and adviser, and often suggests to her how best to help the mortals who implore her aid. Fulla is very beautiful indeed, and has long golden hair, which she wears flowing loose over her shoulders, restrained only by a golden circlet or snood. As her hair is emblematic of the golden grain, this circlet represents the binding of the sheaf. Fulla was also known as Abundia, or Abundantia, in some parts of Germany, where she was considered the symbol of the fullness of the earth.

Hlin, Frigga's second attendant, is the goddess of consolation, sent out to kiss away the tears of mourners and pour balm into hearts wrung by grief. She also listens with ever-open ears to the prayers of mortals, repeats them to her mistress, and advises her at times how best to answer them and give the desired relief.

Gna

Gna is Frigga's swift messenger, who, mounted upon her fleet steed Hofvarpnir (hoof thrower), travels with marvelous rapidity through fire and air, over land and sea, and is therefore considered the personification of the refreshing breeze. Darting thus to and from, Gna sees all that is happening upon earth, and tells her mistress all she knows. On one occasion, as she was passing over Hunaland, she saw King Rerir, a lineal descendant of Odin, sitting mournfully by the shore, bewailing his childlessness. The queen of the Gods, who is also goddess of childbirth, upon hearing this took an apple (the emblem of fruitfulness) from her private store, gave it to Gna, and bade her carry it to the king. With the rapidity of the element she personified, Gna darted away, passed over Rerir's head, and dropped her apple into his lap with a radiant smile.

"'What flies up there, so quickly driving past?'
Her answer from the cloud, as rushing by:
'I fly not, nor do drive, but hurry fast,
Hoof flinger swift through cloud and mist and sky.'"
-ASGARD AND THE GODS (Wagner-Macdowall)

The king, after pondering for a moment upon the meaning of this sudden apparition and gift, returned home, his heart beating high with hope, gave the apple to his wife to eat, and to his intense joy was soon no longer childless, for his wife bore him a son, Volsung, the great Northern hero, who became so famous that he gave his name to all his race.

Lofn

Besides the three above-mentioned attendants, Frigga also has in her train the mild and gracious maiden Lofn (praise or love), whose duty it is to remove all obstacles from the path of lovers.

"My lily tall, from her saddle bearing,
I led then forth through the temple, faring
To th' altar-circle where, priests among,
Lofn's vows she took with unfalt'ring tongue."
-VIKING TALES OF THE NORTH (R. B. Anderson)

Lofn's duty is to incline obdurate hearts to love, to maintain peace and concord among mankind, and to reconcile quarreling husbands and wives. Syn (truth) guards the door of Frigga's palace, refusing to open it to those who are not allowed to come in. When she had once shut the door upon a would-be intruder there was no appeal which would avail to change her decision. She therefore presided over all tribunals and trials, and whenever a thing was to be vetoed the usual formula was to declare that Syn was against it.

Gefjon

Gefjon is also one of the maidens in Frigga's palace, and to her are intrusted all those who died virgins, whom she receives and makes happy forever. According to some mythologists, Gefjon did not always remain a virgin herself, but married one of the giants, by whom she had four sons. This same tradition goes on to declare that Odin sent her ahead of him to visit Gylfi, King of Sweden, and beg for some land which she might call her own. The king, amused at her request, promised her as much land as she could plow around in one day and night. Gefjon, nothing daunted, changed her four sons into oxen, harnessed them to a plow, and began to cut a furrow so wide and deep that the king and his courtiers were amazed. But Gefjon continued her work without giving any signs of fatigue, and when she had plowed all around a large piece of land forcibly wrenched it away, and made her oxen drag it down into the sea, where she made it fast and called it Seeland.

"Gefjun drew from Gylfi,
Rich in stored up treasure,
The land she joined to Denmark.
Four heads and eight eyes bearing,
While hot sweat trickled down them,
The oxen dragged the reft mass
That formed this winsome island."
  -NORSE MYTHOLOGY (R. B. Anderson)

As for the hollow she left behind her, it was quickly filled with water and formed a lake, at first called Logrum (the sea), but now known as Mälar, whose every indentation corresponds with the headlands of Seeland. Gefjon then married Skiold, one of Odin's sons, and became the ancestress of the royal Danish race of Skioldungs, dwelling in the city of Hleidra or Lethra, which she founded, and which became the principal place of sacrifice for the heathen Danes.

Eira, Vara, Vör and Snotra

Eira, also Frigga's attendant, is considered a most skillful physician. She gathers simples all over the earth to cure both wounds and diseases, and it is her province to teach her science to women, who were the only ones to practice medicine among the ancient nations of the North.

"Gaping wounds are bound by Eyra."
  -VALHALLA (J. C. Jones)

Vara hears all oaths and punishes perjurers, while she rewards those who faithfully keep their word. Then there is also Vör (faith), who knows all that is to occur throughout the world, and Snotra, goddess of virtue, who has mastered every kind of study.

With such a band of followers it is no wonder that Frigga is considered an influential goddess; but in spite of the prominent place she occupied in Northern religion, she had no special temple or shrine, and was but little worshiped except in company with Odin.

Holda

While Frigga was not known by this name in southern Germany, there were other goddesses worshiped there, whose attributes were so exactly like hers, that they were evidently the same, although they bore very different names in the various provinces. Among them was the fair goddess Holda (Hulda or Frau Holle) who graciously dispensed many rich gifts, and as she presided over the weather, the people were wont to declare when the snowflakes fell that Frau Holle was shaking her bed, and when it rained, that she was washing her clothes, often pointing to the white clouds as her linen which she had put out to bleach. When long gray strips of clouds drifted across the sky they said she was weaving, for she too was supposed to be a very diligent weaver, spinner, and housekeeper.

This same Holda was also considered the owner of a magic fountain called Quickbom, which rivaled the famed fountain of youth, and of a chariot in which she rode from place to place, inspecting her domain. This wagon having once suffered damage, the goddess bade a wheelwright repair it, and when he had finished told him to keep the chips as his pay. The man, indignant at such a meager reward, kept only a very few; but to his surprise found them on the morrow changed to solid gold.

"Fricka, thy wife —
This way she reins her harness of rams.
Hey! how she whirls
The golden whip;

The luckless beasts
Unboundedly bleat;
Her wheels wildly she rattles;
Wrath is lit in her look."
    -WAGNER (Forman's tr.)

It is said she gave flax to mankind and taught them how to use it, and in Tyrol the following story is told about the way in which she bestowed this invaluable gift:

The Discovery of Flax

There was once a peasant who daily left his wife and children down in the valley to take his sheep up the mountain to pasture; and as he watched his flock graze on the mountain side, he often had the opportunity to use his crossbow and bring down a chamois, whose flesh furnished his larder with food for many a day.

While pursuing some fine game one day he saw it disappear behind a boulder, and when he came to the spot, he was amazed to see a doorway in the neighboring glacier, for in the excitement of the pursuit he had climbed higher and higher until he was now on top of the mountain, where glittered the everlasting snow.
The shepherd boldly passed through the open door, and soon found himself in a wonderful jeweled and stalactite-hung cave, in the center of which stood a beautiful woman, clad in silvery robes, and attended by a host of lovely maidens crowned with Alpine roses.

In his surprise, the shepherd sank to his knees, and as in a dream heard the queenly central figure bid him choose anything he saw to carry away with him. Although dazzled by the glow of the precious stones around him, the shepherd's eyes constantly reverted to a little nosegay of blue flowers which the gracious apparition held in her hand, and he now timidly proffered a request that it might become his. Smiling with pleasure, Holda, for it was she, gave it to him, telling him he had chosen wisely and would live as long as the flowers did not droop and fade. Then giving the shepherd a measure of seed which she told him to sow in his field, the goddess bade him begone; and as the, thunder pealed and the earth shook, the poor man found himself out upon the mountain side once more, and slowly wended his way home to tell his adventure to his wife and show her the lovely blue flowers and the measure of seed.

The woman reproached her husband bitterly for not having brought some of the precious stones which he so glowingly described, instead of the blossoms and seed; nevertheless the man sowed the latter, and often lingered near the field at nightfall to see his new crop grow, for to his surprise the measure had supplied seed enough for several acres.

Soon the little green shoots began to appear, and one moonlight night, while the peasant was gazing upon them, wondering what kind of grain they would produce, he saw a mistlike form hover above the field, with hands outstretched as if in blessing. At last the field blossomed, and countless little blue flowers opened their calyxes to the golden sun. When the flowers had withered and the seed was ripe, Holda came once more to teach the peasant and his wife how to harvest the flax stalks and spin, weave, and bleach the linen they produced. Of course all the people of the neighborhood were anxious to purchase both linen and flaxseed, and the peasant and his wife soon grew very rich indeed, for while he plowed, sowed, and harvested, she spun, wove, and bleached her linen.

When the man had lived to a good old age and seen his grandchildren and great grandchildren grow up around him, he noticed that his carefully treasured bouquet, whose flowers had remained fresh for many a year, had wilted and died.

Knowing that his time had come and that he too must soon die, the peasant climbed the mountain once more, came to the glacier, and found the doorway which he had long vainly sought. He vanished within, and was never seen or heard of again, for the legend states that the goddess took him under her care, and bade him live in her cave, where his every wish was gratified.

Ostara, the Goddess of Spring

The Saxon goddess Eástre, or Ostara, goddess of spring, whose name has survived in the English word Easter, is also identical with Frigga, for she too is considered goddess of the earth, or rather of Nature's resurrection after the long death of winter.

This gracious goddess was so dearly loved by the old Teutons, that even after Christianity had been viciously forced upon the people of the North, they stilt retained a pleasant recollection of her, utterly refused to have her degraded to the rank of a demon, like many of their other divinities, and transferred her name to their great Christian feast. It had long been customary to celebrate this day by the exchange of presents of colored eggs, for the egg is the type of the beginning of life; so the early Christians continued to observe this rule, declaring, however, that the egg is also symbolical of the resurrection. In various parts of Germany, stone altars can still be seen, which are known as Easter-stones, because they were dedicated to the fair goddess Ostara. They were crowned with flowers by the young people, who danced gaily around them by the light of great bonfires, — a species of popular games kept up until the middle of the 19th century, in spite of the priests' denunciations and of the repeatedly published edicts against them.

Bertha, the White Lady

In other parts of Germany, Frigga, Holda, or Ostara is known by the name of Brechta, Bertha, or the White Lady. She is best known under this title in Thuringia, where she was supposed to dwell in a hollow mountain, keeping watch over the Heimchen, the souls of unborn children, and of those who died unbaptized. Here Bertha watched over agriculture, caring for the plants, which her infant troop watered carefully, for each babe was supposed to carry a little jar for that express purpose. As long as the goddess was duly respected and her retreat unmolested, she remained where she was; but tradition relates that she once left the country with her infant train dragging her plow, and settled elsewhere to continue her kind ministrations. Bertha is the legendary ancestress of several noble families, and she is supposed to be the same as the industrious queen of the same name, the mythical mother of Charlemagne, whose era has become proverbial, for in speaking of the golden age in France and Germany it is customary to say, "in the days when Bertha spun."

As this Bertha is supposed to have developed a very large and flat foot, from continually pressing the treadle of her wheel, she is often represented in mediaeval art as a woman with a splay foot, and hence known as la reine pédauque.

As ancestress of the imperial house of Germany, the White Lady is supposed to appear in the palace before a death or misfortune in the family, and this thought was still so rife in 19th century Germany, that the newspapers in 1884 contained the official report of a sentinel, who declared that he had seen her flit past him in one of the palace corridors.

As Bertha was so renowned for her spinning, she naturally was regarded as the special patroness of that branch of female industry, and was said to flit through the streets of every village, at nightfall, during the twelve nights between Christmas and January 6th, peering into every window to ascertain whether the work were all done.

The maidens whose work had all been carefully performed were rewarded by a present of one of her own golden threads or a distaff full of extra-fine flax; but wherever a careless spinner was found, her wheel was broken, her flax soiled, and if she had failed to honor the goddess by eating plenty of the cakes baked at that epoch of the year, she was cruelly punished.

In Mecklenburg, this same goddess is known as Frau Gode, or Wode, the female form of Wotan or Odin, and her appearance is always considered the harbinger of great prosperity. She is also supposed to be a great huntress, and to lead the Wild Hunt, mounted upon a white horse, her attendants being changed into hounds and all manner of wild beasts.

In Holland she was called Vrou-elde, and from her the Milky Way is known by the Dutch as Vrou-elden-straat; while in parts of northern Germany she was called Nerthus (Mother Earth). Her sacred chariot was kept on an island, presumably Rugen, where the priests guarded it carefully until she appeared to take a yearly journey throughout her realm and bless the land. The goddess then sat in this chariot, which was drawn by two cows, her face completely hidden by a thick veil, respectfully escorted by her priests. The people seeing her pass did her homage by ceasing all warfare, laid aside their weapons, donned festive attire, and began no quarrel until the goddess had again retired to her sanctuary. Then both chariot and goddess were bathed in a secret lake (the Schwartze See in Rügen), which swallowed up the slaves who had assisted at the bathing, and once more the priests resumed their watch over the sanctuary and grove of Nerthus or Hlodyn, to await her next apparition.

In Scandinavia, this goddess was also known as Huldra; and boasted of a train of attendant wood nymphs, who sometimes sought the society of mortals, to enjoy a dance upon the village green. They could always be detected, however, by the tip of a cow's tail which trailed from beneath their long snow-white garments. These Huldra folk were the special protectors of the herds of cattle on the mountain sides, and were said to surprise the lonely traveler, at times, by the marvelous beauty of the melodies they sang to beguile their labors.

THOR
God of Thunder

Thor, or Donar, is the son of Odin and by some accounts Jörd (Erda or Earth), while others state that his mother was Frigga, Queen of the Gods. Thor is is known as "The Thunderer", Hammer-God of thunder and lightening, agriculture and craftsmanship. He is the archetype hero/warrior and friend of the common folk. His divine hammer is known as Mjöllnir (the crusher), forged by the Dwarves as remuneration for a crime committed by Loki. He is champion of the Gods and enemy of the Giants and Trolls; protector of Midgard and the common man from the forces of chaos. He dons a magic belt called Megingjardar, which when worn doubles his already miraculous strenght, and drives a chariot pulled by two Giant male goats.

As a child Thor was very remarkable for his great size and strength, and very soon after his birth amazed the assembled gods by playfully lifting and throwing about ten loads of bear skins. Although generally good tempered, Thor occasionally flew into a terrible rage, and as he was very dangerous under these circumstances. His mother, unable to control him, sent him away from home and intrusted him to the care of Vingnir (the winged), and of Hlora (heat). These foster parents, who are also considered as the personification of sheet lightning, soon managed to control their troublesome charge, and brought him up so wisely, that all the gods were duly grateful for their kind offices. Thor himself, recognizing all he owed them, assumed the names of Vingthor and Hlorridi, by which he is also known.

"Cry on, Vingi-Thor,
With the dancing of the ring-mail and the smitten shields of war."
    -SIGURD THE VOLSUNG (William Morris)

Having attained his full growth and the age of reason, Thor was admitted in Asgard among the other gods, where he occupied one of the twelve seats in the great judgment hall. He was also given the realm of Thrud-vang or Thrud-heim, where he built a wonderful palace called Bilskirnir (lightning), the most spacious in all Asgard. It contains five hundred and forty halls for the accommodation of the thralls, who after death are welcomed to his home, where they are treated as well as their masters in Valhalla, for Thor is the patron god of the peasants and lower classes.

"Five hundred halls
And forty more,
Methinketh, hath
Bowed Bilskirnir.
Of houses roofed
There's none I know
My son's surpassing."
    -SÆMUND'S EDDA (Percy's tr.)

As he is the God of Thunder, Thor alone is never allowed to pass over the wonderful bridge Bifröst, lest he should set it aflame by the heat of his presence; and when he daily wishes to join his fellow gods by the Urdar fountain, under the shade of the sacred tree Yggdrasil, he is forced to make his way thither on foot, wading through the rivers Kormt and Ormt, and the two streams Kerlaug, to the trysting place.

Thor, who was honored as the highest god in Norway, came second in the trilogy of all the other countries, and was called "old Thor," because he is supposed by some mythologists to have belonged to an older dynasty of gods, and not on account of his actual age, for he was represented and described as a man in his prime, tall and well formed, with muscular limbs and bristling red hair and beard, from which, in moments of anger, the sparks fairly flew.

"First, Thor with the bent brow,
In red beard muttering low,
Darting fierce lightnings from eyeballs that glow,
Comes, while each chariot wheel
Echoes in thunder peal,
As his dread hammer shock
Makes Earth and Heaven rock,

Clouds rifting above, while Earth quakes below."
-VALHALLA (J. C. Jones)

The Northern races further adorned him with a crown, on each point of which was either a, glittering star, or a steadily burning flame, so that his head was ever surrounded by a kind of halo of fire, his own element.

Thor's Hammer

Thor is the proud possessor of a magic hammer called Mjöllnir (the crusher) which he hurls at his enemies, the frost giants, with destructive power, and which possesses the wonderful property of always returning to his hand, however far away he might hurl it.

"I am the Thunderer!
Here in my Northland,
My fastness and fortress,
Reign I forever!

"Here amid icebergs
Rule I the nations;
This is my hammer,
Mjöllnir the mighty;
Giants and sorcerers
Cannot withstand it!"
-SAGA OF KING OLAF (Longfellow)

As this huge hammer, the emblem of the thunderbolts, is generally red hot, Thor has an iron gauntlet called Iarn-greiper, which enables him to grasp it firmly and hurl it very far, his strength, which was already remarkable, being always doubled when he wears his magic belt called Megingjardar.

"This is my girdle:
Whenever I brace it,
Strength is redoubled!"
-SAGA OF KING OLAF (Longfellow)

Thor's hammer was considered so very sacred by the ancient Northern people, that they were wont to make the sign of the hammer, as the Christians later taught them to make the sign of the cross, to ward off all evil influences, and to secure many blessings. The same sign was also made over the newly born infant when water was poured over its head and a name given it. The hammer was used to drive in boundary stakes, which it was considered sacrilegious to remove, to hallow the threshold of a new house, to solemnize a marriage, and, lastly, to consecrate the funeral pyre upon which the bodies of heroes were burned, together with their weapons and steeds, and, in some cases, with their wives and dependents.

In Sweden, Thor, like Odin, was supposed to wear a broad-brimmed hat, and hence the storm clouds in that country are known as Thor's hat, a name also given to one of the principal mountains in Norway. The rumble and roar of the thunder were called the roll of his chariot, for he alone among the gods never rode on horseback, but walked, or drove in a brazen chariot drawn by two goats, Tanngniostr (tooth cracker), and Tanngrisnr (tooth gnasher), from whose teeth and hoofs the sparks constantly flew

"Thou tamest near the next, O warrior Thor!
Shouldering thy hammer, in thy chariot drawn,
Swaying the long-hair'd goats with silver'd rein."
　　-BALDER DEAD (Matthew Arnold)

When the God thus drove about from place to place, he was called Aku-thor, or Thor the charioteer, and in southern Germany the people, fancying a brazen chariot alone inadequate to furnish all the noise they heard, declared it was loaded with copper kettles, which rattled and clashed, and therefore often called him, with disrespectful familiarity, the kettle vender.

Thor's Family

Thor is twice married; first to the giantess Iarnsaxa (iron stone), who bore him two sons, Magni (strength) and Modi (courage), both destined to survive their father and the twilight of the gods, and rule over the new world which is to rise like a phoenix from the ashes of the first. His second wife is Sif, the golden-haired, who also bore him two children, Lorride, and a daughter named Thrud, a young giantess renowned for her size and strength. By the well-known affinity of contrast, Thrud was wooed by the dwarf Alvis, whom she rather favored; and one evening, when this suitor, who, being a dwarf, could not face the light of day, presented himself in Asgard to sue for her hand, the assembled Gods did not refuse their consent. They had scarcely signified their approbation, however, when Thor, who had been absent, suddenly appeared, and casting a glance of contempt upon the puny lover, declared he would have to prove that his knowledge atoned for his small stature, before he could win his bride.

To test Alvis's mental powers, Thor then questioned him in the language of the Gods, Vanas, elves, and dwarfs, artfully prolonging his examination until sunrise, when. the first beam of light, falling upon the unhappy dwarf, petrified him. There he stood, an enduring example of the Gods' power, and served as a warning to all other dwarfs who would fain have tested it.

"Ne'er in human bosom
Have I found so many
Words of the old time.
Thee with subtlest cunning
Have I yet befooled.
Above ground standeth thou, dwarf,
By day art overtaken,
Bright sunshine fills the hall."
       -SÆMUND'S EDDA (Howitt's version)

Sif, the Golden-haired

Sif, Thor's wife, was very vain of a magnificent head of long golden hair which covered her from head to foot like a brilliant veil; and as she too is a symbol of the earth, her hair is said to represent the long grass, or the golden grain covering the Northern harvest fields. Thor was very proud of his wife's beautiful hair; imagine his dismay, therefore, upon waking one morning, to find her all shorn, and as bald and denuded of ornament as the earth when the grain has all been garnered, and nothing but the stubble remains! In his anger, Thor sprang to his feet, vowing he would punish the perpetrator of this outrage, whom he immediately and rightly conjectured to be Loki, the arch plotter, ever on the lookout for some evil deed to perform. Seizing his hammer, Thor soon overtook Loki in spite of his attempting to evade him by changing form, caught him by the throat, and almost strangled him ere he yielded to his imploring signs, and slightly loosed his powerful grasp. As soon as Loki could catch his breath, he implored forgiveness, but all his entreaties were vain, until he promised to procure for Sif a new head of hair, as beautiful as the first, and as luxuriant in growth.

"And thence for Sif new tresses I'll bring Of gold, ere the daylight's gone,
So that she shall liken a field in spring,
With its yellow-flowered garment on."
    -THE DWARFS, OEHLENSCHLÄGER (Pigott's tr.)

Thor, hearing this, consented to let the traitor go; so Loki rapidly crept down into the bowels of the earth, where Svartalfheim was situated, to beg the dwarf Dvalin to fashion not only the precious hair, but a present for Odin and Frey, whose anger he wished to disarm.

The dwarf soon made the spear Gungnir, which never failed in its aim, and the ship Skidbladnir, which, always wafted by favorable winds, could sail through the air as well as on the water, and was so elastic, that although it could contain the Gods and all their steeds, it could be folded up into the very smallest compass and thrust in one's pocket. Lastly, he spun the very finest golden thread, from which he fashioned the required hair for Sif, declaring that as soon as it touched her head it would grow fast there and become alive.

"Though they now seem dead, let them touch but her head,
Each hair shall the life-moisture fill;
Nor shall malice nor spell henceforward prevail
Sif's tresses to work aught of ill."
    -THE DWARFS, OEHLENSCHLÄGER (Pigott's tr.)

Loki was so pleased with these proofs of the dwarfs' skill that he declared the son of Ivald was the most clever of smiths — words which were overheard by Brock, another dwarf, who exclaimed that he was sure his brother Sindri could produce three objects which would surpass those which Loki held, not only in intrinsic value, but also in magical properties. Loki immediately challenged the dwarf to show his skill, wagering his head against Brock's on the result of the undertaking.

Sindri, apprised of the wager, accepted Brock's offer to blow the bellows, warning him, however, that he must work persistently if he wished to succeed; then he threw some gold in the fire, and went out to bespeak the favor of the hidden powers. During his absence Brock diligently plied the bellows, while Loki, hoping to make him fail, changed himself into a gadfly and cruelly stung his hand. In spite of the pain, the dwarf did not let go, and when Sindri returned, he drew out of the fire an enormous wild boar, called Gullin-bursti, on account of its golden bristles, which had the power of radiating light as he flitted across the sky, for he could travel through the air with marvelous velocity.

"And now, strange to tell, from the roaring fire
Came the golden-haired Gullinbörst,
To serve as a charger the sun-god Frey,
Sure, of all wild boars this the first."
      -THE DWARFS, OEHLENSCHLÄGER (Pigott's tr.)

This first piece of work successfully completed, Sindri flung some more gold on the fire and bade his brother blow, ere he again went out to secure magic assistance. This time Loki, still disguised as a gadfly, stung the dwarf on his cheek; but in spite of the pain Brock worked on, and when Sindri returned, he triumphantly drew out of the flames the magic ring Draupnir, the emblem of fertility, from which eight similar rings dropped every ninth night.

"They worked it and turned it with wondrous skill,
Till they gave it the virtue rare,
That each thrice third night from its rim there fell
Eight rings, as their parent fair."
      -THE DWARFS, OEHLENSCHLÄGER (Pigott's tr.)

Now a lump of iron was cast in the flames, and with a new caution not to forfeit their success by inattention, Sindri passed out, leaving Brock to ply the bellows and wrestle with the gadfly, which this time stung him above the eye until the blood began to flow in such a stream, that it prevented his seeing what he was doing. Hastily raising his hand for a second, Brock dashed aside the stream of blood; but short as was the interruption, Sindri uttered an exclamation of disappointment when he drew his work out of the fire, for the hammer he had fashioned had too short a handle.

"Then the dwarf raised his hand to his brow for the smart,
Ere the iron well out was beat,
And they found that the haft by an inch was too short,
But to alter it then 'twas too late."
        -THE DWARFS, OEHLENSCHLÄGER (Pigott's tr.)

Notwithstanding this mishap, Brock was so sure of winning the wager that he did not hesitate to present himself before the Gods in Asgard, gave Odin the ring Draupnir, Frey the boar Gullin-bursti, and Thor the hammer Mjöllnir, whose power none could resist.

Loki immediately gave the spear Gungnir to Odin, the ship Skidbladnir to Frey, and the golden hair to Thor; but although the latter immediately grew upon Sif's head and was unanimously declared more beautiful than her own locks had ever been, the gods decreed that Brock had won the wager, for the hammer Mjöllnir, in Thor's hands, would prove invaluable against the frost giants on the last day.

"And at their head came Thor, Shouldering his hammer, which the giants know."
        -BALDER DEAD (Matthew Arnold)

Wishing to save his head, Loki fled, but was soon overtaken by Thor, who brought him back and handed him over to Brock, telling him, however, that although Loki's head was rightfully his, he must not touch his neck. Thus hindered from obtaining full vengeance, the dwarf tried to sew Loki's lips together, but, as his sword would not pierce them, he was obliged to borrow his brother's awl. However, Loki, after enduring the Gods' gibes in silence for a little while, managed to cut the string and was soon as loquacious as ever.

In spite of his redoubtable hammer, Thor was never considered as the injurious God of the storm, who destroyed peaceful homesteads and ruined the harvest by sudden hail storms and cloud bursts, for the Northerners fancied he hurled it only against ice giants and rocky walls, reducing the latter to powder to fertilize the earth and make it yield plentiful fruit to the tillers of the soil.

In Germany, where the eastern storms are always cold and blighting, while the western bring warm rains and mild weather, Thor was supposed to journey always from west to east, to wage war against the evil spirits which would fain have enveloped the country in impenetrable veils of mist and have bound it in icy fetters.

Journey to Jötunheim

As the giants from Jötunheim were continually sending out cold blasts of wind to nip the tender buds and hinder the growth of the flowers, Thor once made up his mind to go and force them to better behavior. Accompanied by Loki he therefore set out in his chariot. After riding for a whole day the gods came at nightfall to the confines of the giant-world, where, seeing a peasant's hut, they resolved to spend the night and refresh themselves.

Their host was hospitable but very poor, and Thor seeing that he would scarcely be able to supply the necessary food to satisfy his by no means small appetite, slew both his goats, which he cooked and began to eat, inviting his host and family to partake freely of the food thus provided, but cautioning them to throw all the bones, without breaking them, into the skins spread out on the floor.
The peasant and his family ate heartily, but a youth called Thialfi, encouraged by Loki, ventured to break one of the bones and suck out the marrow, thinking his disobedience would never be detected. On the morrow, however, Thor, ready to depart, struck the goat skins with his hammer Miölnir, and immediately the goats sprang up as lively as before, except that one seemed somewhat lame. Perceiving in a second that his commands had been disregarded, Thor would have slain the whole family in his wrath. The culprit acknowledged his fault, however, and the peasant offered to compensate for the loss by giving the irate god not only his son Thialfi, but also his daughter Roskva, to serve him forever.

Charging the man to take good care of the goats, which he left there until he should return, and bidding the young peasants accompany him, Thor now set out on foot with Loki, and after walking all day found himself at nightfall in a bleak and barren country, which was enveloped in an almost impenetrable gray mist. After seeking for some time, Thor saw through the fog the uncertain outline of what looked like a peculiar-shaped house. Its open portal was so wide and high that it seemed to take up all one side of the house. Entering and finding neither fire nor light, Thor and his companions flung themselves wearily down on the floor to sleep, but were soon disturbed by a peculiar noise, and a prolonged trembling of the ground beneath them. Fearing lest the main roof should fall during this earthquake, Thor and his companions took refuge in a wing of the building, where they soon fell sound asleep. At dawn, the God and his companions passed out, but they had not gone very far ere they saw the recumbent form of a sleeping giant, and perceived that the peculiar sounds which had disturbed their rest were produced by his snores. At that moment the giant awoke, arose, stretched himself, looked about him for his missing property, and a second later he picked up the object which Thor and his companions had mistaken in the darkness for a house. They then perceived with amazement that the wing in which they had all slept was the separate place in a mitten for the giant's great thumb! Learning that Thor and his companions were on their way to Utgard, as the giants' realm was also called, Skrymir, the giant, proposed to be their guide; and after walking with them all day, he offered them the provisions in his wallet ere he dropped asleep. But, in spite of strenuous efforts, neither Thor nor his companions could unfasten the knots which Skrymir had tied.

"*Skrymir's thongs*
Seemed to thee hard,
When at the food thou couldst not get,
When, in full health, of hunger dying."
        -SÆMUND'S EDDA (Thorpe's tr.)

Utgard-loki

Angry because of his snoring, which kept them awake, Thor thrice dealt him fearful blows with his hammer. These strokes, instead of annihilating the monster, merely evoked sleepy comments to the effect that a leaf, a bit of bark, or a twig from a bird's nest overhead had fallen upon his face. Early on the morrow, Skrymir left Thor and his companions, pointing out the shortest road to Utgard-loki's castle, which was built of great ice blocks, with huge glittering icicles as pillars. The gods, slipping between the bars of the great gate, presented themselves boldly before the king of the giants, Utgard-loki, who, recognizing them, immediately pretended to be greatly surprised at their small size, and expressed a wish to see for himself what they could do, as he had often heard their prowess vaunted.

Loki, who had fasted longer than he wished, immediately declared he was ready to eat for a wager with any one. So the king ordered a great wooden trough full of meat to be brought into the hall, and placing Loki at one end and his cook Logi at the other, he bade them see which would win. Although Loki did wonders, and soon reached the middle of the trough, he still found himself beaten, for whereas he had picked the bones clean, his opponent had devoured both them and the trough.

Smiling contemptuously, Utgard-loki said that it was evident they could not do much in the eating line, and so nettled Thor thereby, that he declared if Loki could not eat more than the voracious cook, he felt confident he could drain the biggest vessel in the house, such was his unquenchable thirst. Immediately a horn was brought in, and, Utgard-loki declaring that good drinkers emptied it at one draught, moderately thirsty persons at two, and small drinkers at three, Thor applied his lips to the rim. But, although he drank so deep that he thought he would burst, the liquid still came almost up to the rim when he raised his head. A second and third attempt to empty this horn proved equally unsuccessful. Thialfi then offered to run a race, and a young fellow named Hugi soon outstripped him, although he made remarkably good time.

Thor next proposed to show his strength by lifting great weights, but when challenged to pick up the giant's cat, he tugged and strained, only to succeed in raising one paw from the floor, although he had taken the precaution to enhance his strength as much as possible by tightening his belt Megingjardar.

"Strong is great Thor, no doubt, when Meginjardar
He braces tightly o'er his rock-firm loins."
    -VIKING TALES OF THE NORTH (R. B. Anderson)

An attempt on his part to wrestle with Utgard-loki's old nurse Elli, the only opponent deemed worthy of such a puny fellow, ended equally disastrously, and the Gods, acknowledging they were beaten, were hospitably entertained. On the morrow they were escorted to the confines of Utgard, where the giant politely informed them that he hoped they would never call upon him again, as he had been forced to employ magic against them. He then went on to explain that he was the giant Skrymir, and that had he not taken the precaution to interpose a mountain between his head and Thor's blows, he would have been slain, as deep clefts in the mountain side testified to the god's strength. Next he informed them that Loki's opponent was Logi (wild fire); that Thialfi had run a race with Hugi (thought), than which no swifter runner exists; that Thor's drinking horn was connected with the ocean, where his deep draughts had produced a perceptible ebb ; that the cat was in reality the terrible Midgard serpent encircling the world, which Thor had nearly pulled out of the sea ; and that Elli, his nurse, was old age, whom none can resist. Having finished these explanations and cautioned them never to return or he would defend himself by similar delusions, Utgard-loki vanished, and although Thor angrily brandished his hammer to destroy his castle, such a mist enveloped it that it could not be seen, and the Thunder God was obliged to return to Thrudvang without having accomplished his purpose, the extermination of the race of giants.

"The strong-armed Thor
Full oft against giant Jotunheim did wend,
But spite his belt celestial, spite his gauntlets,
Utgard-Loki still his throne retains;
Evil, itself a force, to force yields never."
           -VIKING TALES OF THE NORTH (R. B. Anderson)

Thor and Hrungnir

As Odin was once dashing through the air on his eight-footed steed Sleipnir, he attracted the attention of the giant Hrungnir, who proposed a race, declaring he was sure his own steed Gullfaxi could rival Sleipnir in speed. In the heat of the race, Hrungnir did not even notice in what direction they were going, and, in the vain hope of overtaking Odin, urged his steed on to the very gates of Valhalla. Discovering where he was, the giant then grew pale with fear, for he knew he had jeopardized his life by venturing into the stronghold of the Gods, his hereditary foes.

The Æsir, however, were too honorable to take even an enemy at such a disadvantage, and, instead of doing him any harm, asked him into their banqueting halls, where he proceeded to indulge in liberal potations of the heavenly mead set before him. He soon grew so excited that he began to boast of his power, declaring he would come some day and take possession of Asgard, which he would destroy, as well as all the Gods, excepting only Freya and Sif, upon whom he gazed with an admiring, drunken leer.

The Gods, knowing he was not responsible, let him talk unmolested; but Thor, coming home just then from one of his journeys, and hearing him propose to carry away his beloved Sif, flew into a terrible rage. He furiously brandished his hammer, intending to annihilate the boaster. This the Gods would not permit, however, and they quickly threw themselves between the irate Thunderer and their guest, imploring the former to respect the sacred rights of hospitality, and not desecrate their peace-stead by shedding blood.

Thor at last consented to bridle his wrath, providing the giant Hrungnir would appoint a time and place for a holmgang, as a Northern duel was generally called. Thus challenged, Hrungnir promised to meet Thor at Griottunagard, the confines of his realm, three days later, and departed somewhat sobered by the fright he had experienced. When his fellow giants heard how rash he had been, they chided him sorely; but hearing he was to have the privilege of being accompanied by a squire, whom Thialfi would engage in fight, they proceeded to construct a creature of clay, nine miles long, and proportionately wide, whom they called Mokerkialfi (mist wader). As they could find no human heart big enough to put in this monster's breast, they secured that of a mare, which, however, kept fluttering and quivering with apprehension. The day of the duel arrived. Hrungnir and his squire were on the ground awaiting the arrival of their respective opponents. The giant had not only a flint heart and skull, but also a shield and club of the same substance, and therefore deemed himself well-nigh invincible. But when he heard a terrible noise, and Thialfi came running up to announce his master's coming, he gladly followed the herald's advice and stood upon his shield, lest the thunder god should come up from the ground and attack him unprotected.

A moment later, however, he saw his mistake, for, while Thialfi attacked Mokerkialfi with a spade, Thor came rushing up and flung his hammer full at his opponent's head. Hrungnir, to ward off the blow, interposed his stone club, which was shivered into pieces, that flew all over the earth, supplying all the flint stones to be found, and one fragment sank deep in Thor's forehead. As the God dropped fainting to the ground, his hammer crashed against the head of Hrungnir, who fell down dead beside him, in such a position that one of his ponderous legs was thrown over the recumbent god.

*"Thou now remindest me
How I with Hrungnir fought,
That stout-hearted Jotun,
Whose head was all of stone;
Yet I made him fall And sink before me."*
   -SÆMUND'S EDDA (Thorpe's tr.)

Thialfi, who, in the mean while, had disposed of the great clay giant with its cowardly mare's heart, now rushed to his master's rescue; but all his efforts and those of the assembled Gods, whom he quickly summoned, could not raise the pinioning leg. While they were standing there, helplessly wondering what they should do next, Thor's little son Magni came up. According to varying accounts, he was then only three days or three years old, but he quickly seized the giant's foot, and, unaided, set his father free, declaring that had he only been summoned sooner he would easily have disposed of both giant and squire. This exhibition of strength upon his part made the gods wonder greatly, and helped them to recognize the truth of the various predictions, which one and all declared that their descendants would be mightier than they, would survive them, and would rule in their turn over the new heaven and earth.

To reward his son for his timely aid, Thor gave him the steed Gullfaxi (golden-maned), to which he had fallen heir by right of conquest, and Magni ever after rode this marvelous horse, which almost equaled the renowned Sleipnir in speed and endurance.

Groa, the Sorceress

After vainly trying to remove the stone splinter from his forehead, Thor sadly returned home to Thrudvang, where Sif's loving efforts were equally unsuccessful. She therefore resolved to send for Groa (green-making), a sorceress, noted for her skill in medicine and for the efficacy of her spells and incantations. Groa immediately signified her readiness to render every service in her power to the god who had so often benefited her, and solemnly began to recite powerful runes, under whose influence Thor felt the stone grow looser and looser. In his delight at the prospect of a speedy deliverance, Thor wished to reward the enchantress. Knowing that nothing could give greater pleasure to a mother than the prospect of seeing a long-lost child, he therefore told her he had recently crossed the Elivagar, or ice streams, to rescue her little son Orvandil (germ) from the frost giants' cruel power, and had succeeded in carrying him off in a basket. But, as the little rogue would persist in sticking one of his bare toes through a hole in the basket, it had been frost bitten, and Thor, accidentally breaking it off, had flung it up into the sky, where it shone as a star, known in the North as "Orvandil's Toe."

Delighted with these tidings, the prophetess paused in her incantations to express her joy, but, having forgotten just where she left off, she was never able to continue her spell, and the flint stone remained imbedded in Thor's forehead, whence it could never be dislodged.

Thor and Thrym

Of course, as Thor's hammer always did him such good service, it was the most prized of all his possessions, and his dismay was very great when he awoke one morning and found it gone. His cry of anger and disappointment soon brought Loki to his side, and to him Thor confided the secret of his loss, declaring that were the giants to hear of it, they would soon attempt to storm Asgard and destroy the Gods.

"Wroth waxed Thor, when his sleep was flown,
And he found his trusty hammer gone;
He smote his brow, his beard he shook,
The son of earth 'gan round him look;
And this the first word that he spoke
'Now listen what I tell thee, Loke;
Which neither on earth below is known,
Nor in heaven above: my hammer's gone.'"
    -THRYM'S QUIDA (Herbert's tr.)

Loki declared he would try to discover the thief and recover the hammer, if Freya would only lend him her falcon plumes, and immediately hastened off to Folkvang to borrow them. In the form of a bird he then winged his flight across the river Ifing, and over the barren stretches of Jotunheim, where he shrewdly suspected the thief was to be found. There he saw Thrym, prince of the frost giants and God of the destructive thunder storm, sitting alone on a hillside, and, artfully questioning him, soon learned that he had stolen the hammer, had buried it deep underground, and would never give it up unless Freya were brought to him, in bridal array, ready to become his wife.

"I have the Thunderer's hammer bound
Fathoms eight beneath the ground;
With it shall no one homeward tread
Till he bring me Freya to share my bed."
         -THRYM'S QUIDA (Herbert's tr.)

Indignant at the giant's presumption, Loki returned to Thrudvang, where Thor, hearing what he had learned, declared it would be well to visit Freya and try to prevail upon her to sacrifice herself for the general good. But when the Æsir told the Goddess of beauty what they wished her to do, she flew into such a passion that even her necklace burst. She told them that she would never leave her beloved husband for any God, and much less to marry an ugly old giant and dwell in Jotunheim, where all was dreary in the extreme, and where she would soon die of longing for the green fields and flowery meadows, in which she loved to roam. Seeing that further persuasions would be useless, Loki and Thor returned home and there devised another plan for recovering the hammer. By Heimdall's advice, Thor borrowed and reluctantly put on all Freya's clothes and her necklace, and enveloped himself in a thick veil. Loki, having attired himself as a handmaiden, then mounted with him in the goat-drawn chariot, to ride to Jötunheim, where they intended to play the respective parts of the Goddess of beauty and of her attendant.

"Home were driven
Then the goats,
And hitched to the car;
Hasten they must —
The mountains crashed,
The earth stood in flames:
Odin's son
Rode to Jötunheim."
         -NORSE MYTHOLOGY (R. B. Anderson)

Thrym welcomed his guests at the palace door, overjoyed at the thought that he was about to secure undisputed possession of the Goddess of beauty, for whom he had long sighed in vain. He quickly led them to the banquet hall, where Thor, the bride elect, almost disgraced himself by eating an ox, eight huge salmon, and all the cakes and sweets provided for the women, washing down these miscellaneous viands with two whole barrels of mead.

The giant bridegroom watched these gastronomic feats with amazement, and was not even reassured when Loki confidentially whispered to him that the bride was so deeply in love with him that she had not been able to taste a morsel of food for more than eight days. Thrym then sought to kiss the bride, but drew back appalled at the fire of her glance, which Loki explained as a burning glance of love. The giant's sister, claiming the usual gifts, was not even noticed; so Loki again whispered to the wondering Thrym that love made people absent-minded. Intoxicated with passion and mead, which he, too, had drunk in liberal quantities, the bridegroom now bade his servants produce the sacred hammer to consecrate the marriage, and as soon as it was brought he himself laid it in the pretended Freya's lap. The next moment a powerful hand closed over the short handle, and the weapon, rapidly hurled by Thor, soon slew the giant, his sister, and all the invited guests.

"'Bear in the hammer to plight the maid;
Upon her lap the bruiser lay,
And firmly plight our hands and fay.'
The Thunderer's soul smiled in his breast;
When the hammer hard on his lap was placed,
Thrym first, the king of the Thursi, he slew,
And slaughtered all the giant crew."
    -THRYM'S QUIDA (Herbert's tr.)

Leaving a smoking heap of ruins behind them, the Gods then drove rapidly back to Asgard, where the borrowed garments were given back to Freya, and the Æsir all rejoiced at the recovery of the precious hammer. When next Odin glanced towards that part of Jötunheim from the top of his throne Hlidskialf, he saw the ruins covered with tender green shoots, for Thor, having conquered his enemy, had taken possession of his land, which no longer remained barren and desolate as before, but brought forth fruit in abundance.

Thor and Geirrod

Loki, in search of adventures, once borrowed Freya's falcon garb and flew off to another part of Jötunheim, where he perched on top of the gables of Geirrod's house, and, gazing about him, soon attracted the attention of this giant, who bade one of his servants catch the bird. Amused at the fellow's clumsy attempts to secure him, Loki flitted about from place to place, only moving just as the giant was about to lay hands upon him, until, miscalculating his distance, he suddenly found himself a captive.

Geirrod, gazing upon the bird's bright eyes, shrewdly suspected that it was a god in disguise, and to force him to speak, locked him up in a cage, where he kept him for three whole months without food or drink. Conquered at last by hunger and thirst, Loki revealed his identity, and obtained his release by promising that he would induce Thor to visit Geirrod without his hammer, pelt, or magic gauntlet. Loki then flew back to Asgard, and told Thor that he had been royally entertained, and that his host had expressed a strong desire to see the powerful Thunder God, of whom Loki had told him such wonderful tales. Flattered by this artful speech, Thor was soon brought to consent to a journey to Jötunheim, and immediately set out, leaving his three marvelous weapons at home. He and Loki had not gone very far, however, ere they came to the house of the giantess Grid, one of Odin's many wives, who, seeing Thor disarmed, lent him her own girdle, staff, and glove, warning him to beware of treachery. Some time after leaving her, Thor and Loki came to the river Veimer, which the Thunder God, accustomed to wading, coolly prepared to ford, bidding Loki and Thialfi cling fast to his belt if they would come safe across.

In the middle of the stream, however, a sudden cloudburst and freshet overtook them; the waters began to rise and roar, and although Thor leaned heavily upon his staff, he was almost swept away by the force of the raging current.

"Wax not, Veimer,
Since to wade I desire
To the realm of the giants!
Know, if thou waxest,
Then waxes my asamight
As high as the heavens."
   -NORSE MYTHOLOGY (R. B. Anderson)

Looking up the stream, Thor now became aware of the presence of Geirrod's daughter Gialp, and rightly suspected that she was the cause of the storm. He picked up a huge bowlder, which he flung at her, muttering that the best place to dam a river was at its source. The rock had the desired effect, for the giantess fled, the waters abated, and Thor, exhausted but safe, pulled himself up on the opposite bank by a little shrub, the mountain-ash or sorb, which has since been known as "Thor's salvation," and considered gifted with occult powers. After resting awhile the God resumed his journey; but upon arriving at Geirrod's house he was so exhausted that he sank wearily down upon the only chair in sight. To his surprise, however, he felt it rise beneath him, and fearing lest he should be crushed against the rafters, he braced the borrowed staff against the ceiling and forced the chair downward with all his might. A terrible cracking, sudden cries, and moans of pain proved that he had broken the backs of the giant's daughters, Gialp and Greip, who had slipped under his chair and had treacherously tried to slay him.

"Once I employed
My asamight
In the realm of giants,
When Gialp and Greip,
Geirrod's daughters,
Wanted to lift me to heaven."
  -NORSE MYTHOLOGY (R. B. Anderson)

Geirrod now challenged Thor to show his strength and skill, and without waiting for the preconcerted signal, flung a red-hot wedge at him. Thor, quick of eye and a practiced catcher, caught the missile with the giantess's iron glove, and hurled it back at his opponent. Such was the force of the god, that the missile passed, not only through the pillar behind which the giant had taken refuge, but through him and the wall of the house, and buried itself deep in the earth without.
Thor then marched up to the giant's corpse, which at the blow from his weapon had been changed into stone, and set it up in a conspicuous place, as a monument of his strength and of the victory he had won over his redoubtable foes, the mountain giants.

Worship of Thor

Thor's name has been given to many of the places he was wont to frequent, such as the principal harbor of the Faroe Islands, Tórshavn, and to families which claim to be descended from him. It is still extant in such names as Thunderhill in Surrey, and in the family names of Thorburn and Thorwaldsen, but is most conspicuous in the name of one of the days of the week, Thor's day or Thursday.

"Over the whole earth
Still is it Thor's day!"
      -SAGA OF KING OLAF (Longfellow)

Thor was considered a preeminently benevolent deity, and it was for that reason that he was so widely worshiped and that his temples arose at Moeri, Hlader, Godey, Gothland, Upsala, and other places, where the people never failed to invoke him for a favorable year at Yule-tide, his principal festival. It was customary on this occasion to burn a great log of oak, his sacred tree, as an emblem of the warmth and light of summer, which would soon come to drive away the darkness and cold of winter.

Brides invariably wore red, Thor's favorite color, which was considered emblematical of love, and for the same reason betrothal rings in the North were almost always set with a red stone.

Thor's temples and statues, like Odin's, were fashioned of wood, and the greater number of them were destroyed during the reign of King Olaf the Saint. According to ancient chronicles, this monarch forcibly converted his subjects. He was specially incensed against the inhabitants of a certain province, because they worshiped a rude image of Thor, which they decked with golden ornaments, and before which they set food every evening, declaring the God ate it, as no trace of it was left in the morning.

The people, being called upon in 1030 to renounce this idol in favor of a "true" foreign god, promised to consent if the morrow were cloudy; but when after a whole night spent in ardent prayer, Olaf rapturously beheld a cloudy day, the obstinate people declared they were not yet convinced of his god's power, and would only believe if the sun shone on the following day.

Once more Olaf spent the night in prayer, but at dawn his chagrin was great to see the sky overcast. Nevertheless, determined to gain his end he assembled the people near Thor's statue, and after secretly bidding his principal attendant smash the idol with his battle ax if the people turned their eyes away but for a moment, he began to address them. Suddenly, while all were listening to him, Olaf pointed to the horizon, where the sun was slowly breaking its way through the clouds, and exclaimed, "Behold God!" While the people one and all turned to see what he meant, the attendant broke the idol, and began the process of a forced conversion to the alien middle-eastern based Christianity.

BALDER
Best Loved of the Gods

Odin and Frigga were parents of twin sons as dissimilar in character and physical appearance as it was possible to be; for while Hodur, god of darkness, was somber, taciturn, and blind; Balder, the beautiful, was the pure and radiant god of innocence and light. The snowy brow and golden locks of this Asa seemed to send out beams of sunshine to gladden the hearts of Gods and men, by whom he was equally beloved.

"Of all the twelve round Odin's throne,
Balder, the Beautiful, alone,
The Sun-god, good, and pure, and bright,
Was loved by all, as all love light."
         -VALHALLA (J. C. Jones)

Nanna

Balder, attaining his full growth with marvelous rapidity, was admitted to the council of the Gods, and married Nanna (blossom), the daughter of Nip (bud), a beautiful and charming young goddess, with whom he lived in perfect unity and peace. He took up his abode in the palace of Breidablik, whose silver roof rested upon golden pillars, and whose purity was such that nothing common or unclean was ever allowed within its precincts.

The God of light was well versed in the science of runes which were carved on his tongue; he knew the various virtues of the simples, one of which, the camomile, was always called "Balder's brow," because its flower was just as immaculately pure as his forehead. The only thing hidden from Balder's radiant eyes, at first, was the perception of his own ultimate fate.

*"His own house
Breidablik, on whose columns Balder graved
The enchantments that recall the dead to life.
For wise he was, and many curious arts,
Postures of runes, and healing herbs he knew;
Unhappy! but that art he did not know,
To keep his own life safe, and see the sun."*
  -BALDER DEAD (Matthew Arnold)

As Balder the beautiful was always smiling and happy, the Gods were greatly troubled when they finally saw the light die out of his blue eyes, a careworn look come into his face, and his step grow heavy and slow. Odin and Frigga, seeing their beloved son's evident depression, tenderly implored him to reveal the cause of his silent grief. Balder, yielding at last to their anxious entreaties, confessed that his slumbers, instead of being peaceful and restful as of yore, had been strangely troubled of late by dark and oppressive dreams, which, although he could not clearly remember them when he awoke, constantly haunted him with a vague feeling of fear.

*"To that god his slumber
Was most afflicting;
His auspicious dreams
Seemed departed."*
  -LAY OF VEGTAM (Thorpe's tr.)

When Odin and Frigga heard this, they were troubled indeed, but declared they were quite sure nothing would harm their son, who was so universally beloved. Yet, when the anxious Father and Mother had returned home, they talked the matter over, acknowledged that they also were oppressed by strange forebodings, and having learned from the giants that Balder really was in danger, they proceeded to take measures to avert it.

Frigga, therefore, sent out her servants in every direction, bidding them make all living creatures, all plants, metals, stones — in fact, every animate and inanimate thing — register a solemn vow not to do any harm to Balder. All creation readily took the oath, for all things loved the radiant god, and basked in the light of his smile. So the servants soon returned to Frigga, telling her that all had been duly sworn except the mistletoe, growing upon the oak stem at the gate of

Valhalla, which, they added, was such a puny, inoffensive thing that no harm could be feared from it.

"On a course they resolved:
That they would send
To every being,
Assurance to solicit,
Balder not to harm.
All species swore
Oaths to spare him;
Frigg received all
Their vows and compacts."
      -SÆMUND'S EDDA (Thorpe's tr.)

The Vala's Prophecy

Frigga now resumed her spinning with her usual content, for she knew no harm could come to the child she loved best of all. Odin, in the mean while, also sorely troubled, and wishing to ascertain whether there was any cause for his unwonted depression, resolved to consult one of the dead Valas or prophetesses. He therefore mounted his eight-footed steed Sleipnir, rode over the tremulous bridges Bifröst and Giallar, came to the entrance of Nifiheim, and passing the Helgate and the dog Garm, penetrated into Hel's dark abode.

"Uprose the king of men with speed,
And saddled straight his coal-black steed;
Down the yawning steep he rode,
That leads to Hela's drear abode."
      -DESCENT OF ODIN (Gray)

To his surprise, he noticed that a feast was being spread in this dark realm, and that the couches had all been covered with tapestry and rings of gold, as if some highly honored guest were expected before long. Hastening on, Odin finally reached the grave where the Vala had rested undisturbed for many a year, and solemnly began to chant the magic spell and trace the runes which had the power of raising the dead.

"Thrice pronounc'd, in accents dread,
The thrilling verse that wakes the dead:

Till from out the hollow ground
Slowly breath'd a sullen sound."
      -DESCENT OF ODIN (Gray)

Suddenly the grave opened, and the prophetess slowly rose, inquiring who he was and why he thus came to trouble her long rest. Odin, not wishing her to know that he was King of the Gods, replied that he was Vegtam, Valtam's son, and that he had awakened her to inquire for whom Hel was spreading her couches and preparing a festive meal. In hollow tones, the prophetess now confirmed all his fears by telling him that the expected guest was Balder, who would shortly be slain by Hodur, his brother, the blind God of darkness.

"Hodur will hither
His glorious brother send;
He of Balder will
The slayer be,
And Odin's son
Of life bereave.
By compulsion I have spoken;
Now I will be silent."
      -SÆMUND'S EDDA (Thorpe's tr.)

But in spite of these sad tidings, and of the Vala's evident reluctance to answer any other questions, Odin was not yet satisfied, and forced her to tell him who would avenge the murdered man by calling his assassin to account — a spirit of revenge and retaliation being considered a sacred duty among the races of the North.

Then the prophetess told him, as Rossthiof had predicted before, that Rinda, the earth-goddess, would bear a son to Odin, and that this divine emissary, Vali, would neither wash his face nor comb his hair until he had avenged Balder and slain Hodur.

"In the caverns of the west,
By Odin's fierce embrace comprest,
A wondrous boy shall Rinda bear,
Who ne'er shall comb his raven hair,
Nor wash his visage in the stream,
Nor see the sun's departing beam,
Till he on Hoder's corse shall smile

Flaming on the fun'ral pile."
      -DESCENT OF ODIN (Gray)

Having discovered this from the reluctant Vala, Odin, who, thanks to his visit to the Urdar fountain, already knew much of the future, now incautiously revealed some of his knowledge by inquiring who would refuse to weep at Balder's death. When the prophetess heard this question, she immediately knew that it was Odin who had called her out of her grave, and, refusing to speak another word, she sank back into the silence of the tomb, declaring that none would ever be able to lure her out again until the end of the world had come.

"Hie thee hence, and boast at home,
That never shall inquirer come
To break my iron sleep again,
Till Lok has burst his tenfold chain;
Never, till substantial Night
Has reassum'd her ancient right
Till wrapt in flames, in ruin hurl'd,
Sinks the fabric of the world."
      -DESCENT OF ODIN (Gray)

Odin had questioned the greatest prophetess the world had ever known, and had learned Orlog's (fate's) decrees, which he knew could not be set aside. He therefore remounted his steed, and sadly wended his way back to Asgard, thinking of the time, no longer far distant, when his beloved son would no more be seen in the heavenly abodes, and when the light of his presence would have vanished forever.

On entering Glads-heim, however, Odin was somewhat cheered when he heard of the precautions taken by Frigga to insure their darling's safety, and soon, feeling convinced that if nothing would slay Balder he would surely continue to gladden the world with his presence, he cast aside all care and ordered games and a festive meal.

The Gods at Play

The Gods resumed their wonted occupations, and were soon casting their golden disks on the green plain of Ida, which was called Idavold, the playground of the Gods. At last, wearying of this pastime, and knowing that no harm could come to their beloved

Balder, they invented a new game and began to use him as a target, throwing all manner of weapons and missiles at him, certain that no matter how cleverly they tried, and how accurately they aimed, the objects, having sworn not to injure him, would either glance aside or fall short. This new amusement was so fascinating that soon all the Gods were assembled around Balder, at whom they threw every available thing, greeting each new failure with prolonged shouts of laughter. These bursts of merriment soon excited the curiosity of Frigga, who sat spinning in Fensalir; and seeing an old woman pass by her dwelling, she bade her pause and tell what the Gods were doing to provoke such great hilarity. The old woman, who was Loki in disguise, immediately stopped at this appeal, and told Frigga that all the gods were throwing stones and blunt and sharp instruments at Balder, who stood smiling and unharmed in their midst, daring them to touch him.

The Goddess smiled, and resumed her work, saying that it was quite natural that nothing should harm Balder, as all things loved the light, of which he was the emblem, and had solemnly sworn not to injure him. Loki, the personification of fire, was greatly disappointed upon hearing this, for he was jealous of Balder, the sun, who so entirely eclipsed him and was generally beloved, while he was feared and avoided as much as possible; but he cleverly concealed his chagrin, and inquired of Frigga whether she were quite sure that all objects had joined the league.

Frigga proudly answered that she had received the solemn oath of all things, except of a harmless little parasite, the mistletoe, which grew on the oak near Valhalla's gate, and was too small and weak to be feared. Having obtained the desired information, Loki toddled off; but as soon as he was safely out of sight, he resumed his wonted form, hastened to Valhalla, found the oak and mistletoe indicated by Frigga, and by magic arts compelled the parasite to assume a growth and hardness hitherto unknown.

The Death of Balder

From the wooden stem thus produced he deftly fashioned a shaft ere he hastened back to Idavold, where the Gods were still hurling missiles at Balder, Hodur alone leaning mournfully against a tree, and taking no part in the new game. Carelessly Loki approached him, inquired the cause of his melancholy, and twitted him with pride and indifference, since he would not condescend to take part in the new game. In answer to these remarks, Hodur pleaded his blindness; but when Loki put the mistletoe in his hand, led him into the midst of the circle, and indicated in what direction the novel target stood, Hodur threw his shaft boldly. Instead of the loud shout of laughter which he expected to hear, a shuddering cry of terror fell upon his ear, for Balder the beautiful had fallen to the ground, slain by the fatal blow.

"So on the floor lay Balder dead; and round
Lay thickly strewn swords, axes, darts, and spears,
Which all the Gods in sport had idly thrown
At Balder, whom no weapon pierced or clove;
But in his breast stood fixed the fatal bough
Of mistletoe, which Lok, the Accuser, gave
To Hoder, and unwitting Hoder threw —
'Gainst that alone had Balder's life no charm."
     -BALDER DEAD (Matthew Arnold)

Anxiously the Gods all crowded around him, but alas! life was quite extinct, and all their efforts to revive the fallen Sun-God were vain. Inconsolable at their loss, they turned angrily upon Hodur, whom they would have slain had they not been restrained by the feeling that no willful deed of violence should ever desecrate their peace steads. At the loud sound of lamentation the Goddesses came in hot haste, and when Frigga saw that her darling was dead, she passionately implored the Gods to go to Niflheim and entreat Hel to release her victim, for the earth could not live happy without him.

Hermod's Errand

As the road was rough and painful in the extreme, none of the Gods at first volunteered to go; but when Frigga added that she and Odin would reward the messenger by loving him most of all the Æsir, Hermod signified his readiness to execute the commission. To help him on his way, Odin lent him Sleipnir, and bade him good speed, while he motioned to the other Gods to carry the corpse to Breidablik, and directed them to go to the forest and cut down huge pines to make a worthy pyre for his son.

"But when the Gods were to the forest gone,
Hermod led Sleipnir from Valhalla forth
And saddled him; before that, Sleipnir brook'd

No meaner hand than Odin's on his mane,
On his broad back no lesser rider bore;
Yet docile now he stood at Hermod's side,
Arching his neck, and glad to be bestrode,
Knowing the God they went to seek, how dear.
But Hermod mounted him, and sadly fared
In silence up the dark untravel'd road
Which branches from the north of Heaven, and went
All day; and daylight waned, and night came on.
And all that night he rode, and journey'd so,
Nine days, nine nights, toward the northern ice,
Through valleys deep-engulph'd by roaring streams.
And on the tenth morn he beheld the bridge
Which spans with golden arches Giall's stream,
And on the bridge a damsel watching, arm'd,
In the straight passage, at the further end,
Where the road issues between walling rocks."
   -BALDER DEAD (Matthew Arnold)

While Hermod was traveling along the cheerless road to Niflheim, the Gods hewed and carried down to the shore a vast amount of fuel, which they placed upon the deck of Balder's favorite vessel, Ringhorn, constructing an elaborate funeral pyre, which, according to custom, was decorated with tapestry hangings, garlands of flowers, vessels and weapons of all kinds, golden rings, and countless objects of value, ere the immaculate corpse was brought and laid upon it in full attire.

One by one, the Gods now drew near to take a last farewell of their beloved companion, and as Nanna bent over him, her loving heart broke, and she fell lifeless by his side. Seeing this, the Gods reverently laid her beside her husband, that she might accompany him even in death; and after they had slain his horse and hounds and twined the pyre with thorns, the emblems of sleep, Odin, the last of the Gods, drew near.

The Funeral Pyre

In token of affection for the dead and of sorrow for his loss, all laid their most precious possessions upon his pyre, and Odin, bending down, now added to the offerings his magic ring Draupnir. The assembled gods then perceived that he was whispering in his dead son's ear, but none were near enough to hear what word he said.

These preliminaries ended, the Gods now prepared to launch the ship, but found it so heavily laden with fuel and treasures that their combined efforts could not make it stir an inch. The mountain giants, witnessing the sad scene from afar, and noticing their quandary, said that they knew of a giantess called Hyrrokin, who dwelt in Jötunheim, and was strong enough to launch the vessel without any other aid. The Gods therefore bade one of the storm giants hasten off to summon Hyrrokin, who soon appeared, riding a gigantic wolf, which she guided by a bridle made of writhing live snakes. Riding down to the shore, the giantess dismounted and haughtily signified her readiness to give them the required aid, if in the mean while they would but hold her steed. Odin immediately dispatched four of his maddest Berserkers to fulfill this task; but, in spite of their phenomenal strength, they could not hold the monstrous wolf until the giantess had thrown and bound it fast.

Hyrrokin, seeing them now able to manage her refractory steed, marched down the beach, set her shoulder against the stern of Balder's ship Ringhorn, and with one mighty shove sent it out into the water. Such was the weight of the burden she moved, however, and the rapidity with which it shot down into the sea, that all the earth shook as if from an earthquake, and the rollers on which it glided caught fire from the friction. The unexpected shock almost made the Gods lose their balance, and so angered Thor that he raised his hammer and would have slain the giantess had he not been restrained by his fellow Gods. Easily appeased, as usual — for Thor's violence, although quick, was evanescent — he now stepped up on the vessel once more to consecrate the funeral pyre with his sacred hammer. But, as he was performing this ceremony, the dwarf Lit managed to get into his way so provokingly that Thor, still slightly angry, kicked him into the fire, which he had just kindled with a thorn, where the dwarf was burned to ashes with the corpses of the faithful pair.

As the vessel drifted out to sea, the flames rose higher and higher, and when it neared the western horizon it seemed as if sea and sky were all on fire. Sadly the Gods watched the glowing ship and its precious freight, until it suddenly plunged into the waves and disappeared; nor did they turn aside and go back to their own homes until the last spark of light had vanished, and all the world was enveloped in darkness, in token of mourning for Balder the good.

"Soon with a roaring rose the mighty fire,
And the pile crackled; and between the logs
Sharp quivering tongues of flame shot out, and leapt
Curling and darting, higher, until they lick'd
The summit of the pile, the dead, the mast,
And ate the shriveling sails; but still the ship
Drove on, ablaze above her hull with fire.
And the gods stood upon the beach, and gazed;
And while they gazed, the sun went lurid down
Into the smoke-wrapt sea, and night came on.
Then the wind fell with night, and there was calm;
But through the dark they watch'd the burning ship
Still carried o'er the distant waters, on
Farther and farther, like an eye of fire.
So show'd in the far darkness, Balder's pile;
But fainter, as the stars rose high, it flared;
The bodies were consumed, ash choked the pile.
And as, in a decaying winter fire,
A charr'd log, falling, makes a shower of sparks —
So, with a shower of sparks, the pile fell in,
Reddening the sea around; and all was dark."
    -BALDER DEAD (Matthew Arnold)

Sadly the Gods entered Asgard, where no sounds of merriment or feasting were heard, but all hearts were filled with despair, for they knew the end was near, and shuddered at the thought of the terrible Fimbul-winter, which was to herald their death.

Frigga alone cherished some hope, and anxiously watched for the return of her messenger, Hermod the swift, who in the mean while had ridden over the tremulous bridge, along the dark Helway, and on the tenth night had crossed the rushing tide of the river Gioll. Here he was challenged by Mödgud, who inquired why the Giallar-bridge trembled more beneath his horse's tread than when a whole army passed, and asked why he, a live man, was attempting to penetrate into the dreaded realm of Hel.

"Who art thou on thy black and fiery horse
Under whose hoofs the bridge o'er Giall's stream

Rumbles and shakes? Tell me thy race and home.
But yestermorn five troops of dead pass'd by,
Bound on their way below to Hela's realm,
Nor shook the bridge so much as thou alone.
And thou hast flesh and color on thy cheeks,
Like men who live, and draw the vital air;
Nor look'st thou pale and wan, like man deceased,
Souls bound below, my daily passers here."
      -BALDER DEAD (Matthew Arnold)

Hermod explained to Mödgud the reason of his coming, and, having ascertained that Balder and Nanna had ridden over the bridge before him, he hastened on, until he came to the gate of hell, which rose forbiddingly before him.
Nothing daunted by this barrier, Hermod dismounted on the smooth ice, tightened the girths of his saddle, remounted, and burying his spurs deep into Sleipnir's sleek sides, he made him take a prodigious leap, which landed him safely on the other side of Hel-gate.

"Thence on he journey'd o'er the fields of ice
Still north, until he met a stretching wall
Barring his way, and in the wall a gate.
Then he dismounted, and drew tight the girths,
On the smooth ice, of Sleipnir, Odin's horse,
And made him leap the gate, and came within."
      -BALDER DEAD (Matthew Arnold)

Riding onward, Hermod came at last to Hel's banquet hall, where he found Balder, pale and dejected, lying upon a couch, his wife Nanna beside him, gazing fixedly at the mead before him, which he had no heart to drink.

Hermod's Quest

In vain Hermod informed his brother that he had come to redeem him; Balder sadly shook his head, saying that he knew he must remain in this cheerless abode until the last day should come, but imploring him to take Nanna back with him, as the home of the shades was no place for such a bright and beautiful young creature. But when Nanna heard this request she clung more closely still to her husband's side, vowing that nothing would ever induce her to part from him, and that she would stay with him, even in Niflheim, forever.

The whole night was spent in close conversation, ere Hermod sought Hel and implored Balder's release. The churlish Goddess listened silently to his request, and finally declared that she would let her victim go providing all things animate and inanimate should prove their sorrow for his loss by shedding a tear.

"Come then I if Balder was so dear beloved,
And this is true, and such a loss is Heaven's —
Hear, how to Heaven may Balder be restored.
Show me through all the world the signs of grief!
Fails but one thing to grieve, here Balder stops!
Let all that lives and moves upon the earth
Weep him, and all that is without life weep;
Let Gods, men, brutes, beweep him; plants and stones!
So shall I know the lost was dear indeed,
And bend my heart, and give him back to Heaven."
    -BALDER DEAD (Matthew Arnold)

Having received this answer, the ring Draupnir, which Balder sent back to Odin, an embroidered carpet from Nanna for Frigga, and a ring for Fulla, Hermod cheerfully made his way out of Hel's dark realm, whence he hoped soon to rescue Balder the good, for well he knew all Nature sincerely mourned his departure and would shed unlimited tears to win him back.

The assembled Gods crowded anxiously around him as soon as he returned, and when he had delivered his messages and gifts, the Æsir sent out heralds to every part of the world to bid all things animate and inanimate weep for Balder.

"Go quickly forth through all the world, and pray
All living and unliving things to weep
Balder, if haply he may thus be won!"
    -BALDER DEAD (Matthew Arnold)

These orders were rapidly carried out, and soon tears hung from every plant and tree, the ground was saturated with moisture, and metals and stones, in spite of their hard hearts, wept too.

On their way home the messengers passed a dark cave, in which they saw the crouching form of a giantess named Thok, whom some suppose to have been Loki in disguise; when they asked her also to shed a tear, she mocked them and fled into the dark recesses of her cave, declaring that she would never weep and that Hel might retain her prey forever.

"Thok she weepeth
With dry tears
For Balder's death —
Neither in life, nor yet in death,
Gave he me gladness.
Let Hel keep her prey."
        -ELDER EDDA (Howitt's version)

As soon as the returning messengers arrived in Asgard, all the Gods crowded around them to know the result of their mission; but their faces, all alight with the joy of anticipation, soon grew dark with despair when they heard that, as one creature refused the tribute of tears, they should behold Balder on earth no more.

"Balder, the Beautiful, shall ne'er
From Hel return to upper air!
Betrayed by Loki, twice betrayed,
The prisoner of Death is made;
Ne'r shall he 'scape the place of doom
Till fatal Ragnarok be come!"
        -VALHALLA (J. C. Jones)

The sole consolation left Odin was to fulfill the decree of fate. He therefore departed and achieved the difficult courtship of Rinda, which we have already described. She bore Vali, the Avenger, who, coming into Asgard on the very day of his birth, slew Hodur with his sharp arrow. Thus he punished the murderer of Balder according to the true Northern creed.

The physical explanation of this tale is either the daily setting of the sun (Balder), which sinks beneath the western waves, driven away by darkness (Hodur), or the end of the short Northern summer and reign of the long winter season. "Balder represents the bright and clear summer, when twilight and daylight kiss each other and go hand in hand in these Northern latitudes."

"Balder's pyre, of the sun a mark,
Holy hearth red staineth;
Yet, soon dies its last faint spark,
Darkly then Hoder reigneth."
      -VIKING TALES OF THE NORTH (R. B. Anderson)

"His death by Hodur is the victory of darkness over light, the darkness of winter over the light of summer; and the revenge by Vali is the breaking forth of new light after the wintry darkness."

Loki, the fire, is jealous of the pure light of heaven, Balder, who alone among the Northern Gods never fought, but was always ready with words of conciliation and peace.

"But from thy lips, O Balder, night or day,
Heard no one ever an injurious word
To God or Hero, but thou keptest back
The others, laboring to compose their brawls."
      -BALDER DEAD (Matthew Arnold)

The tears shed by all things for the beloved God are symbolical of the spring thaw, setting in after the hardness and cold of winter, when every tree and twig, and even the stones drip with moisture; Thok (coal) alone shows no sign of tenderness, as she is buried deep within the dark earth and needs not the light of the sun.

"And as in winter, when the frost breaks up,
At winter's end, before the spring begins,
And a warm west wind blows, and thaw sets in —
After an hour a dripping sound is heard
In all the forests, and the soft-strewn snow
Under the trees is dibbled thick with holes,
And from the boughs the snow loads shuffle down;
And, in fields sloping to the south, dark plots
Of grass peep out amid surrounding snow,
And widen, and the peasant's heart is glad —
So through the world was heard a dripping noise
Of all things weeping to bring Balder back;
And there fell joy upon the Gods to hear."
      -BALDER DEAD (Matthew Arnold)

From the depths of their underground prison, the sun (Balder) and vegetation (Nanna) try to cheer heaven (Odin) and earth (Frigga) by sending them the ring Draupnir, the emblem of fertility, and the flowery tapestry, symbolical of the carpet of verdure which will again deck the earth and enhance her charms with its beauty.

The ethical signification of the tale is no less beautiful, for Balder and Hodur are symbols of the conflicting forces of good and evil, while Loki impersonates the tempter.

"But in each human soul we find
That night's dark Hoder, Balder's brother blind,
Is born and waxeth strong as he;
For blind is ev'ry evil born, as bear cubs be,
Night is the cloak of evil; but all good
Hath ever clad in shining garments stood.
The busy Loke, tempter from of old,
Still forward treads incessant, and doth hold
The blind one's murder hand, whose quick-launch'd spear
Pierceth young Balder's breast, that sun of Valhal's sphere!"
        -VIKING TALES OF THE NORTH (R. B. Anderson)

The Worship of Balder

One of the most important festivals was held at the summer solstice, or midsummer's eve, in honor of Balder the good, for it was considered the anniversary of his death and of his descent into the lower world. On that day, the longest in the year, all the people congregated out of doors, made great bonfires, and watched the sun, which in extreme Northern latitudes merely touches the horizon ere it rises upon a new day. From midsummer, the days gradually grow shorter, and the sun's rays less warm, until the winter solstice, which was called the "Mother night," as it was the longest in the year. Midsummer's eve, once celebrated in honor of Balder, was usurped by the alien Christian subjugators and was from then on called St. John's day, that saint used to entirely supplant Balder the Good.

TYR
God of War

 Tyr, Tiu, or Ziu is the son of Odin, and according to some accounts, his mother is Frigga, Queen of the Gods. He is the god of martial honor, God of defense and victory, bravest of the Gods and one of the twelve principal deities of Asgard. Although he appears to have no special dwelling there, he is always welcome to Vingolf or Valhalla, and occupies one of the twelve thrones in the great council hall of Glads-heim.

"The hall Glads-heim, which is built of gold;
Where are in circle ranged twelve golden chairs,
And in the midst one higher, Odin's throne."
      -BALDER DEAD (Matthew Arnold)

Tyr is regarded also as the God of courage and of war, and therefore frequently invoked by the various nations of the North, who cried to him as well as to Odin to obtain victory. That he ranked next to Odin and Thor is proved by his name, Tiu, having been given to one of the days of the week, Tiu's day, which in modern English has become Tuesday. Under the name of Ziu, Tyr was the principal divinity of the Suabians, who originally called their capital, the modern Augsburg, Ziusburg. This people, venerating the God as they did, were wont to worship him under the emblem of a sword, his distinctive attribute, and in his honor held great sword dances, where various figures were carried out.

Sometimes the participants forming two long lines, crossed their swords, point upwards, and challenged the boldest among their number to take a flying leap over them. At other times the warriors joined their sword points closely together in the shape of a rose or wheel, and when this figure was complete invited their chief to stand on the navel thus formed of flat, shining steel blades, and then they bore him upon it through the camp in triumph. The sword point was further considered so sacred that it became customary to register oaths upon it.

"... Come hither, gentlemen,
And lay your hands again upon my sword;
Never to speak of this that you have heard,
Swear by my sword."
      -HAMLET (Shakespeare)

A distinctive feature of the worship of this God among the Franks and some other Northern nations was that the priests called Druids or Godi offered up human sacrifices upon his altars. These sacrifices were made upon rude stone altars called dolmens, which can still be seen in Northern Europe. As Tyr was considered the patron god of the sword, it was deemed indispensable to engrave the sign or rune representing him upon the blade of every sword — an observance which the Edda enjoined upon all those who were desirous of obtaining victory.

"Sig-runes thou must know,
If victory (sigr) thou wilt have,
And on thy sword's hilt rist them;
Some on the chapes,
Some on the guard,
And twice name the name of Tyr."
      -LAY OF SIGDRIFA (Thorpe's tr.)

Tyr, whose name was synonymous with bravery and wisdom, was also considered by the ancient Northern people to have the white-armed Valkyries, Odin's attendants, at his beck and call, and to designate the warriors whom they had best transfer to Valhalla to aid the gods on the last day.

"The god Tyr sent
Gondul and Skogul
To choose a king
Of the race of Ingve,
To dwell with Odin

In roomy Valhal."
    -NORSE MYTHOLOGY (R. B. Anderson)

The Story of Fenris

Loki, the arch deceiver, went to Jötunheim and secretly married the hideous giantess Angur-boda (anguish boding), who bore him three monstrous children — the wolf Fenris, Hel, the party-colored goddess of death, and Jörmungandr, a terrible serpent. He kept the existence of these monsters secret as long as he could; but they speedily grew so large that they could no longer remain confined in the cave where they had come to light. Odin, from the top of his throne Hlidskialf, soon became aware of their existence, and also of the frightful rapidity with which they increased in size. Fearing lest the monsters, when they had gained a little more strength, should invade Asgard and destroy the Gods, Allfather determined to get rid of them, and, striding off to Jötunheim, flung Hel down into the depths of Niflheim, where he told her she could reign over the dismal worlds of the dead. He threw Jörmungandr into the sea, where he stretched himself and grew until he encircled all the earth and could bite his own tail.

"Into mid-ocean's dark depths hurled,
Grown with each day to giant size,
The serpent soon inclosed the world,
With tail in mouth, in circle-wise;
Held harmless still
By Odin's will."
    -VALHALLA (J. C. Jones)

None too well pleased that the serpent should have attained such fearful dimensions in his new element, Odin resolved to lead Fenris to Asgard, where he hoped, by kindly treatment, to make him gentle and tractable. But the Gods one and all shrank back in dismay when they saw the wolf, and none dared approach to give him food except Tyr, whom nothing ever daunted. Seeing that Fenris daily increased in size, strength, voracity, and fierceness, the Gods assembled in council to deliberate how they might best dispose of him. They unanimously decided that it would desecrate their peace-steads to slay him, and resolved to bind him fast so that he could work them no harm.

With that purpose in view, they ordered a strong chain named Læding, and, going out into the yard with it, playfully proposed to Fenris to bind it about him, to see whether his vaunted strength could burst it asunder. Confident in his ability to release himself, Fenris patiently allowed them to bind him fast, but when all stood aside, he shook and stretched himself and easily broke the chain to pieces.

Concealing their chagrin, the Gods praised his strength, but soon left him to order a much stronger fetter, Droma, which, after some persuasion, the wolf allowed them to fasten around him also. A short, sharp struggle sufficed, however, to burst this bond too; so it has become proverbial in the North to use the figurative expressions, "to get loose out of Lading," and "to dash out of Drama," whenever great difficulties have to be surmounted.

"Twice did the Æsir strive to bind,
Twice did they fetters powerless find;
Iron or brass of no avail,
Naught, save through magic, could prevail."
    -VALHALLA (J. C. Jones)

The Gods, perceiving now that ordinary bonds, however strong, would never prevail against the Fenris wolf's great strength, bade Skirnir, Frey's servant, go down to Svartalfheim and bid the dwarfs fashion a bond which nothing could sever.

By magic arts the dark elves manufactured a slender silken rope out of such impalpable materials as the sound of a cat's footsteps, a woman's beard, the roots of a mountain, the longings of the bear, the voice of fishes, and the spittle of birds, and when it was finished they gave it to Skirnir, assuring him that no strength would avail to break it, and that the more it was strained the stronger it would become.

"Gleipnir, at last,
By Dark Elves cast,
In Svart-alf-heim, with strong spells wrought,
To Odin was by Skirnir brought:
As soft as silk, as light as air,
Yet still of magic power most rare."
    -VALHALLA (J. C. Jones)

Armed with this bond, called Gleipnir, the Gods went with Fenris to the Island of Lyngvi, in the middle of Lake Amsvartnir, and again proposed to test his strength. But although Fenris had grown still stronger, he mistrusted the bond which looked so slight. He therefore refused to allow himself to be bound, unless one of the Æsir would consent to put his hand in his mouth, and leave it there, as a pledge of good faith, and that no magic arts were to be used against him.

The Gods heard this condition with dismay, and all drew back except Tyr, who, seeing that the others would not venture to comply with this request, boldly stepped forward and thrust his hand between the monster's jaws. The Gods now fastened Gleipnir around Fenris's neck and paws, shouting and laughing with glee when they saw that his utmost efforts to free himself were fruitless. Tyr, however, could not share their joy, for the wolf, finding himself captive, snapped his teeth together for rage, biting off the god's hand at the wrist, which since then has been known as the wolf's joint.

LOKI:

"Be silent, Tyr!
Thou couldst never settle
A strife 'twixt two;
Of thy right hand also
I must mention make,
Which Fenris from thee took.

TYR:

I of a hand am wanting
But thou of honest fame;
Sad is the lack of either.
Nor is the wolf at ease
He in bonds must bide
Until the gods' destruction."
    -SÆMUND'S EDDA (Thorpe's tr.)

Deprived of his right hand, Tyr was now forced to use the maimed arm for his shield, and to wield his sword with his left hand; but such was his dexterity that he slew just as many enemies as before.

The Gods, in spite of all the wolf's struggles, now drew the end of the fetter Gelgia through the rock Gioll, and fastened it to the boulder Thviti, which was sunk deep in the ground. Opening wide his fearful jaws, Fenris uttered such terrible howls that the Gods, to silence him, thrust a sword into his mouth, the hilt resting upon his lower jaw and the point against his palate. The blood then began to pour out in such streams that it formed a great river, called Von. The wolf was condemned to remain thus chained fast until the last day, when his bonds would burst and he would find himself free to avenge his wrongs.

"The wolf Fenrir,
Freed from the chain,
Shall range the earth."
    -DEATH-SONG OF HÂKON (W. Taylor's tr.)

While some mythologists see in this myth an emblem of crime restrained and made innocuous by the power of the law, others see the underground fire, which kept within bounds can injure no one, but which unfettered fills the world with destruction and woe. Just as Odin's second eye is said to rest in Mimir's well, so Tyr's second hand (sword) is found in Fenris's jaws, as he has no more use for two weapons than the sky for two suns.

Historical Tyr

Tyr was identical with the Saxon god Saxnot (from sax, a sword), and with Er, Heru, or Cheru, the chief divinity of the Cheruski, who also considered him God of the sun, and deemed his shining sword blade an emblem of its rays.

"This very sword a ray of light
Snatched from the Sun!"
    -VALHALLA (J. C. Jones)

According to an ancient legend, Cheru's sword, which had been fashioned by the dwarfs, sons of Ivald — the same who had also made Odin's spear — was held very sacred by his people, to whose care he had intrusted it, declaring that those who possessed it were sure to have the victory over their foes. But although carefully guarded in the temple, where it was hung so that it reflected the first beams of the morning sun, it suddenly and mysteriously disappeared one night. A Vala, druidess, or prophetess, consulted by the priests, revealed that the Norns had decreed that whoever wielded it would conquer the world and come to his death by it; but in spite of all entreaties she refused to tell who had taken it or where it might be found. Some time after this occurrence a tall and dignified stranger came to Cologne, where Vitellius, the Roman prefect, was feasting, called him away from his beloved dainties, gave him the sword, telling him it would bring him glory and renown, and hailed him as emperor. This cry was taken up by the assembled legions, and Vitellius, without making any personal effort to secure the honor, found himself elected Emperor of Rome.

The new ruler, however, was so absorbed in indulging his taste for food and drink that he paid but little heed to the divine weapon. One day while leisurely making his way towards Rome he carelessly left it hanging in the antechamber to his apartments. A German soldier seized this opportunity to substitute in its stead his own rusty blade. The besotted emperor went on, and was so busily engaged in feasting that he did not notice the exchange. When he arrived at Rome, he learned that the Eastern legions had named Vespasian emperor, and that he was even then on his way home to claim the throne.

Searching for the sacred weapon to defend his rights, Vitellius now discovered the theft, and, overcome by superstitious fears, did not even attempt to fight. He crawled away into a dark corner of his palace, whence he was ignominiously dragged by the enraged populace to the foot of the Capitoline Hill. There the prophecy was duly fulfilled, for the German soldier, who had joined the opposite faction, coming along at that moment, cut off Vitellius' head with the sacred sword.

The German soldier now changed from one legion to another, and traveled over many lands; but wherever he and his sword were found, victory was assured. After winning great honor and distinction, this man, having grown old, retired from active service to the banks of the Danube, where he secretly buried his treasured weapon, building his hut over its resting place to guard it as long as he lived. But although implored, when he lay on his deathbed, to reveal where he had hidden it, he persistently refused to do so, saying that it would be found by the man who was destined to conquer the world, but that he would not be able to escape the curse. Years passed by. Wave after wave the tide of barbarian invasion swept over that part of the country, and last of all came the terrible

Huns under the leadership of Attila, the "Scourge of God." As he passed along the river, he saw a peasant mournfully examining his cow's foot, which had been wounded by some sharp instrument hidden in the long grass, and when search was made the point of a buried sword was found sticking out of the soil.

Attila, seeing the beautiful workmanship and the fine state of preservation of this weapon, immediately exclaimed that it was Cheru's sword, and brandishing it above his head announced that he was about to conquer the world. Battle after battle was fought by the Huns, who, according to the Saga, were everywhere victorious, until Attila, weary of warfare, settled down in Hungary, taking to wife the beautiful Burgundian princess Ildico, whose father he had slain. This princess, resenting the murder of her kin and wishing to avenge it, took advantage of the king's state of intoxication upon his wedding night to secure possession of the divine sword, with which she slew him in his bed, once more fulfilling the prophecy uttered so many years before.

The magic sword again disappeared for a long time, only to be unearthed once more and wielded by the Duke of Alva, Charles V's general, who shortly after won the victory of Mühlberg (1547). Since then nothing more has been heard of the sword of the god Cheru, in whose honor the Franks were wont to celebrate yearly martial games; but it is said that when the heathen Gods were, through vicious persecution, renounced in favor of Christianity, the priests transferred many of their attributes to the saints, and that this sword became the property of the Archangel St. Michael.

Tyr's worship is commemorated in sundry places (such as Tübingen, in Germany), which bear more or less modified forms of his name. It has also been given to the aconite, a plant known in Northern countries as "Tyr's helm."

HEIMDALL
Watchman of the Gods

Heimdall, "Heaven's Mount", is also called "the Son of the Waves". Heimdall is the Asa-God of Light and the rainbow, the Watchman of the Gods, "The White God", and the the Guardian of Bifrost bridge.

Odin was once walking along the seashore when he beheld the nine beautiful wave maidens, Gialp, Greip, Egia, Augeia, Ulfrun, Aurgiafa, Sindur, Atla, and Iarnsaxa, sound asleep on the white sand. To secure possession of these charming girls was not much trouble for the God of the Sky, who married all nine of them at once, and was very happy indeed when they simultaneously bore him a son called Heimdall.

"Born was I of mothers nine, Son I am of sisters nine."
  -SÆMUND'S EDDA (Thorpe's tr.)

The nine mothers now proceeded to nourish this babe on the strength of the earth, the moisture of the sea, and the heat of the sun, which singular diet proved so strengthening that the new god acquired his full growth in a remarkably short space of time, and hastened to join his father in Asgard. There he found the Gods proudly contemplating the rainbow bridge Bifrost, which they had just constructed out of fire, water, and air, which three materials can still plainly be seen in its long arch, where glow the three primary colors: the red representing the fire, the blue the air, and the green the cool depths of the sea.

The Guardian of the Rainbow

Fearing lest their enemies, the frost giants, should make their way over this bridge, which, connecting heaven and earth, ended under the shade of the mighty world tree Yggdrasil, close beside the fountain where Mimir kept guard, the Gods bade the white-clad Heimdall watch it night and day.

"Bifrost i' th' east shone forth in brightest green;
On its top, in snow-white sheen,
Heimdal at his post was seen."
      -OEHLENSCHLÄGER (Pigott's tr.)

To enable their watchman to detect the approach of any enemy from afar, the assembled Gods gifted him with very keen senses, for he is said to be able to hear the grass grow on the hillside, and the wool on the sheep's back, to see plainly one hundred miles off by night as well as by day, and to require less sleep than a bird.

"'Mongst shivering giants wider known
Than him who sits unmoved on high,
The guard of heaven, with sleepless eye."
      -LAY OF SKIRNER (Herbert's tr.)

Heimdall was further provided with a flashing sword and a marvelous trumpet, called Gjallarhorn, which the Gods bade him blow whenever he saw their enemies draw near, declaring that its sound would rouse all creatures in heaven, earth, and Niflheim; would announce that the last day had come and that the great battle was about to be fought.

"To battle the gods are called
By the ancient
Gjallar-horn.
Loud blows Heimdall,
His sound is in the air."
      -SÆMUND'S EDDA (Thorpe's tr.)

To keep this instrument, which was a symbol of the moon crescent, ever at hand, Heimdall either hangs it on a branch of Yggdrasil above his head or sinks it in the waters of Mimir's well, where it lay side by side with Odin's eye, which is also an emblem of the moon at its full.

Heimdall's palace, called Himinbiorg, was placed on the highest point of the bridge, and here the Gods often visit him to quaff the delicious mead which he sets before them.

*"'Tis Himminbjorg called
Where Heimdal, they say,
Hath dwelling and rule.
There the gods' warder drinks,
In peaceful old halls,
Gladsome the good mead."*
      -NORSE MYTHOLOGY (R. B. Anderson)

Heimdall, always clad in resplendent white armor, is therefore called the bright God, as well as the light, innocent, and graceful God, all which titles he fully deserves, for he is as good as beautiful, and all the Gods love him.

Connected on his mothers' side with the sea, he was sometimes counted among the Vanas; and as the ancient Northerners, and especially the Icelanders, to whom the surrounding sea appeared the most important element, fancied that all things had risen out of it, they attributed to him a knowledge of all things and imagined him particularly wise.

*"Then said Heimdall,
Of Æsir the brightest —
He well foresaw
Like other Vanir."*
      -SÆMUND'S EDDA (Thorpe's tr.)

This God is further distinguished by his golden teeth, which flash when he smiles, and won for him the surname of Gullintani (golden-toothed). He is also the proud possessor of a swift, golden-maned steed called Gull-top, which transports him to and fro over the quivering rainbow bridge. This he crosses many times a day, but particularly in the early morn, when he is considered a herald of the day and bore the name of Heim-dellinger.

*"Early up Bifrost
Ran Ulfrun's son,
The mighty hornblower
Of Himinbiörg."*
      -SÆMUND'S EDDA (Thorpe's tr.)

Loki and Freya

Owing to his extreme acuteness of hearing, Heimdall was greatly disturbed one night by hearing soft, catlike footsteps in the direction of Freya's palace, Folkvang. Gazing fixedly towards that side with his eagle eyes, Heimdall soon perceived, in spite of the darkness, that the sound was produced by Loki, who stealthily entered the palace as a fly, stole to Freya's bedside, and strove to purloin her shining golden necklace Brisinga-men, the emblem of the fruitfulness of the earth.

As it happened, however, the Goddess had turned in her sleep in such a way that he could not possibly unclasp the necklace without awaking her. Loki stood hesitatingly by the bedside for a few moments, and then rapidly began to mutter the runes which enabled the Gods to change their form at will. As he was doing this, Heimdall saw him shrivel up until he was changed to the size and form of a flea, when he crept under the bedclothes and bit Freya's side, thus making her change her position without really rousing her.

The clasp was now free, and Loki, cautiously unfastening it, secured the coveted ornament, with which he proceeded to steal away. Heimdall immediately started out in pursuit of the midnight thief, and drawing his sword from its scabbard, was about to cut off his head when the God suddenly transformed himself into a flickering blue flame. Quick as thought, Heimdall changed himself into a cloud and sent down a deluge of rain to quench the fire; but Loki as promptly altered his form to that of a huge polar bear, and opened wide his jaws to swallow the water. Heimdall, nothing daunted, then assumed the form of a bear also, and fought fiercely with him; but the combat threatening to end disastrously for Loki, he changed himself into a seal, and, Heimdall imitating him, a last struggle took place, at the end of which Loki, vanquished, was forced to give up the necklace, which was duly restored to Freya.

In this tale, Loki is an emblem of the drought, or of the baleful effects of the too ardent heat of the sun, which comes to rob the earth (Freya) of its most cherished ornament (Brisinga-men). Heimdall is a personification of the gentle rain and dew, which, after struggling for a while with his foe the drought, manages to conquer him and force him to relinquish his prize.

Heimdall's Names

Heimdall has several other names, among which we find those of Hallinskide and Irmin, for at times he takes Odin's place and is identified with that god, as well as with the other sword-gods, Er, Heru, Cheru, and Tyr, who are all noted for their shining weapons. He, however, is most generally known as warder of the rainbow, God of heaven, and of the fruitful rains and dews which bring refreshment to the earth.

This god also shared with Bragi the honor of welcoming heroes to Valhalla, and, under the name of Riger, was considered the ancestor of the various classes which compose the human race, as is set forth in the following myth:

"Sacred children,
Great and small,
Sons of Heimdall!"
    -SÆMUND'S EDDA (Thorpe's tr.)

The Story of Riger

One day Heimdall left his place in Asgard to wander down upon the earth as the Gods were wont to do. He had not gone very far ere he came to a poor hut on the seashore, where he found Ai (great grandfather) and Edda (great grandmother), a poor but worthy couple, who hospitably invited him to share their meager meal of porridge. Heimdall, who gave his name as Riger, gladly accepted this invitation, and remained with them three whole days, teaching them many things. At the end of that time he left them to resume his journey. Some time after his visit, Edda bore a dark-skinned, thickset male child, whom she called Thrall.

Thrall soon showed uncommon physical strength and a great aptitude for all heavy work; and having attained marriageable age, he took to wife Thyr, a heavily built girl with sunburnt hands and flat feet, who labored early and late, and bore him many children, from whom all the Northern serfs or thralls are descended.

"They had children,
Lived and were happy;

. . . .

They laid fences,
Enriched the plow-land,
Tended swine,
Herded goats,
Dug peat."
      -RIGSMÁL *(Du Chaillu's version)*

Riger, in the mean while, had pursued his journey, and leaving the barren seacoast had pushed inland, where ere long he came to cultivated fields and a thrifty farmhouse. He entered, and found Afi (grandfather) and Amma (grandmother), who hospitably invited him to sit down and share their plain but bountiful fare.

Riger accepted this invitation also, remained three days with them, and imparted all manner of useful knowledge to his hosts. After his departure from their house, Amma gave birth to a blue-eyed sturdy boy, whom she called Karl. He soon revealed great skill in all agricultural pursuits, and married a buxom and thrifty wife named Snor, who bore him many children, from whom all husbandmen are descended.

"He did grow
And thrive well;
He broke oxen,
Made plows;
Timbered houses,
Made barns,
Made carts,
And drove the plow."
      -RIGSMÁL *(Du Chaillu's version)*

After leaving the house of this second couple, Riger went on until he came to a hill, upon which a stately castle was perched, and here he was received by Fadir (father) and Modir (mother), who, delicately nurtured and luxuriously clad, received him cordially, and set before him dainty meats and rich wines.

Riger tarried three days with them ere he returned to Himinbiorg to resume his post as guardian of the Asa-bridge; and the lady of the castle bore a handsome, slenderly built little son, whom she called Jarl. This child early showed a great taste for the hunt and all manner of martial exercises, learned to understand runes, and lived to do great deeds of valor which brought added glory to his name and race. Having attained manhood, Jarl married Erna, an aristocratic, slender-waisted maiden, who ruled his household wisely and bore him many children, all born to rule, the youngest of which, Konur, became the first king of Denmark according to this tale, which is illustrative of the marked sense of classes among the Northern races.

"Up grew
The sons of Jarl;
They brake horses,
Bent shields,
Smoothed shafts,
Shook ash spears.
But Kon, the young,
Knew runes,
Everlasting runes
And life runes."
   -RIGSMÁL (Du Chaillu's version)

VIDAR
The Silent God

Vidar is the brother of Vali, and the son of Odin and Grid. Vidar is known as the Silent God and will avenge Odin's death by slaying the Fenris wolf at Ragnarok.

Odin once saw and fell in love with the beautiful Grid, who dwelt in a cave in the desert, and, wooing her, prevailed upon her to become his wife. The offspring of this union between Odin (mind) and Grid (matter) was a son as strong as taciturn, named Vidar, whom the ancients considered a personification of the primeval forest or of the imperishable forces of Nature.

As the Gods, through Heimdall, were intimately connected with the sea, they were also bound by close ties to the forests and Nature in general by Vidar, surnamed "The Silent," who was destined to survive their destruction and rule over the regenerated earth. This God has his home in Landvidi (the wide land), a palace decorated with green boughs and fresh flowers, situated in the midst of an impenetrable primeval forest where reigns the deep silence and solitude which he loves.

"Grown over with shrubs
And with high grass
Is Vidar's wide land."
    -NORSE MYTHOLOGY (R. B. Anderson)

This old Scandinavian conception of the silent Vidar is very grand and poetical indeed, and was inspired by the rugged Northern scenery. "Who has ever wandered through such forests, in a length of many miles, in a boundless expanse, without a path, without a goal, amid their monstrous shadows, their sacred gloom, without being filled with deep reverence for the sublime greatness of Nature above all human agency, without feeling the grandeur of the idea which forms the basis of Vidar's essence?"

Vidar's Shoe

Vidar is tall, strong, and handsome, has a broad-bladed sword, and besides his armor wears a great leather shoe. Vidar's "thick shoe" consists of all the leather waste pieces that Northern cobblers have cut from their own shoes at the toe and heel, collected by the God throughout all time. As it was very important that the shoe should be large and strong enough to resist the Fenris wolf's sharp teeth at the last day, it became a matter of religious observance among Northern shoe-makers to give away as many odds and ends of leather as possible.

The Norns' Prophecy

One day, when Vidar had joined his peers in Valhalla, they welcomed him gaily, for they all loved him and placed their reliance upon him, for they knew he would use his great strength in their favor in time of need. But after he had quaffed the golden mead, Allfather bade him accompany him to the Urdar fountain, where the Norns were busy weaving their web. When questioned by Odin concerning his future and Vidar's destiny, the three sisters answered oracularly each by the following short sentences:

"Early begun."
"Further spun."
"One day done."

To which their mother, Wyrd, the primitive goddess of fate, added: "With joy once more won."

These mysterious answers would have remained totally unintelligible to the Gods, had she not gone on to explain that time progresses, that all must change, but that even if the father fell in the last battle, his son Vidar would be his avenger, and would live to rule over a regenerated world, after having conquered all his enemies.

*"There sits Odin's
Son on the horse's back;*

He will avenge his father."
 -NORSE MYTHOLOGY (R. B. Anderson)

At Wyrd's words the leaves of the world tree began to flutter as if agitated by a breeze, the eagle on its topmost bough flapped its wings, and the serpent Nidhug for a moment suspended its work of destruction at the roots of the tree. Grid, joining the father and son, rejoiced with Odin when she heard that their son was destined to survive the older Gods and to rule over the new heaven and earth.

"There dwell Vidar and Vale
In the gods' holy seats,
When the fire of Surt is slaked."
 -NORSE MYTHOLOGY (R. B. Anderson)

Vidar, however, said not a word, but slowly wended his way back to his palace Landvidi, in the heart of the primeval forest, where, sitting down upon his throne, he pondered long about eternity, futurity, and infinity. If he fathomed their secrets he never revealed them, for the ancients averred that he was "as silent as the grave" — a silence which indicated that no man knows what awaits him in the life to come.

Vidar is not only a personification of the imperishability of Nature, but he is also a symbol of resurrection and renewal, proving that new shoots and blossoms are always ready to spring forth to replace those which have fallen into decay.
The shoe he wears is to be his defense against the wolf Fenris, who, having destroyed Odin, would turn his entire wrath upon him, and open wide his terrible jaws to devour him. But the old Northerners declared that Vidar would brace the foot thus protected against the monster's lower jaw, and, seizing the upper, would struggle with him until he had rent him to pieces.

IDUN
Goddess of Youth

Idun, "She Who Renews" is the Goddess of spring, immortal youth and eternal life. According to some, Idun, who had no birth and is never to taste death, was also warmly welcomed by the Gods when she made her appearance in Asgard with Bragi. To win their affections she promised them a daily taste of the marvelous apples which she bore in her casket, which had the power of conferring immortal youth and loveliness upon all who partook of them.

*"The golden apples
Out of her garden
Have yielded you dower of youth,
Ate you them every day."*
   -WAGNER (Forman's tr.)

Thanks to this magic fruit, the Gods, who are not all immortal, ward off the approach of old age and disease, and remain vigorous, beautiful, and young throughout the countless ages. These apples are therefore considered very precious indeed, and Idun carefully treasures them in her magic casket. But no matter how many she draws out, the same number always remain for distribution at the Feast of the Gods, to whom alone she offers a taste, although dwarfs and giants are eager to obtain possession of this fruit.

*"Bright Iduna, Maid immortal!
Standing at Valhalla's portal,
In her casket has rich store
Of rare apples, gilded o'er;
Those rare apples, not of Earth,
Ageing Æsir give fresh birth."*
   -VALHALLA (J. C. Jones)

Thiassi, the Storm Giant

One day, Odin, Hoenir, and Loki started out upon one of their usual excursions to earth, and, after wandering for a long while, found themselves in a deserted region, where they could discover no hospitable dwelling. Weary and very hungry, the Gods perceiving a herd of oxen, slew one, kindled a fire, and sat down beside it to rest while waiting for their meat to cook.

To their surprise, however, in spite of the roaring flames the meat remained quite raw. Realizing that some magic must be at work, they looked about them to discover what could hinder their cookery. They finally perceived an eagle perched upon a tree above them. The bird addressed them and declared that the spell would be removed and the meat done to a turn in a very short time if they would only give him as much food as he could eat. The Gods agreed to do this, and the eagle, swooping downwards, fanned the flames with his huge wings, and soon the meat was cooked. But as he was about to carry off three quarters of the ox as his share, Loki seized a great stake lying near at hand, and began to belabor the voracious bird, forgetting that it was versed in magic arts. To his great dismay one end of the stake stuck fast to the eagle's back, the other to his hands, and he found himself dragged over stones and through briers, flying through the air, his arms almost torn out of their sockets. In vain he cried for mercy and implored the eagle to let him go; the bird flew on, until he promised any ransom his ravisher could ask in exchange for his release.

The bird, who was the storm giant Thiassi in eagle guise, let him go only upon one condition. He made him promise upon the most solemn of oaths that he would lure Idun out of Asgard, so that the giant might obtain possession of her and of her magic fruit.

Released at last, Loki returned to join Odin and Hoenir, to whom, however, he was very careful not to confide the condition upon which he had obtained his freedom; and when they had returned to Asgard he began to plan how he might entice Idun outside of the Gods' abode. A few days later, Bragi being absent on one of his minstrel tours, Loki sought Idun in the groves of Brunnaker, where she had taken up her abode, and by artfully describing some apples which grew at a short distance from there, and which he mendaciously declared were exactly like hers, he lured her away from home with a crystal dish full of fruit, which she intended to compare with that which he extolled. No sooner had Idun left Asgard, however, than the deceiver Loki forsook her, and ere she could return home the storm giant Thiassi swept down from the north on his eagle wings, caught her up in his cruel talons, and bore her swiftly away to his barren and desolate home of Thrymheim.

"Thrymheirn the sixth is named,
Where Thiassi dwelt,
That all-powerful Jötun."
    -LAY OF GRIMNIR (Thorpe's tr.)

There she pined, grew pale and sad, but persistently refused to give him the smallest bite of her magic fruit, which, as he well knew, would make him beautiful and renew his strength and youth.

"All woes that fall
On Odin's hall
Can be traced to Loki base.
From out Valhalla's portal
'Twas he who pure Iduna lured, —
Whose casket fair
Held apples rare
That render gods immortal, —
And in Thiassi's tower immured."
    -VALHALLA (J. C. Jones)

Time passed. The Gods, thinking that Idun had accompanied her husband and would soon return, at first paid no heed to her departure, but little by little the beneficial effect of their last apple feast passed away. They gradually felt themselves grow old and stiff, and saw their youth and beauty disappear; so they became alarmed and began to search for the missing Goddess of perpetual youth. Close investigation very soon revealed the fact that she had last been seen in Loki's company, and when Odin sternly called him to account, this God was forced to reveal that he had betrayed her into the storm giant's power.

"By his mocking, scornful mien,
Soon in Valhal it was seen
'Twas the traitor Loki's art
Which had led Idun apart
To gloomy tower
And Jotun power."
    -VALHALLA (J. C. Jones)

The Gods now indignantly bade Loki undo the harm he had done and immediately bring the goddess back, warning him that unless he complied with this command he would forfeit his life.

Thus adjured, Loki promised to do all he could, and, borrowing Freya's falcon plumage, flew off to Thrymheim, where he found Idun alone, sadly mourning her exile from Asgard and her beloved Bragi. Changing the fair Goddess into a nut according to some accounts, or according to others, into a swallow, Loki held her tightly between his claws, and rapidly winged his way back to Asgard, hoping he would reach the shelter of its high walls ere Thiassi returned from his fishing excursion in the Northern seas.

The Gods, assembled on the ramparts of the heavenly city, were watching for his return with far more anxiety than they had for Odin when he went in search of Odhroerir, and, remembering the success of their ruse on that occasion, they had gathered great piles of fuel, which they were ready to set on fire at any moment.

The Return of Idun

Suddenly they saw Loki coming, but descried in his wake the giant Thiassi, who, in eagle plumes, was striving to overtake him and claim his prey. Loki, knowing his life depended upon the success of his venture, made such great efforts to reach the goal ere Thiassi overtook him that he cleared the wall and sank exhausted in the midst of the gods, who, setting fire to the accumulated fuel, singed Thiassi's wings, blinded him with smoke, and, when he dropped stunned in their midst, ruthlessly fell upon and slew him.

The Æsir were overjoyed at the recovery of Idun, — who hastened to deal out her apples to them all. Feeling their wonted strength and good looks return with every mouthful they ate, they good-naturedly declared that it was no wonder even the giants longed to taste the apples of perpetual youth. They therefore vowed they would place Thiassi's eyes as constellations in the heavens, in order to soften any feeling of anger which his relatives might experience upon learning how he had been slain.

*"Up I cast the eyes
Of Allvaldi's son
Into the heaven serene
They are signs the greatest
Of my deeds."*
  -LAY OF HARBARD (Thorpe's tr.)

The Goddess of Spring

The physical explanation of this tale is obvious. Idun, the emblem of vegetation, is forcibly carried away in autumn, when Bragi is absent and the singing of the birds has ceased. The cold wintry wind, Thiassi, detains her in the frozen, barren north, where she cannot thrive, until Loki, the south wind, brings back the seed or the swallow, which are both precursors of the returning spring. The youth, beauty, and strength conferred by Idun are symbolical of Nature's resurrection in spring after winter's sleep, when color and vigor return to the earth, which has grown wrinkled and gray.

As the disappearance of Idun (vegetation) was a yearly occurrence, the old scalds were not content with this one tale, but also invented another, which, unfortunately, has come down to us only in a fragmentary and very incomplete form. According to this account, Idun was once sitting upon the branches of the sacred ash Yggdrasil, when, growing suddenly faint, she loosed her hold and dropped down on the ground beneath, to the lowest depths of Niflheim. There she lay, pale and motionless, gazing with fixed and horror-struck eyes upon the grewsome sights of Hels realm, trembling violently all the while, as if overcome by the penetrating cold.

*"In the dales dwells
The prescient Dîs,
From Yggdrasil's
Ash sunk down,
Of alfen race,
Idun by name,
The youngest of Ivaldi's
Elder children.
She ill brooked
Her descent
Under the hoar tree's
Trunk confined.*

*She would not happy be
With Norvi's daughter,
Accustomed to a pleasanter
Abode at home."*
　　　-ODIN'S RAVENS' SONG (Thorpe's tr.)

Seeing that she did not rouse herself and return, Odin finally bade Bragi, Heimdall, and another of the Gods go in search of her, giving them a white wolfskin to envelop her in, so that she should not suffer from the cold, and bidding them make every effort to rouse her from her stupor.

*"A wolf's skin they gave her,
In which herself she clad."*
　　　-ODIN'S RAVENS' SONG (Thorpe's tr.)

But although Idun passively allowed them to wrap her up in the warm wolfskin, she persistently refused to speak or move, and the Gods sadly suspected she foresaw great ills, for the tears continually rolled down her pallid cheeks. Bragi, seeing her unhappiness, bade the other Gods return to Asgard without him, vowing that he would remain beside her until she was ready to leave Hel's dismal realm. But the sight of her woe oppressed him so sorely that he had no heart for his usual merry songs, and the strings of his harp remained entirely mute.

*"That voice-like zephyr o'er flow'r meads creeping,
Like Bragi's music his harp strings sweeping."*
　　　-VIKING TALES OF THE NORTH (R. B. Anderson)

In this tale Idun's fall from Yggdrasil is symbolical of the autumnal falling of the leaves, which lie limp and helpless on the cold bare ground until they are hidden from sight under the snow, represented by the wolfskin, which Odin, the sky, sends down to keep them warm; and the cessation of the birds' songs is further typified by Bragi's silent harp.

VALI
God of Vengeance and Rebirth

Vali, as told in the *Skaldskaparmal*, is the "son of Odin and Rind, stepson of Frigg, brother of the Æsir, Baldr's avenging As, enemy of Hod and his slayer, father's homestead-inhabiter." We also learn that Vali is among the twelve Æsir seated as judges at Ægir's banquet. He is not only seen as a God of vengeance, but truly one of the Æsir, seated with the others at table and drink. He is referenced for his courage and his accuracy with the bow, and is one of the inheritors of Asgard after Ragnarok.

The Wooing of Rinda

Billing, the king of the Ruthenes, was greatly dismayed when he heard that a great force was about to invade his kingdom, for he was too old to fight as of yore, and his only child, a daughter named Rinda, although she was of marriageable age, obstinately refused to choose a husband among her many suitors, and thus give her father the assistant he so sorely needed.

While Billing was musing disconsolately in his hall, a stranger suddenly entered his palace. Looking up, the king beheld a middle-aged man wrapped in a wide cloak, with a broad-brimmed hat drawn down over his forehead to conceal the fact that he had but one eye. The stranger courteously inquired the cause of his evident depression, and as soon as he had learned it, volunteered to command the army of the Ruthenes.

His services being joyfully accepted, Odin — for it was he — soon won a signal victory for the aged king, and, returning in triumph, asked permission to woo his daughter Rinda to be his wife. Billing, hoping that his daughter would lend a favorable ear to this suitor, who appeared very distinguished in spite of his years, immediately signified his consent. So Odin, still unknown, presented himself before the princess, who scornfully rejected his proposal, and rudely boxed his ears when he attempted to kiss her.

Forced to withdraw, Odin nevertheless clung to his purpose to make Rinda his wife, for he knew, thanks to Rossthiof's prophecy, that none but she could bear the destined avenger of his murdered son. Assuming the form of a smith, Odin therefore soon came back to Billing's hall, fashioned costly ornaments of silver and gold, and so artfully multiplied these precious metals that the king joyfully acquiesced when he inquired whether he might pay his addresses to the princess. The smith Rosterus was, however, as summarily dismissed by Rinda as the successful old general had been; but although his ear tingled with the force of her blow, he was more determined than ever to make her his wife.

A third time Odin now presented himself before the capricious fair one, disguised this time as a dashing warrior, thinking a young soldier might perchance touch the maiden's heart; but when he again attempted to kiss her, she pushed him back so suddenly that he stumbled and fell upon one knee.

"Many a fair maiden,
When rightly known,
Towards men is fickle
That I experienced,
When that discreet maiden I
Strove to win
Contumely of every kind
That wily girl
Heaped upon me;
Nor of that damsel gained I aught."
       -SÆMUND'S EDDA (Thorpe's tr.)

This third insult so enraged Odin that he drew his magic rune stick out of his breast, pointed it at Rinda, and uttered such a terrible spell that she fell back into the arms of her attendants rigid and apparently lifeless.

When Rinda came to life again, the suitor had disappeared, but the king discovered with great dismay that she had entirely lost her senses and was melancholy mad. In vain all the physicians were summoned and all their simples tried; the maiden remained as passive and sad as before, and her distracted father was only too glad when an old woman called Vecha, or Vak, appeared, offering to undertake the cure of the princess. The old woman, who was Odin in disguise, first prescribed a footbath for the patient; but as this did not appear to have any very marked effect, she declared she would be forced to try a severe treatment. This could only be administered if the patient were intrusted to her exclusive care, securely bound so that she could not offer the least resistance. Billing, anxious to save his child, consented to all the strange attendant proposed; and when Odin had thus gained full power over Rinda, he compelled her to marry him, releasing her from bonds and spell only when she had faithfully promised to be his wife.

The Birth of Vali

The prophecy made by Rossthiof was duly fulfilled, for Rinda bore a son named Vali (Ali, Bous, or Beav), a personification of the lengthening days, who grew with such marvelous rapidity, that in the course of a single day he attained his full stature. Without even taking time to wash his face or comb his hair, this young God hastened off to Asgard with bow and arrow to avenge the death of Balder, God of light, by slaying his murderer, Hodur, the blind God of darkness.

"But, see! th' avenger, Vali, come,
Sprung from the west, in Rindas' womb,
True son of Odin! one day's birth!
He shall not stop nor stay on earth
His locks to comb, his hands to lave,
His frame to rest, should rest it crave,
Until his mission be complete,
And Baldur's death find vengeance meet."
   -VALHALLA (J. C. Jones)

In this tale, Rinda, a personification of the hard-frozen rind of the earth, resists the warm wooing of the sun, Odin, who vainly points out that spring is the time for warlike exploits, and offers the adornments of golden summer. She only yields when, after a shower (the footbath), a thaw set in. Conquered then by the sun's irresistible might, the earth yields to his embrace, is freed from the spell (ice) which made her hard and cold, and brings forth Vali the nourisher, or Bous the peasant, who emerges from his dark hut when the pleasant days have come. The slaying of Hodur by Vali is therefore emblematical of "the breaking forth of new light after wintry darkness."

Vali, who ranked as one of the twelve deities occupying seats in the great hall of Gladsheim, shared with his father the dwelling called Valaskialf, and was destined, even before birth, to survive the last battle and twilight of the Gods, and to reign with Vidar over the regenerated earth.

Worhip of Vali

Vali is God of eternal light, just as Vidar of imperishable matter; and as beams of light were often called arrows, he is always represented and worshiped as an archer. For that reason his month in Norwegian calendars is designated by the sign of the bow, and is called Liosberi, the light-bringing. As it falls between the middle of January and of February, the early Christians dedicated this month to St. Valentine, who was also a skillful archer, and was said, like Vali, to be the harbinger of brighter days, the awakener of tender sentiments, and the patron of all lovers.

NJÖRD
Stiller of Storms

Njörd, or Niord, is the Vana-God of seafaring. He is known as the "Stiller-of-Storms" and controls wind, stills sea and fire. He is the son of Nott (Night) and his first wife was Nerthus, with whom he had his most famous children, Freyr and Freyja. After the terrible war between the Æsir and Vanas, hostages were exchanged, and that while Hoenir, Odin's brother, went to live in Vanaheim, Njörd, with his two children, Frey and Freya, definitely took up his abode in Asgard.

"In Vana-heim
Wise powers him created,
And to the gods a hostage gave."
        -LAY OF VAFTHRDDNIR (Thorpe's tr.)

As ruler of the winds, and of the sea near the shore, Njörd was given the palace of Nôatûn, near the seashore, where we are told he stilled the terrible tempests stirred up by Ægir, god of the deep sea.

"Njörd, the god of storms, whom fishers know;
Not born in Heaven — he was in Van-heim rear'd,
With men, but lives a hostage with the gods;
He knows each frith, and every rocky creek
Fringed with dark pines, and sands where sea fowl scream."
        -BALDER DEAD (Matthew Arnold)

He also extended his special protection over commerce and fishing, which two occupations could be pursued with advantage only during the short summer months, of which he was in a measure considered the personification.

The God of Summer

Njörd is represented in art as a very handsome god, in the prime of life, clad in a short green tunic, with a crown of shells and seaweed upon his head, or a broad-brimmed hat adorned with eagle or heron plumes. As personification of the summer, he was invoked to still the raging storms which desolated the coasts during the winter months. He was also implored to hasten the vernal warmth and thereby extinguish the winter fires.

As agriculture was practiced only during the summer months, and principally along the fiords or sea inlets, Njörd was also invoked for favorable harvests, for he was said to delight in prospering those who placed their trust in him.

Njörd's first wife, according to some authorities, was Nerthus, Mother Earth, who in Germany was identified with Frigga, as we have seen, but in Scandinavia was considered a separate divinity. He was, however, obliged to part with her when summoned to Asgard, where he occupied one of the twelve seats in the great council hall, and was present at all the assemblies of the gods, withdrawing to Nôatûn only when his services were not required by the Æsir.

"Nôatûn is the eleventh;
There Njörd has
Himself a dwelling made,
Prince of men;
Guiltless of sin,
He rules o'er the high-built fane."
   -LAY OF GRIMNIR *(Thorpe's tr.)*

In his own home by the seashore, Njörd delighted in watching the gulls fly to and fro, and in observing the graceful movements of the swans, his favorite birds, which were held sacred to him. He spent many an hour, too, considering the gambols of the gentle seals, which came to bask in the sunshine at his feet.

Skadi, Goddess of Winter

Shortly after Idun's recovery from Thrymheim, and Thiassi's death within the bounds of Asgard, the assembled Gods were greatly surprised and dismayed to see Skadi, the giant's daughter, appear one day in their midst, demanding satisfaction for her father's death. Although the daughter of an ugly old Hrim-thurs, Skadi, the Goddess of Winter, was very beautiful indeed, in her silvery armor, with her glittering spear, sharp-pointed arrows, short white hunting dress, white fur leggings, and broad snowshoes, and as she confronted the Gods they could not but recognize the justice of her claim, and offered the usual fine in atonement. Skadi, however, was so very angry that she at first refused this compromise, and sternly demanded a life for a life, until Loki, wishing to appease her wrath, and thinking that if he could only make those proud lips unbend enough to smile the rest would be easy, began to play all manner of pranks. Fastening a goat to himself by an invisible cord, he went through a series of antics, grotesquely reproduced by the goat; and this sight was so very comical that all the Gods fairly shouted with merriment, and even Skadi was seen to smile.

Taking advantage of this softened mood, the Gods pointed to the firmament where her father's eyes glowed like radiant stars in the northern hemisphere. They told her they had placed them there to show him all honor, and finally added that she might select as husband any of the Gods present at the assembly, providing she were content to judge of their attractions by their naked feet.
Blindfolded, so that she could see only the feet of the gods standing in a circle around her, Skadi looked about her until she saw a pair of beautifully formed feet. She felt sure they must belong to Balder, the god of light, whose bright face had charmed her, and she designated their owner as her choice.

But when the bandage was removed, she discovered to her secret chagrin that she had chosen Njörd, to whom her troth was plighted, and with whom she nevertheless spent a very happy honeymoon in Asgard, where all seemed to delight in doing her honor. This time passed, however; Njörd took his bride home to Nôatûn, where the monotonous sound of the waves, the shrieking of the gulls, and the cries of the seals so disturbed Skadi's slumbers that she finally declared it was quite impossible for her to remain there any longer, and implored her husband to take her back to her native Thrym-heim.

*"Sleep could I not
On my sea-strand couch,
For screams of the sea fowl.*

There wakes me,
When from the wave he comes,
Every morning the mew (gull)."
      -NORSE MYTHOLOGY (R. B. Anderson)

Njörd, anxious to please his new wife, consented to take her to Thrymheim and dwell there with her nine nights out of every twelve, providing she would spend the remaining three with him at Nôatûn; but when he reached the mountain region, the soughing of the wind in the pines, the thunder of the avalanches, the cracking of the ice, the roar of the waterfalls, and the howling of the wolves appeared to him as unbearable as the sound of the sea had seemed to his wife, and he could not but rejoice when his time of exile was ended, and he once more found himself domiciled at Nôatûn.

"Am weary of the mountains;
Not long was I there,
Only nine nights;
The howl of the wolves
Methought sounded ill
To the song of the swans."
      -NORSE MYTHOLOGY (R. B. Anderson)

Parting of Njörd and Skadi

For some time, Njörd and Skadi, who are the personifications of summer and winter, alternated thus, the wife spending the three short summer months by the sea, and he reluctantly remaining with her in Thrymheim during the nine long winter months. But, finding at last that their tastes would never agree, they decided to part forever, and returned to their respective homes, where each could follow the occupations which custom had endeared.

"Thrymheim it's called,
Where Thjasse dwelled,
That stream-mighty giant;
But Skade now dwells,
Pure bride of the gods,
In her father's old mansion."
      -NORSE MYTHOLOGY (R. B. Anderson)

Skadi now resumed her wonted pastime of hunting, leaving tier realm again only to marry the semi-historical Odin, to whom she bore a son called Saeming, the first king of Norway, and the supposed founder of the royal race which long ruled that country.

According to other accounts, however, Skadi eventually married Uller, the winter-god. As Skadi was a skillful markswoman, she is represented with bow and arrow, and, as Goddess of the chase, she is generally accompanied by one of the wolf-like dogs so common in the North. Skadi was invoked by hunters and by winter travelers, whose sleighs she guided over the snow and ice, thus helping them to reach their destination in safety.

Skadi's anger against the Gods, who had slain her father, the storm giant, is an emblem of the unbending rigidity of the ice-enveloped earth, which, softened at last by the frolicsome play of Loki (the heat lightning), smiles, and permits the embrace of Njörd (summer). His love, however, cannot hold her for more than three months of the year (typified in the myth by nights), as she is always secretly longing for the wintry storms and her wonted mountain amusements.

The Worship of Njörd

As Njörd was supposed to bless the vessels passing in and out of port, his temples were situated by the seashore; it was there that the oaths in his name were commonly sworn, and his health was drunk at every banquet, where he was invariably named with his son Frey.

As all aquatic plants were supposed to belong to him, the marine sponge was known in the North as "Njörd's glove," a name which was retained until lately, when the same plant has been popularly called the "Virgin's hand."

FREYA
Goddess of Love

Freya, the fair Northern goddess of beauty and love, is the sister of Frey and the daughter of Njörd and Nerthus, or Skadi. She is the most beautiful and best beloved of all the Goddesses, and while in Germany she was identified with Frigga, in Norway, Sweden, Denmark, and Iceland she was considered a separate divinity. Freya, having been born in Vanaheim, was also known as Vanadis, the Goddess of the Vanas, or as Vanabride.

As soon as she reached Asgard, the gods were so charmed by her beauty and grace that they bestowed upon her the realm of Folkvang and the great hall Sessrymnir (the roomy-seated), where they assured her she could easily accommodate all her guests.

"Folkvang 'tis called,
Where Freyja has right
To dispose of the hall-seats.
Every day of the slain
She chooses the half,
And leaves half to Odin."
    -NORSE MYTHOLOGY
    (R. B. Anderson)

Queen of the Valkyries

Although Goddess of love, Freya is not soft and pleasure-loving only, for the ancient Northern races said that she has very martial tastes, and that as Valfreya she often leads the Valkyries down to the battlefields, choosing and claiming one half the heroes slain. She is therefore often represented with corselet and helmet, shield and spear, only the lower part of her body being clad in the usual flowing feminine garb.

Freya transports the chosen slain to Folkvang, where they are duly entertained, and where she also welcomes all pure maidens and faithful wives, that they might enjoy the company of their lovers and husbands even after death. The joys of her abode were so enticing to the heroic Northern women that they often rushed into battle when their loved ones were slain, hoping to meet with the same fate; or they fell upon their swords, or were voluntarily burned on the same funeral pyre as the beloved remains.

As Freya is inclined to lend a favorable ear to lovers' prayers, she is often invoked by them, and it is customary to indite love songs in her honor, which are sung on all festive occasions, her very name in Germany being used as the verb "to woo."

Freya and Odur

Freya, the golden-haired and blue-eyed goddess, was also, at times, considered a personification of the earth. She therefore married Odur, a symbol of the summer sun, whom she dearly loved, and by whom she had two daughters, Hnoss and Gersemi, so beautiful that all things lovely and precious were called by their names.

So long as Odur lingered contentedly at her side, Freya was smiling and perfectly happy; but, alas! this God was a rover, and, wearying of his wife's company, he suddenly left home and wandered far out into the wide world. Freya, sad and forsaken, wept abundantly, and her tears fell down upon the hard rocks, which softened at their contact. We are even told that they trickled down to the very center of the stones, where they were transformed to drops of gold. The tears which fell into the sea, however, were changed into translucent amber.

Weary of her widowed condition, and longing to clasp her beloved in her arms once more, Freya finally started out in search of him, passing through many lands, where she was called by different names, such as Mardel, Horn, Gefn, Syr, Skialf, and Thrung, inquiring of all she met whether her husband had passed that way, and shedding so many tears that gold can be found in all parts of the earth.

"And Freya next came nigh, with golden tears;
The loveliest Goddess she in Heaven, by all
Most honor'd after Frea, Odin's wife.
Her long ago the wandering Oder took
To mate, but left her to roam distant lands;
Since then she seeks him, and weeps tears of gold.
Names hath she many; Vanadis on earth
They call her, Freya is her name in Heaven."
      -BALDER DEAD (Matthew Arnold)

Far away in the sunny South, under the flowering myrtle trees, Freya found Odur at last, and her love being restored to her, she grew happy and smiling once more, and as radiant as a bride. It is perhaps because Freya found her husband beneath the flowering myrtle, that Northern brides, to this day, wear myrtle in preference to the conventional orange wreath.

Hand in hand, Odur and Freya now gently wended their way home once more, and in the light of their happiness the grass grew green, the flowers bloomed, and the birds sang, for all Nature sympathized as heartily with Freya's joy as it had mourned with her when she was in sorrow.

"Out of the morning land,
Over the snowdrifts,
Beautiful Freya came
Tripping to Scoring.
White were the moorlands,
And frozen before her;
Green were the moorlands,
And blooming behind her.
Out of her gold locks
Shaking the spring flowers,
Out of her garments
Shaking the south wind,
Around in the birches
Awaking the throstles,
And making chaste housewives all
Long for their heroes home,
Loving and love-giving,
Came she to Scoring."
      -THE LONGBEARDS' SAGA (Charles Kingsley)

The prettiest plants and flowers in the North were called Freya's hair or Freya's eye dew, while the butterfly was called Freya's hen. This Goddess is also supposed to have a special affection for the fairies, whom she loves to watch dancing in the moonbeams, and for whom she reserves her daintiest flowers and sweetest honey. Odur, Freya's husband, besides being considered a personification of the sun, is also regarded as an emblem of passion, or of the intoxicating pleasures of love; so the ancients declared that it was no wonder his wife could not be happy without him.

As Goddess of beauty, Freya is very fond of glittering adornments and of precious jewels. One day, while she was in Svartalfheim, the underground kingdom, she saw four dwarfs carefully fashioning the most wonderful necklace she had ever seen. Almost beside herself with longing to possess this treasure, which was called Brisinga-men, and was an emblem of the stars, or of the fruitfulness of the earth, Freya implored the dwarfs to give it to her; but they obstinately refused to do so unless she would promise to grant them her favor. Having secured the necklace at this price, Freya hastened to put it on, and its beauty so enhanced her charms that the Goddess wore it night and day, and only occasionally could be persuaded to loan it to the other divinities. Thor, however, wore this necklace when he personated Freya in Jötunheim, and Loki coveted and would have stolen it, had it not been for the watchfulness of Heimdall.

Freya is also the proud possessor of a falcon garb, or falcon plumes, which enables the wearer to flit through the air like a bird; and this garment is so invaluable that it was twice borrowed by Loki, and was used by Freya herself when in search of the missing Odur.

"Freya one day
Falcon wings took, and through space hied away;
Northward and southward she sought her
Dearly-loved Odur."
   -FRIDTHIOF'S SAGA, TEGNÉR (Stephens's tr.)

As Freya is also considered Goddess of fecundity, she is sometimes represented as riding about with her brother Frey in the chariot drawn by the golden-bristled boar, scattering, with lavish hands, fruits and flowers to gladden the hearts of all mankind. She also has a chariot of her own, however, in which she generally travels, which is drawn by cats, her favorite animals, the emblems of caressing fondness and sensuality, or the personifications of fecundity.

"Then came dark-bearded Niörd, and after him
Freyia, thin robed, about her ankles slim
The gray cats playing."
         -LOVERS OF GUDRUN (William Morris)

Frey and Freya were held in such high honor throughout the North that their names, in modified forms, are still used for "master" and "mistress," and one day of the week is called Freya's day, or Friday, even by the English-speaking race. Freya's temples were very numerous indeed, and were long maintained by her votaries, the last in Magdeburg, Germany, being destroyed by order of Charlemagne.

Story of Ottar and Angantyr

The Northern people were wont to invoke her not only for success in love, prosperity, and increase, but also at times for aid and protection. This she vouchsafed to all who served her truly, as is proved by the story of Ottar and Angantyr, two men who, after disputing for some time concerning their rights to a certain piece of property, laid their quarrel before the Thing. In that popular assembly it was soon decreed that the man who could prove that he had the longest line of noble ancestors would be the one to win, and a special day was appointed to hear the genealogy of each claimant.

Ottar, unable to remember the names of more than a few of his progenitors, offered up sacrifices to Freya, entreating her aid. The Goddess graciously heard his prayer, appeared before him, changed him into a boar, and rode off upon his back to the dwelling of the sorceress Hyndla, the most renowned witch of the day. By threats and entreaties, Freya compelled this old woman to trace Ottar's genealogy back to Odin, naming every individual in turn, and giving a synopsis of his achievements. Then, fearing lest her votary's memory should prove treacherous, Freya further compelled Hyndla to brew a potion of remembrance, which she gave him to drink.

"He shall drink
Delicious draughts.
All the Gods I pray

To favor Ottar."
   -SÆMUND'S EDDA (Thorpe's tr.)

Thus prepared, Ottar presented himself before the Thing on the appointed day, glibly recited his pedigree, and by naming many more ancestors than Angantyr could recollect, obtained possession of the property he coveted.

"A duty 'tis to act
So that the young prince
His paternal heritage may have
After his kindred."
   -SÆMUND'S EDDA (Thorpe's tr.)

Freya was so beautiful that all the gods, giants, and dwarfs longed for her love and in turn tried to secure her as wife. But Freya scorned the ugly old giants and refused to belong even to Thrym, when urged to accept him by Loki and Thor. She was not so obdurate where the Gods themselves were concerned, if the various mythologists are to be believed, for as the personification of the earth she is said to have married Odin, the sky, Frey, the fruitful rain, Odur, the sunshine, etc., until it seems as if she deserved the accusation hurled against her by the archfiend Loki, of having loved and married all the Gods in turn.

Worship of Freya

It was customary on solemn occasions to drink Freya's health with that of the other Gods, and when Christianity was imposed by force in the North this toast was transferred to the Virgin or to St. Gertrude; Freya herself, like all the heathen divinities, was declared a demon or witch by the invading christians, and banished to the mountain peaks of Norway, Sweden, or Germany, where the Brocken is pointed out as her special abode, and the general trysting place of her demon train on Valpurgisnacht.

CHORUS OF WITCHES

"On to the Brocken the witches are flocking —
Merry meet — merry part — how they gallop and drive,
Yellow stubble and stalk are rocking,

And young green corn is merry alive,
With the shapes and shadows swimming by.
To the highest heights they fly,
Where Sir Urian sits on high —
Throughout and about,
With clamor and shout,
Drives the maddening rout,
Over stock, over stone;
Shriek, laughter, and moan,
Before them are blown."
    -GOETHE'S FAUST (Anster's tr.)

As the swallow, cuckoo, and cat were held sacred to Freya in heathen times, these creatures were turned into ones having demoniacal properties by the alien forces of Christianity, and to this day witches are always depicted with coal-black cats close beside them.

FREY
God of Fertility

Frey, or Fro as he was called in Germany, is the God of Frith; peace, fertility, nature and plenty. He is the son of Njörd and Nerthus, or of NJörd and Skadi, and was born in Vanaheim. He therefore belongs to the race of the Vanas, the divinities of water and air, but was warmly welcomed in Asgard when he came thither as hostage with his father. As it was customary among the Northern nations to bestow some valuable gift upon a child when he cut his first tooth, the sir gave the infant Frey the beautiful realm of Alfheim, the home of all the Light Elves.

"Alf-heim the gods to Frey
Gave in days of yore
For a tooth gift."
         -SÆMUND'S EDDA (Thorpe's tr.)

Here Frey, the God of the golden sunshine and the warm summer showers, took up his abode, charmed with the company of the elves and fairies, who implicitly obeyed his every order, and at a sign from him flitted to and fro, doing all the good in their power, for they were preeminently beneficent spirits.

Frey received from the Gods a marvelous sword (an emblem of the sunbeams), which had the power of fighting successfully, and of its own accord, as soon as it was drawn from its sheath. Because he carried this glittering weapon, Frey has sometimes been confounded with the sword-god Tyr or Saxnot, although he wielded it principally against the frost giants, whom he hated almost as much as did Thor.

"With a short-shafted hammer fights conquering Thor;
Frey's own sword but an ell long is made."
      -VIKING TALES OF THE NORTH (R. B. Anderson)

The dwarfs from Svartalfheim gave Frey the golden-bristled boar Gullin-bursti (the golden-bristled), a personification of the sun. The radiant bristles of this animal are considered symbolical either of the solar rays, of the golden grain, which at his bidding waved over the harvest fields of Midgard, or of agriculture, for the boar (by tearing up the ground with his sharp tusk) is supposed to have first taught mankind how to plow.

"There was Frey, and sat
On the gold-bristled boar, who first, they say,
Plowed the brown earth, and made it green for Frey."
      -LOVERS OF GUDRUN (William Morris)

Frey sometimes rides astride of this marvelous boar, whose celerity is very great, and at other times harnesses him to his golden chariot, which is said to contain the fruits and flowers which he lavishly scatters abroad over the face of the earth.

Frey is, moreover, the proud possessor, not only of the dauntless steed Blodug-hofi, which dashes through fire and water at his command, but also of the magic ship Skidbladnir, a personification of the clouds. This vessel, navigating over land and sea, is always wafted along by favorable winds, and is so elastic that, while it can assume large enough proportions to carry the gods, their steeds, and all their equipments, it can also be folded up like a napkin and thrust out of sight.

"Ivaldi's sons
Went in days of old
Skidbladnir to form,
Of ships the best,
For the bright Frey,
Niörd's benign son."
      -LAY OF GRIMNIR (Thorpe's tr.)

The Wooing of Gerda

It is related in one of the lays of the Edda that Frey once ventured to ascend Odin's throne Hlidskialf, and from this exalted seat cast a glance over all the wide earth. Gazing towards the frozen North, he saw a beautiful young maiden enter the house of the frost giant Gymir, and as she raised her hand to lift the latch her radiant beauty illuminated sea and sky.

A moment later, this lovely creature, whose name was Gerda, and who is considered as a personification of the flashing Northern lights, vanished within her father's house, and Frey pensively wended his way back to Alfheim, his heart oppressed with longing to make this fair maiden his wife. Being deeply in love, he was melancholy and absentminded in the extreme, and began to behave so strangely that his father, Njörd, became greatly alarmed about his health, and bade his favorite servant, Skirnir, discover the cause of this sudden change. After much persuasion, Skirnir finally won from Frey an account of his ascent of Hlidskialf, and of the fair vision he had seen. He confessed his love and especially his utter despair, for as Gerda was the daughter of Gymir and Angur-boda, and a relative of the murdered giant Thiassi, he feared she would never view his suit with favor.

"In Gymer's court I saw her move,
The maid who fires my breast with love;
Her snow-white arms and bosom fair
Shone lovely, kindling sea and air.
Dear is she to my wishes, more
Than e'er was maid to youth before;
But gods and elves, I wot it well,
Forbid that we together dwell."
        -SKIRNER'S LAY (Herbert's tr.)

Skirnir, however, consolingly replied that he could see no reason why his master should take such a despondent view of the matter, and proposed to go and woo the maiden in his name, providing Frey would lend him his steed for the journey, and give him his glittering sword in reward.

Overjoyed at the mere prospect of winning the beautiful Gerda, Frey handed Skirnir the flashing sword, and bade him use his horse, ere he resumed his interrupted day-dream; for ever since he had fallen in love he had frequently indulged in revery. in his absorption he did not even notice that Skirnir was still hovering near him, and did not perceive him cunningly steal the reflection of his face from the surface of the brook near which he was seated, and imprison it in his drinking horn, intending "to pour it out in Gerda's cup, and by its beauty win the heart of the giantess for the lord" for whom he was about to go a-wooing. Provided with this portrait, with eleven golden apples, and with the magic ring Draupnir, Skirnir now rode off to Jötunheim, to fulfill his embassy. As soon as he came near Gymir's dwelling he heard the loud and persistent howling of his watch dogs, which were personifications of the wintry winds. A shepherd, guarding his flock in the vicinity, told him, in answer to his inquiry, that it would be impossible for him to approach the house, on account of the flaming barrier which surrounded it; but Skirnir, knowing that Blodug-hofi would dash through any fire, merely set spurs to his steed, and, riding up to the giant's door, soon found himself ushered into the presence of the lovely Gerda.

To induce this fair maiden to lend a favorable ear to his master's proposals, Skirnir showed her the purloined portrait, and proffered the golden apples and magic ring, which she haughtily refused to accept, declaring that her father had gold enough and to spare.

"I take not, I, that wondrous ring,
Though it from Balder's pile you bring.
Gold lack not I, in Gymer's bower;
Enough for me my father's dower."
    -SKIRNER'S LAY (Herbert's tr.)

Indignant at her scorn, Skirnir now threatened to use his magic sword to cut off her head; but as this threat did not in the least frighten the maiden, and she calmly defied him, he had recourse to magic arts. Cutting runes in his stick, he told her that unless she yielded ere the spell was ended, she would be condemned either to eternal celibacy, or to marry some hideous old frost giant whom she could never love.

Terrified into submission by the frightful description he gave of her cheerless future in case she persisted in her refusal, Gerda finally consented to become Frey's wife, and dismissed Skirnir, promising to meet her future spouse on the ninth night, in the land of Buri, the green grove, where she would dispel his sadness and make him happy.

*"Burri is hight the seat of love;
Nine nights elapsed, in that known grove
Shall brave Niorder's gallant boy
From Gerda take the kiss of joy."*
    -SKIRNER'S LAY (Herbert's tr.)

Delighted with his success, Skirnir hurried back to Alfheim, where Frey eagerly came to meet him, and insisted upon knowing the result of his journey. When he learned that Gerda had consented to become his wife, his face grew radiant with joy; but when Skirnir further informed him that he would have to wait nine nights ere he could behold his promised bride, he turned sadly away, declaring the time would appear interminable.

*"Long is one night, and longer twain;
But how for three endure my pain?
A month of rapture sooner flies
Than half one night of wishful sighs."*
    -SKIRNER'S LAY (Herbert's tr.)

In spite of this loverlike despondency, however, the time of waiting came to an end, and Frey joyfully hastened to the green grove, where he met Gerda, who became his happy wife, and proudly sat upon his throne beside him.

*"Frey to wife had Gerd;
She was Gymir's daughter,
From Jotuns sprung."*
    -SÆMUND'S EDDA (Thorpe's tr.)

According to some mythologists, Gerda is not a personification of the aurora borealis, but of the earth, which, hard, cold, and unyielding, resists the Spring-God's proffers of adornment and fruitfulness (the apples and ring), defies the flashing sunbeams (Frey's sword), and only consents to receive his kiss when it learns that it will else be doomed to perpetual barrenness, or given over entirely into the power of the giants (ice and snow). The nine nights of waiting are typical of the nine winter months, at the end of which the earth becomes the bride of the sun, in the groves where the trees are budding forth into leaf and blossom.

Frey and Gerda, we are told, became the parents of a son called Fiolnir, whose birth consoled Gerda for the loss of her brother Beli.

The latter had attacked Frey and had been slain by him, although the Sun-God, deprived of his matchless sword, had been obliged to defend himself with a stag horn which he hastily snatched from the wall of his dwelling.

The Historical Frey

Snorro-Sturleson, in his "Heimskringla," or chronicle of the ancient kings of Norway, states that Frey was an historical personage who bore the name of Ingvi-Frey, and ruled in Upsala after the death of the semi-historical Odin and Njörd. Under his reign the people enjoyed such prosperity and peace that they declared their king must be a god. They therefore began to invoke him as such, carrying their enthusiastic admiration for him to such lengths that when he died the priests, not daring to reveal the fact, laid him in a great mound instead of burning his body, as had been customary until then. They then informed the people that Frey — whose name was the Northern synonym for "master" — had "gone into the mound," an expression which eventually became the Northern phrase for death.

Only three years later the people, who had continued paying their taxes to the king by pouring the gold, silver, and copper coin into the mound by three different openings, discovered that Frey was dead. As their peace and prosperity had remained undisturbed, they decreed that his corpse should never be burned, and thus inaugurated the custom of mound burial, which in due time supplanted the funeral pyre in many places. One of the three mounds near Gamla Upsala still bears this god's name. His statues were placed in the great temple there, and his name was duly mentioned in all solemn oaths, of which the usual formula was, "So help me Frey, Njörd, and the Almighty Asa" (Odin).

Worship of Frey

No weapons were ever admitted in Frey's temples, the most celebrated of which were at Throndhjeim, and at Thvera in Iceland, where oxen or horses were offered up in sacrifice to him, and where a heavy gold ring was dipped in the victim's blood ere the above-mentioned oath was solemnly taken upon it.

Frey's statues, like those of all the other Northern divinities, were roughly hewn blocks of wood, and the last of these sacred images seems to have been destroyed by Olaf the Saint, who forcibly converted many of his subjects. Besides being God of Sunshine, fruitfulness, peace, and prosperity, Frey was considered the patron of horses and horsemen, and the deliverer of all captives.

"Frey is the best
Of all the chiefs
Among the gods.
He causes not tears
To maids or mothers:
His desire is to loosen the fetters
Of those enchained."
　　　　-NORSE MYTHOLOGY (R. B. Anderson)

The Yule Feast

One month of every year, the Yule month, or Thor's month, was considered sacred to Frey as well as to Thor, and began on the longest night of the year, which bore the name of Mother Night. This month was a time of feasting and rejoicing, for it heralded the return of the sun. The festival was called Yule (wheel) because the sun was supposed to resemble a wheel rapidly revolving across the sky. This resemblance gave rise to a singular custom in England, Germany, and along the banks of the Moselle. Until within late years, the people were wont to assemble yearly upon a mountain, to set fire to a huge wooden wheel, twined with straw, which, all ablaze, was then sent rolling down the hill and plunged with a hiss into the water.

"Some others get a rotten Wheele, all worn and cast aside,
Which, covered round about with strawe and tow, they closely hide;
And caryed to some mountaines top, being all with fire light,
They hurle it down with violence, when darke appears the night;
Resembling much the sunne, that from the Heavens down should fal,
A strange and monstrous sight it seemes, and fearful to them all;
But they suppose their mischiefs are all likewise throwne to hell,
And that, from harmes and dangers now, in safetie here they dwell."
　　　　-NAOGEORGUS

All the Northern races considered the Yule feast the greatest of the year, and were wont to celebrate it with dance, feasting, and drinking, each God being pledged by name. The missionaries, perceiving the extreme popularity of this feast, thought best to encourage drinking to the health of the Lord and his twelve apostles when they first began to convert the Northern heathens. In honor of Frey, boar's flesh was eaten on this occasion. Crowned with laurel and rosemary, the animal's head was brought into the banquet hall with much ceremony — a custom long after observed at Oxford, where the following lines were sung:

"Caput apri defero
Reddens laude Domino.
The boar's head in hand bring I,
With garlands gay and rosemary.
I pray you all sing merrily
Qui estis in convivio."
   -QUEEN'S COLLEGE CAROL, OXFORD

The father of the family then laid his hand on this dish, which was called "the boar of atonement," swearing he would be faithful to his family, and would fulfill all his obligations — an example which was followed by all present, from the highest to the lowest. This dish could be carved only by a man of unblemished reputation and tried courage, for the boar's head was a sacred emblem which was supposed to inspire every one with fear. For that reason a boar's head was frequently used as ornament for the helmets of Northern kings and heroes whose bravery was unquestioned.

God of Conjugal Happiness

As Frey's name of Fro is phonetically the same as the word used in German for gladness, he was considered the patron of every joy, and was invariably invoked by married couples who wished to live in harmony. Those who succeeded in doing so for a certain length of time were publicly rewarded by the gift of a piece of boar's flesh, for which, in later times, the English and Viennese substituted a flitch of bacon or a ham.

"You shall swear, by custom of confession,
If ever you made nuptial transgression,
Be you either married man or wife
If you have brawls or contentious strife;
Or otherwise, at bed or at board,
Offended each other in deed or word;
Or, since the parish clerk said Amen,

You wish'd yourselves unmarried again;
Or, in a twelvemonth and a day
Repented not in thought any way,
But continued true in thought and desire
As when you join'd hands in the quire.
If to these conditions, with all feare,
Of your own accord you will freely sweare,
A whole gammon of bacon you shall receive,
And bear it hence with love and good leave
For this our custom at Dunmow well known —
Though the pleasure be ours, the bacon's your own."
   -BRANDS POPULAR ANTIQUITIES

At Dunmow, England, and in Vienna, Austria, this custom was kept up very long indeed, the ham or flitch of bacon being hung over the city gate, whence the successful candidate was expected to bring it down, after he had satisfied the judges that he lived in peace with his wife, but was not under petticoat rule. It is said that in Vienna this ham once remained for a long time unclaimed until at last a worthy burgher presented himself before the judges, bearing his wife's written affidavit that they had been married twelve years and had never disagreed — a statement which was confirmed by all their neighbors. The judges, satisfied with the proofs laid before them, told the candidate that the prize was his, and that he only need climb the ladder placed beneath it and bring it down. Rejoicing at having secured such a fine ham, the man obeyed; but as he was about to reach upwards, he noticed that the ham, exposed to the noonday sun, was beginning to melt, and that a drop of fat threatened to fall upon and stain his Sunday coat. Hastily beating a retreat, he pulled off his coat, jocosely remarking that his wife would scold him roundly were he to stain it, a confession which made the bystanders roar with laughter, and which cost him his ham.

Another Yule-tide custom was the burning of a huge log, which had to last all night or it was considered of very bad omen indeed. The charred remains of this log were carefully collected, and treasured up to set fire to the log of the following year.

"With the last yeeres brand
Light the new block, and
For good successe in his spending,
On your psaltries play,

*That sweet luck may
Come while the log is a-tending."*
    -HESPERIDES (Herrick)

This festival was so popular in Scandinavia, where it was celebrated in January, that King Olaf, seeing how dear it was to the Northern heart, transferred most of its observances to Christmas day, thereby doing much to reconcile the people to their change of religion.

As God of peace and prosperity, Frey is supposed to have reappeared upon earth many times, and to have ruled the Swedes under the name of Ingvi-Frey, whence his descendants were called Inglings. He also governed the Danes under the name of Fridleef. In Denmark he is said to have married the beautiful maiden Freygerda, whom he had rescued from a dragon. By her he had a son named Frodi, who, in due time, succeeded him as king.

This Frodi ruled Denmark in the days when there was "peace throughout all the world," and because all his subjects lived in amity, he was generally known as Peace Frodi.

How the Sea Became Salt

This king once received from Hengi-kiaptr a pair of magic millstones, called Grotti, which were so ponderous that none of his servants nor even his strongest warriors could turn them. As Peace Frodi knew that the mill was enchanted and would grind anything he wished, he was very anxious indeed to set it to work, and, during a visit to Sweden, saw and purchased as slaves the two giantesses Menia and Fenia, whose powerful muscles and frames had attracted his attention.
On his return home, Peace Frodi led these women to the mill, and bade them turn the grindstones and grind out gold, peace, and prosperity — a wish which was immediately fulfilled. Cheerfully the women worked on, hour after hour, until the king's coffers were overflowing with gold and his land with prosperity and peace.

*"Let us grind riches to Frothi!
Let us grind him, happy
In plenty of substance,
On our gladdening Quern."*
    -GROTTA-SAVNGR (Longfellow's tr.)

But when Menia and Fenia would fain have rested awhile, the king, whose greed had been excited, bade them work on. In spite of their cries and entreaties he forced them to labor hour after hour, allowing them only as much time to rest as was required for the singing of a verse in a song, until, exasperated by his cruelty, the giantesses resolved to have their revenge. Once while Frodi slept they changed their song, and grimly began to grind an armed host, instead of prosperity and peace. By their spells they induced the Viking Mysinger to land with his troops, surprise the Danes, who were wrapped in slumber, and slay them all.

*"An army must come
Hither forthwith,
And burn the town
For the prince."*
        -GROTTA-SAVNGR (Longfellow's tr.)

This Viking then placed the magic millstones Grotti and the two slaves on board his vessel, and bade the women grind for him, saying that he wanted salt, as it was a very valuable staple of commerce at that time. The women obeyed; the millstones went round, grinding salt in abundance; but the Viking, as cruel as Frodi, kept the women persistently at work, until they ground such an immense quantity of salt that its weight sunk the ship and all on board.

The ponderous millstones sank straight down into the sea in the Pentland Firth, or off the northwestern coast of Norway, making a deep round hole. The waters, rushing into the vortex and gurgling in the holes in the center of the stones, produced the great whirlpool, which is known as the Maelstrom. As for the salt, it soon melted; but such was the quantity ground by the giantesses that it tainted all the waters of the sea, which have ever since been very salt indeed.

40
The Rite of Self Profession for Odinism

This ceremony/rite may be as simple or as elaborate as one elects to construct it. It is the Odinist version of a baptism and initiation. It also serves as an act/rite of purification and it may be employed as thus at any time one feels the need to do it, beyond the initial rite.

One may dress however one elects, for this rite, albeit keeping with Heathen Pagan tradition, nudity is best as it evokes a sense of ridding one's self of the alien dogma and religion and its stain upon the Sál (soul), thereby purifying the initiate.

Rainwater (skywater) is best employed for this rite. But regular water from the tap and consecrated to the Gods will suffice.

1) Perform the Hammer blessing/raise the shield wall as in all other Blótar/Rites.

2) Meditate upon your purpose for a few moments, face North and take the boli (bowl) of water up, and intone:

> Wise and Elder Gods
> Of my Folk, great and
> Mighty Æsir and Vanir.
> In Odin's holy name
> May this holy water cleanse
> From me all alien stain
> May it purify my mind and soul,
> My heart and being,
> so that with the Gods of
> my Ancestors, I shall
> remain true.

3) Now dip the fingers of the right hand (the Hammer hand) into the water and make a clenched fist and touch your forehead while intoning;

> "Odin, give me wit and wisdom"

Next, touch your heart and say;

> "Balder, grace me with boldness and goodness."

Next, touch your left shoulder and say;

> "Frey and Freya, bless me with joy, harmony and lust for life."

Next, touch your right shoulder and say;

> "Thor, bless me with might, main and fortitude."

Meditate for a few moments about the rite you preformed and the Oath you are about to take.
Then swear your Oath…

"I oath this day/night to remain ever true to the Gods of my Ancestors, the true Gods of my Folk! The Northern Path of Odinism is ever more my Siðr (way/religion). This do I freely Oath. Heil the Gods in Odin's name."

> This rite is now done.

Photo Courtesy of D. Anastasion
Associate Producer National Geographic Television

ABOUT THE AUTHOR

Casper Odinson Cröwell has been an Odinist/Heathen for thirty-four years in which time he has been associated with numerous Odinist, Ásatrú and Folk oriented organizations. He is the author of Ek Einherjar: Hammer of the Gods, published in 2009. He is the Chieftain/Herjan and co-founder of the Vinland Kindred of the Order of the Sacred Circle of the Sons of Odin, 1519. He is also the co-founder of the HOLY NATION of ODIN, Inc., where he is the Chief Court Gothi and Director of Religious Services. He has dual Ph.D.'s in the fields of Comparative Religion and Metaphysics, as well as a Doctorate of Divinity in Odinist Theology and a minor law degree. He is also the National Chairman of the Vinland Folk Resistance

At age 50, he remains confined within the California State Prison System. A Political Prisoner, Dr. Cröwell is serving a life sentence for his Folkish beliefs and Patriotism.

www.ingramcontent.com/pod-product-compliance
Lightning Source LLC
Chambersburg PA
CBHW060454090426
42735CB00011B/1980